D0909969

THE LOEB CLASSICAL LIBRARY

FOUNDED BY JAMES LOEB

CICERO

XXII

LCL 7

CICERO

LETTERS TO ATTICUS

VOLUME I

EDITED AND TRANSLATED BY

D. R. SHACKLETON BAILEY

HARVARD UNIVERSITY PRESS
CAMBRIDGE, MASSACHUSETTS
LONDON, ENGLAND
1999

Library of Congress Cataloging-in-Publication Data

Cicero, Marcus Tullius.
[Ad Atticum. English)
Letters to Atticus / Cicero ; edited and translated by
D.R. Shackleton Bailey.
p. cm.—(Loeb classical library ; 7-8, 97, 491)
Includes bibliographical references and index.
ISBN 0-674-99571-6 (v. 1). — ISBN 0-674-99572-4 (v. 2). —
ISBN 0-674-99573-2 (v. 3). — ISBN 0-674-99540-6 (v. 4)
1. Cicero, Marcus Tullius—Correspondence. 2. Latin
letters— Translations into English. 3. Atticus, Titus
Pomponius—Correspondence.
4. Statesmen—Rome—Correspondence.
5. Authors, Latin—Correspondence. I. Atticus, Titus
Pomponius. II. Shackleton Bailey, D. R. (David Roy), 1917–
III. Title. IV. Series. PA6308.E6B3 1998
937′.05′092—dc2l [b] 98-8779

CONTENTS

INTRODUCTION

The Roman, at any rate the upper-class Roman, was a letter writer. In ancient Greece a man's circle was apt to be mainly confined to a single small town and the countryside adjoining. But the well-to-do Roman might well have connections up and down Italy as well as in the provinces. He himself spent much time in his country houses (villas). Business, public or private, might take him abroad for long periods. Although there was no postal system, bearers could usually be found—his own slaves, his friends' slaves, casual travellers, or the couriers of business companies.

Hardly any specimens of this activity survive except for Cicero's correspondence, consisting almost entirely of private letters written without any idea of future publication and published, as it seems, almost exactly as they stood. (The omission in one letter to Atticus of a scandalous story about Cicero's nephew may have been deliberate, but it is hard to find any other evidence of expurgation, let alone falsification.) As such they are uniquely interesting even apart from their value as a source of historical and other kinds of information. To Atticus in particular Cicero reveals himself as to no other of his correspondents except his brother. Here the modern reader comes close to the writer's personality and lives in his remote yet familiar world.

What remains of Cicero's correspondence has come down in two large collections, the Letters to Atticus and the so-called Letters to Friends, and two much smaller ones, to his brother Q. Cicero and to M. Brutus. Many more were extant in antiquity of which only stray fragments now survive. Except for a few of the earliest letters to Atticus they were all written in the last twenty years of Cicero's life. We know from Cornelius Nepos[1] that Atticus preserved Cicero's letters dating from his Consulship in 63[2] in eleven papyrus rolls and that friends were allowed to read them. What happened after his death is unknown, but they were probably not published until the middle of the first century A.D., though the rest of the correspondence seems to have come out much earlier. For the most part the Atticus letters as they stand in the manuscripts are in chronological order, but the departures are of a nature to suggest that some which Atticus himself had for various reasons not included were found in his remains and incorporated so as to make the existing sixteen 'books.'[3] Successive commentators and translators have changed the manuscript order so as to conform with chronology as best that could be determined. For convenience I here adhere to the arrangement in my Cambridge edition of the Let-

[1] A younger friend of Atticus. The short biography of Atticus in his *Lives of Illustrious Men* contains almost everything known about its subject apart from what Cicero's letters provide.

[2] Henceforward all dates are to be understood as B.C. unless otherwise stated.

[3] As explained in the introduction to my Cambridge edition of the Letters to Atticus, pp. 69–73.

ters, even in a few cases (to be noted in their place) where it calls for revision.[4]

Cicero's letters only come fully to life against a historical and biographical background, though a bare outline is all that can be attempted here.

Historical Background

Marcus Tullius Cicero was born on 3 January 106 B.C. at his family home near the hill town of Arpinum (still Arpino) about seventy miles to the east of Rome. For nearly a century the Arpinates had been citizens of Rome, a status attained by most of Italy south of the Po only after the bloody 'Social War' of 90–88. The family was old and well-to-do, and like many locally prominent Italian families, had good Roman connections; but from the standpoint of a Roman aristocrat Cicero was a nobody, a 'new man,' a fact of lasting practical and psychological importance.

About ten years after Cicero's birth his father took up residence in a fashionable part of Rome. Cicero and his younger brother received the best education money could buy, and he is said to have easily outshone his socially superior classmates. On coming of age at sixteen or seventeen he served for a short time in the Roman army against the insurgent Italian allies. He lived in stormy times. Ro-

[4] J. T. Ramsey in *The Comet of 44 B.C.* (American Classical Studies no. 39, 1997, with A. Lewis Licht, 19–40) has proposed new and convincing dates for Letters 335–336 and 350–352, assigning the former to July 13–14 and the latter, written from Astura, to July 25–30 instead of August 27–30.

man political institutions were turning out to be inadequate for the government of an already large empire. The authority of the Senate, the only permanent governing body, had been seriously shaken in the last three decades of the second century. The career of the great general Marius, also a native of Arpinum and a family connection of the Ciceros, had pointed the way to future army commanders who were to build positions of personal power on the loyalty of their troops.

The Social War was followed by the terrible internal struggles of the eighties. In 88 the Consul Sulla, a brilliant general from an impoverished noble family who combined conservative sympathies with a contempt for constitutional forms, set a fateful precedent by marching his army on the capital in rebuttal of a personal injustice. His chief opponents were killed or, like Marius, escaped into exile. But Sulla had business elsewhere. Later in the year he left for the East to deal with a foreign enemy, the redoubtable Mithridates of Pontus. Turmoil ensued. Rome stood a siege before being captured again by the forces of the anti-Sullan Consul Cinna and old Marius, emerging from banishment like an avenging ghost. The resulting massacre was the bloodiest of its kind so far known in Roman history. Marius died a few months later, but Rome and Italy remained under the control of Cinna and his associates for the next four years.

In 83 Sulla brought his victorious legions home. Fighting followed up and down the peninsula, and Rome had another Marian bloodbath before Sulla came out master of the situation. His ruthless reprisals left a grim memory, but to people of traditional outlook he was the restorer of

the Republic. As Dictator he produced a new constitution guaranteeing control of affairs to an enlarged Senate, and, this task completed, he retired voluntarily into private life (79). His work was not wholly undone for thirty years.

Despite close Marian connections Cicero seems to have disliked and despised Cinna's regime and only began his public career, as an advocate, after Sulla's victory. He scored a sensational triumph with his defence of a certain Roscius, the victim of persecution by an influential freedman of Sulla's, and his services in court became much in demand. But in 79 his voice was suffering from overstrain and for this and perhaps other reasons he left Rome for three years of travel in Greece and Asia Minor. After a fresh start in 76 his star rose rapidly and steadily. The next thirteen years brought him the two great objects of his ambition, primacy at the Roman bar and a political career culminating in the Consulship. Without one setback he climbed the official ladder, elected Quaestor, Plebeian Aedile, and Praetor by handsome majorities and at the earliest age allowed by law. The Consulship at this period was almost a preserve of the nobility, consisting of descendants of Consuls, though now and again a man of praetorian family was let in. For more than a generation before Cicero's candidature in 64 new men had been excluded. Nevertheless he easily topped the poll.

His year of office would not have been particularly memorable but for a timely attempt at a coup d'état by his unsuccessful fellow candidate Catiline, a patrician champion of the bankrupt and disinherited. The plot was discovered and suppressed by Cicero. Catiline had left Rome to join his armed followers, and had to be defeated and

killed next year, but five of his chief associates were arrested and brought before the Senate. After a memorable debate they were executed under Cicero's supervision. In and out of the Senate he was hailed as the saviour of Rome, but the legality of the action was disputed, and it brought him into lasting unpopularity with the have-nots.

Cicero's prestige had reached a peak (from which it gradually declined), but the principal figure of the Roman world was not in Rome. Gnaeus Pompeius Magnus (Pompey the Great) rose early to fame by his brilliant military exploits against the adversaries of Sulla. His reputation was consolidated by years of finally successful warfare against the Marian leader Sertorius in Spain and the suppression of Spartacus' slave revolt in Italy. In 70 he became Consul in defiance of legal qualifications as to age and previous offices. Three years later, against the opposition of the senatorial leaders, he received an extraordinary commission to clear the Mediterranean of piracy. Prompt and complete success was followed by something even bigger — an overall command in the East where Mithridates and his ally the King of Armenia were still defying the empire. Pompey's campaigns established Roman control over a vast area of western Asia, which he reorganized as he saw fit. In 62 he returned to Italy and, to the relief of the home authorities, at once disbanded his army.

Pompey had two demands, both reasonable: ratification of his arrangements in the East and land for his veteran soldiers. But the senatorial conservatives, now tending to centre around a strong-minded young nobleman called M. Porcius Cato, distrusted his intentions and resented a career so conspicuously out of conformity with oligarchical norms. Several, in particular his predecessor in the eastern

command, L. Lucullus, and a Metellus (Creticus) who had fallen foul of him in Crete, nursed bitter personal grudges. Their unwisely stubborn obstructiveness resulted in a coalition between Pompey and two prominent politicians, both out of sympathy with the post-Sullan establishment: C. Julius Caesar and M. Licinius Crassus. The former, son of a Marian Praetor and former son-in-law of Cinna, was a favourite with the city populace, none the less so because he came from one of Rome's most ancient families; the latter, also a nobleman and Pompey's colleague in 70, was, next to Pompey himself, the richest man in Rome. This alliance, often called the First Triumvirate though it had no official status, dominated the scene for years to come. Cicero could have made a fourth, but although much dissatisfied with the 'optimates,' who were apt to remember his origins rather than the public services of which he so often reminded them, his principles would not let him take part in a conspiracy against the constitution.

In 59 Caesar became Consul. Almost literally over the dead body of his optimate colleague Bibulus, in defiance of senatorial opposition and constitutional procedures, he pushed through a legislative program which satisfied his two associates and gave himself a five-year command in northern Italy and Gaul. In the event it lasted until 49 and enabled him to annex modern France (apart from the old Roman province in the south) and Belgium to the Roman empire. There were even expeditions across the Rhine and the English Channel. Before leaving Rome he had arranged for the elimination of Cicero, who had rejected several tempting overtures. Early in 58 the patrician demagogue and Tribune P. Clodius Pulcher, following a personal vendetta, was allowed to drive him into exile with the pas-

sive connivance of Pompey, despite earlier professions of friendship and support. Distraught and desperate, Cicero fled to Greece. Eighteen months later the tide had turned. Clodius had fallen out with Pompey, who, with Caesar's rather reluctant consent, arranged for a triumphal restoration. For a while thereafter Cicero tried to play an independent political hand, taking advantage of rifts in the triumviral solidarity. But these were patched up at the Conference of Luca (Lucca) in 56, and Cicero received a sharp warning from Pompey, which took prompt effect. A eulogy of Caesar's victories in the Senate, described by himself as a palinode, was his last important political gesture for several years. He continued active forensically, but his choice of clients now had to include creatures of the dynasts, some of them enemies of his own. Meanwhile his personal relations with Caesar developed a new cordiality, and in 54 his brother Quintus went to Gaul to make a military reputation and, as he hoped, his fortune as one of Caesar's lieutenant generals.

The year 55 saw Pompey and Crassus together again in the Consulship. Caesar's tenure in Gaul was extended for another quinquennium, and the Consuls were appointed to commands in Spain and Syria for a like period (Pompey remained in Italy, governing Spain through deputies). But the later fifties produced a realignment. Pompey was the devoted husband of Caesar's daughter Julia; she died in 54 and in the following year Crassus was defeated and killed by the Parthians. Caesar and Pompey were left in what began to look like confrontation. After the conquest of Gaul Pompey could no longer feel secure in his position of senior while at the same time Cato and his friends were

losing their hostility to Pompey in face of the threat from Caesar. The rapprochement between Pompey and Senate, which Cicero had once unsuccessfully tried to promote, came about under the pressure of events. In 52, at the behest of the Catonians, Pompey took power as sole Consul (the term Dictator was avoided) to restore law and order, which had broken down in a welter of street warfare and electoral corruption. This accomplished with no less efficiency than the clearance of the seas in 67, the question of Caesar's future came uppermost. After protracted maneuvring the upshot was another civil war, which broke out at the beginning of 49, when Caesar led his troops across the river Rubicon into the homeland. Hardly more than two months later, after Caesar had encircled and captured a large republican army at Corfinium, Pompey, the Consuls, and a large part of the Senate crossed the Adriatic with their remaining troops, leaving Caesar in undisputed control of Italy and Rome.

Cicero had missed the political preliminaries. In 51 he found himself unexpectedly saddled with the government of a province (a thing he had twice avoided in the past), namely Cilicia, comprising almost all the southern seaboard of Asia Minor and a large part of the interior, together with the island of Cyprus. He entered it at the end of July for his year's tenure. He proved an excellent, if reluctant, governor and with the assistance of his brother and other experienced military men on his staff he even campaigned against the untamed people of the mountains with enough success to win the title of Imperator from his troops and a Supplication (Thanksgiving) from the Senate — the usual preliminaries to a Triumph. Arriving in Italy

during the final stage of the crisis he pleaded for peace in public and in private. When that failed, after many waverings recorded in almost daily letters to Atticus, he sailed from Italy in June and is next heard of early the following year in Pompey's camp near Dyrrachium (Durazzo).

Caesar's victory at Pharsalia[5] in August 48 was virtually the end of Pompey, who was killed shortly afterwards in Egypt, but it was not the end of the Civil War. Thinking it was, Cicero accepted Caesar's invitation (conveyed through his own son-in-law Dolabella) to return to Italy and spent an unhappy year in Brundisium (Brindisi) pending decisions on his future, while Caesar was involved in Egypt and Asia. On Caesar's return in September 47 his anxieties were relieved in a gracious interview and he was able to take up life again in Rome.

It was almost entirely a private life. Caesar showed him much kindness and he was on outwardly friendly social terms with most of Caesar's principal followers, but his advice was not required and he rarely appeared in the Forum or the Senate House. Paradoxically he now had most to fear from a republican victory. For Cato and others had established a new position of strength in Africa, where Caesar's lieutenant Curio had lost his life and army early in the war; and after that was destroyed by another Caesarian victory at Thapsus in April 46, Pompey's sons were able to fight another day in Spain. Even their defeat in the hard-fought battle of Munda (March 45) was not the end.

[5] 'Pharsalus, the modern title of the battlefield, is not merely in itself an error both gross and gratuitous; it is implicated with another that is more serious still': J. P. Postgate; see his discussion in *Lucan*, De Bello Civili VIII (Cambridge 1917), Excursus C.

Meanwhile, especially after his daughter's death in February 45, Cicero took refuge in literary work. In his young days he had published verse, with temporary acclaim, and many carefully edited speeches. The works *On the Orator* and *On the Republic* appeared in the fifties. In 46–44 he turned to philosophy. Without any pretensions to original thought, he put the ideas he found in his Greek sources into elegant Latin in a rapid succession of treatises which made a greater impact on the minds of men to come than perhaps any other secular writings of antiquity.

Cicero had no prior knowledge of the conspiracy against Caesar's life in 44, though its leader M. Brutus was his intimate friend. But when Caesar fell in the Senate House on the Ides of March, Brutus waved his bloodstained dagger and shouted Cicero's name. Certainly the act had Cicero's wholehearted approval. But a little while later he ruefully recognized that though the king was dead the monarchy survived. The conspirators, an assortment of republican loyalists and disgruntled place-seekers, had not planned ahead, and the Consul Mark Antony, who in Cicero's opinion ought to have been eliminated along with his colleague Caesar, soon made it evident that he intended to take Caesar's place. The 'liberators' were driven out of Rome by mob violence.

Disgusted at the scene, Cicero set out in July for Greece, where his son was a student in Athens, but reports from Rome made him turn back. On 2 September he delivered in the Senate the first of a series of attacks on Antony which he jestingly called Philippics, after Demosthenes' speeches against Philip of Macedon. There were no immediate consequences and for some time Cicero again lay low. But by the end of the year the situ-

ation had been transformed. Antony was at Mutina (Modena) besieging the legal governor of Cisalpine Gaul, Decimus Brutus, who was one of Caesar's assassins. Soon he found himself opposed by three republican armies. Their commanders were the two Consuls of 43, Hirtius and Pansa, both Caesarians but hostile to Antony's ambitions, and Caesar's youthful grandnephew and adopted son, Caesar Octavianus, who had returned to Italy the previous April and emerged as Antony's rival for the loyalty of Caesar's veterans. At this time Cicero professed complete confidence in Octavian's loyalty to the Republic. Meanwhile, he himself had taken the lead in Rome as the acknowledged embodiment of the Senate and People's will to resist the new despotism. M. Brutus and his brother-in-law and co-conspirator Cassius had left for the East, where they succeeded in taking over the entire Roman empire east of the Adriatic in the republican interest. The West, however, was in the hands of four Caesarian governors, none of whom, except perhaps Cornificius in Africa, was wholly reliable from Cicero's standpoint. It was his business to make the Senate a focus for their loyalties and to maintain a stream of hortatory correspondence.

In April the situation at Mutina was resolved. Antony suffered two heavy defeats and was forced to raise the siege and escape westwards. But both Consuls lost their lives in the fighting. The game in Italy now lay in Octavian's hands, but Antony was not finished. Joined by a large contingent under his lieutenant Ventidius he crossed the Alps into southern Gaul, now governed by Caesar's former Master of the Horse, M. Lepidus. The news that they had joined forces caused consternation in Rome, where the war had seemed as good as won. In northern Gaul Cicero's family

friend L. Plancus professed loyalty and was joined by Decimus Brutus. But the armies remained inactive until August or September, when Plancus, along with Pollio, the governor of Further Spain, joined the opposition. Decimus' men deserted and he was killed in flight.

In Italy Octavian had begun to assert himself, demanding the vacant Consulship—at nineteen years old! When the Senate refused, he marched his army on Rome and occupied the city without bloodshed. His election followed on 19 August. Then came a meeting with Antony and Lepidus in October at which a common front was established. The three dynasts became 'Triumvirs for the Constitution of the Republic' and parcelled out the western part of the empire between them. Funds were raised and vengeance satisfied by a revival of Sulla's Proscriptions. The victims were numerous, many of them eminent, and Cicero was naturally among the first. After an abortive attempt to escape by sea he was hunted down and killed at his villa near Formiae on 7 December 43. His brother and nephew met a similar fate.

In 42 the republican cause finally went down to defeat at Philippi, where Brutus and Cassius perished. Eleven years later monarchy was established by Octavian's victory over Antony at Actium.

The complexities of Cicero's career and personality hardly appear in a mere summary of events. In his various phases he became what circumstances made him, sometimes paltry, sometimes almost heroic. His ambition was rooted in insufficiency. Carrying all his life a set of traditional ideas which he never consciously questioned, he seldom ignored his code, but was easily swayed and per-

plexed by side issues and more or less unacknowledged personal inducements. His agile mind moved on the surface of things, victim of their complexity. Always the advocate, he saw from ever-shifting angles, and what he saw he rarely analysed.

Often confused himself, he perplexes us. He failed to realise that self-praise can defeat its end. Alongside the image of the wise and dauntless patriot which he tried to project into posterity has arisen the counterimage of a windbag, a spiteful, vainglorious egotist. And that is not because, as some of his admirers have urged, the survival of his private correspondence has placed him at a disadvantage. His published speeches reveal him to a generation intolerant of his kind of cliché. The flabbiness, pomposity, and essential fatuity of Ciceronian rhetoric at its too frequent worst does him more damage than any epistolary 'secrets.' No other antique personality has inspired such venomous dislike. In antiquity Asinius Pollio's son wrote a book comparing Cicero with his own father to the disadvantage of the former. This may have criticized him mainly as an orator and stylist, like another production entitled 'Cicero whipped.' His modern enemies hate and despise him as a man—from titanic Mommsen, obsessed by scorn of political inadequacy, romantic worshipper of 'complete and perfect' Caesar, to Kingsley Amis' young schoolmaster who had the bad luck to be reading the Second Philippic in class.[6] The living Cicero was hated by

[6] 'For a man so long and thoroughly dead it was remarkable how much boredom, and also how precise an image of nasty silliness, Cicero could generate.' (*Take a Girl Like You,* Chapter V.)

some, but not despised. His gifts, matching the times, were too conspicuous. And many opponents were disarmed; Mommsen himself might have capitulated to a dinner party at Tusculum.

Cicero's Family

In later life, after the death of his parents and a cousin, Lucius Cicero, to whom he was much attached, Cicero's family circle at one time or other included the following.

1. His wife Terentia. She was rich and well connected, possibly even of noble family; we hear only of a half-sister, a Vestal Virgin who probably belonged to the patrician Fabii. The marriage apparently worked well for many years, but after Cicero's return from exile there are signs of strain. The differences seem to have mainly had to do with money. In 46 they ended in divorce. Terentia is alleged to have lived to 103 and twice remarried.

2. His daughter Tullia. Probably born in 76 or 75 rather than 79 or 78, as usually supposed. Cicero was devoted to her and distraught with grief at her death in February 45. On her marriages see items 7–9.

3. His son Marcus, born in 65. He turned out a disappointment to his father, an unremarkable young man who was happier commanding a troop of cavalry than studying philosophy. He escaped the Proscriptions, being in Greece at the time, and served in Brutus' army. Later Octavian made him Augur, Consul in 30, and governor of Asia. He also gained a reputation as the hardest drinker in Rome.

4. A brother Quintus, about two years his junior. Following in Cicero's wake he held the usual offices up to

Praetor and was Proconsul in Asia from 61 to 59. In 54 he took service under Caesar in Gaul, but like his brother followed Pompey in the Civil War. Pardoned by Caesar after Pharsalia, he perished in the Proscriptions of 43. His relations with his brother were close and generally affectionate until 48. The story of their quarrel and superficial reconciliation can be found in Chapter 19 of my biography. A number of Cicero's letters to him written between 59 and 54 survive.

5. Quintus' wife Pomponia, sister of Atticus. The marriage took place in 70 or thereabouts and ended with divorce in 45. It was never a success. Pomponia was several years older than her husband and apparently of a shrewish disposition. Cicero's letters contain many references to their domestic difficulties.

6. Their son, the younger Q. Cicero, born about the end of 67. Much more gifted intellectually than his cousin, he grew up to be a thorn in his elders' flesh. Like his father and uncle he perished in the Proscriptions.

7. Tullia had three husbands, all young men of noble family. She was betrothed to the first, C. Calpurnius Piso Frugi, in 67 and married in 62. He was Quaestor in 58, but died the following year before Cicero's return. He seems to have been a model son-in-law, and Cicero writes warmly of his loyalty in the bad times.

8. Tullia married Furius Crassipes in 55. They were divorced within a few years, but nothing is known of the circumstances.

9. Tullia married P. Cornelius Dolabella in 50, a rake and a Caesarian. Divorce followed in 46, but Cicero remained on good terms with him until he allied himself with

Antony, having succeeded Caesar as Consul in 44. He committed suicide in the East in 42 to avoid capture by Cassius.

10. In January 45 Tullia bore a son, who lived only a few months. He was called Lentulus after Dolabella's adoptive name.

11. Not long after divorcing Terentia Cicero married his young and wealthy ward, Publilia. Another divorce followed after a few months. She had a brother(?), Publilius, and a mother living.

12. Pomponia's brother, T. Pomponius Atticus. He married Pilia in 56; her brother, Pilius Celer, was a noted speaker and a Caesarian. Their daughter, Caecilia Attica, was probably born in 51.

Atticus

Titus Pomponius (the cognomen Atticus being a personal acquisition) was born about November 110. His family was, like Cicero's, equestrian, but Roman as far back as it could be traced. Their friendship began in his school days. After his father's death in 86 or a little later, the young Pomponius made his home in Athens for about twenty years, though often returning to Rome on visits. In 79 he was joined by the Cicero brothers and their cousin Lucius, but after six months of study and contact with the philosophical and rhetorical celebrities of the 'university city' Cicero passed on to further travels. From his long residence in Athens and his love of things Hellenic Pomponius came to be called Atticus, 'the Athenian.'

In 65 or thereabouts Rome again became his permanent domicile, though he made frequent and lengthy visits

to an estate in Epirus, opposite the island of Corcyra (Corfu). It is to these absences and to Cicero's sojourns in his Italian villas and abroad that we owe their correspondence. Atticus' life was spent in cultural and antiquarian pursuits (he was the author of a work on Roman history and several chronicles of Roman noble families), on the management of his large fortune, and on obliging his friends. Much has sometimes been made of his adherence to the philosophy of Epicurus. No doubt it appealed to his temperament, though he was certainly no fervent disciple like his contemporary Lucretius. The Epicureans attached great importance to friendship. Despite (or perhaps to some extent because of) wide differences of nature and circumstance, his friendship with Cicero stood the test of time and his services were innumerable, especially in matters of business and in the dissemination of Cicero's literary works through his staff of slave copyists. In a sense we may regard him as Cicero's publisher, and it is to this aspect of their relationship, often referred to in the letters, that we owe most of our information about Cicero's literary activity, especially in 46–43. But nothing suggests any financial arrangement.

It may be relevant that Epicurus also discouraged involvement in politics. Atticus' wealth, social status, and friendships with men of birth and influence, especially Cato and his connections, would have made him a natural candidate for public office. But he avoided overt political activity, apart from a demonstration of support for Cicero in the Catilinarian crisis; it seems he did not even like voting at elections. He aimed at keeping on good terms with everybody, though his personal sympathies were

steadily conservative. In 'Caesar's war' he stayed in Italy and in 43 he befriended Antony's family and friends in Rome. But in the background he followed events closely, and could intervene when there was an axe to be ground. During his own absences from Rome Cicero largely depended on Atticus for news and views.

After Cicero's death Atticus lived on until 32 in excellent relations with both Octavian and Antony. His daughter, Caecilia Attica, married the former's right-hand man, M. Agrippa, and their daughter Vipsania was the first wife of the future Emperor Tiberius and mother of his ill-fated son.[7]

It is easy to be less than fair to a man who made so bland a success of safe living in troubled times and who, unlike Montaigne, has left no self-portrait to engage posterity in his favour. There was more in Atticus than 'the quintessence of prudent mediocrity' (Tyrrell and Purser). The basis of his many friendships must have been a singularly attractive personality. Its hallmark was the *humanitas* which Cicero so often associates with him, that untranslatably Roman amalgam of kindness and culture, width of mind, and tact of manner. Atticus never quarrelled with Pomponia in his life and spoke Greek as though Athenian born. A delightful talker, who liked to walk as he talked, he loved sparkle in others and doubtless evoked it. Many a Roman frown, even Brutus' 'solemn old countenance,' will have relaxed when Atticus thought it time to say 'halis

[7] The history of Atticus' relations with Cicero is traced at length in the Introduction to my Cambridge edition. The following estimate is based upon Cicero's letters and the biography of Atticus by Cornelius Nepos.

spoudēs' ('no more gravity,' 'trêve de sérieux'). Intellectually omnivorous, he was as ready to take an interest in a treatise on Homeric accentuation as in the latest city scandal. His social qualities were finished by a palatable salt of idiosyncrasy—some quaint turns of speech, his rich man's 'nearness' excused by good taste, his exaggerated cult of antiquity and *mos maiorum*. Moving much among his social superiors, he deferred to no man's arrogance. There was a formidable side to Atticus, and Nepos' testimony that his friends respected quite as much as they loved him can be read between the lines of many a letter. 'He never told a lie and could not tolerate lying in others': that too we can believe, though Atticus' conception of lying did not include prudent dissimulation. The reader of Cicero's correspondence needs no pious biographer to tell him that Atticus was a man of his word, indefatigable in pursuit of whatever he undertook. His moral code, however limited, was steadily and strictly observed: 'In the things that really matter—uprightness, integrity, conscientiousness, fidelity to obligation—I put you second neither to myself nor to any other man.' Cicero could flatter, but this does not sound like flattery. That deficiency in 'noble rage' which in modern estimates has tended to discount so many virtues might have gone unnoticed in a smaller epoch. But greatness had not yet deserted the air that fed Roman blood and made Latin speech. All evasions notwithstanding, Cicero had his portion, which no Mommsenian spleen shall take away; in the end he ran his risks and 'glaubte an Glauben.' Atticus, with his comity and learning, his business morals and sagacious benevolence, his warm heart and cool head, represents a meaner species.

Translation

The present translation of the Atticus letters is basically one that originally appeared as part of my edition in Cambridge Classical Texts and Commentaries (7 vols., Cambridge University Press, 1965–1970). It was reprinted in Penguin Classics (*Cicero's Letters to Atticus,* 1978) and has now been revised throughout. The notes, largely taken from the latter, aim to give some help in passages where a mere translation leaves the reader guessing. There is plenty in these letters to puzzle even specialists, written as they are to an intimate friend for whom everything did not have to be spelled out; and Atticus had the advantage of knowing what *he* had written to Cicero.

Two special problems of translation call for a word of comment. Cicero was a famous wit and regarded jokes as an essential ingredient of familiar letter writing. Most of them take the form of puns or other wordplays which can only seldom be satisfactorily reproduced in another language. One does one's best and hopes for tolerance. The second difficulty is Cicero's habit, especially when writing to his friend 'the Athenian,' of interlarding his Latin with scraps of Greek, sometimes quotations from Homer or other writers, sometimes not. In the latter case a translation which simply ignores the change of language robs the letters of one of their most characteristic elements. To use French (or some other foreign language) systematically, as was done by G. E. Jeans, leads to grotesque results. I compromised. When I could think of no convenient French (or Latin) expression I let Cicero's Greek go unmarked (the quotations, of course, mark themselves); occasionally, by

way of compensation, I used such an expression when Cicero uses Latin.

Manuscripts and Text

The extant manuscripts of the letters to Atticus are late and corrupt, the earliest dating from the end of the fourteenth century. Moreover, some of them break off long before the end, so that the situation gets worse and worse as the series goes on. We have a few fragments of earlier manuscripts, and, importantly, reports from a variety of sources, one of which disappeared in the sixteenth century, the Tornesianus, representing a superior tradition. For a full account see the introduction to my Cambridge edition.

In my critical notes I have not particularized the manuscript sources, but rather aimed to give warning where the reading in my text has little or no manuscript support (excluding some as too obvious and generally accepted to need mention). The notes in such a case give the manuscript reading followed in parenthesis by the name of the corrector. The siglum ς indicates inferior manuscript(s) or early edition(s). The fullest apparatus criticus is in H. Sjögren's edition (Uppsala, 1916–1960), but for most purposes Watt's Oxford Text of Books I–VIII or my Teubner or Beaujeu's Budé in the later Books (see below) will serve.

In the textual criticism and interpretation of the correspondence W. S. Watt's Oxford Text of the letters to Quintus and Brutus (1958) began a new era. Succeeding decades saw advances which might be hard to match within

the twentieth century for any Latin author except Manilius. The following editions of *Ad Atticum* incorporate much that had already appeared separately in periodicals, also my monograph *Towards a Text of Cicero Ad Atticum* (Cambridge, 1959):

D. R. Shackleton Bailey, *Ciceronis Epistulae ad Atticum IX–XVI* (Oxford Classical Text, 1961).

———*Cicero's Letters to Atticus* (with translation and commentary) 7 vols. (Cambridge, 1965–1970). Cited as *CLA* in notes to this translation.

———*M. Tullius Cicero, Epistulae ad Atticum* 2 vols. (Stuttgart, Bibliotheca Teubneriana, 1987–1988).

W. S. Watt, *Ciceronis Epistulae ad Atticum I–VIII* (Oxford Classical Text, 1965).

The editions of the later Books in the Budé series, vols. VI–XI (1980–1996), by the late J. Beaujeu are valuable not only for their admirable introductions and notes but for a text which, if containing little of original importance, deserves praise for thorough scholarship and independent and open-minded judgment. I have reviewed it volume by volume in *Gnomon*. Also noteworthy is the series of *Gnomon* reviews by F. R. D. Goodyear (1962–1986). They can be found in his posthumously collected *Papers on Latin Literature* (Duckworth, 1992).

The text of this Loeb Classical Library edition is almost the same as in the Teubner, differences (mostly promotions of conjectures from its apparatus) being indicated by an asterisk in my critical notes.

It has of course been impossible in this edition to argue controversial readings and interpretations. The dating of the letters too raises many difficult problems not to be

discussed here, especially in the twelfth and thirteenth Books.

Bibliographical Note

A list of relevant literature might fill a volume. What follows can represent only a beginning.

As a general history of the period T. Rice Holmes, *The Roman Republic* (3 vols., Oxford University Press, 1923), can still be recommended. Mommsen's *History of Rome*, however outmoded its ideological bias, keeps its fascination as a work of genius. R. Syme's *Roman Revolution* (Oxford University Press, 1939) is an established classic (largely, however, concerned with the period after Cicero's death). Anything by E. Badian and P. A. Brunt is of value, but much of their work is for specialists. The same goes for E. S. Gruen's challenging *Last Generation of the Roman Republic* (University of California Press, 1974). Notable for penetrating analysis of the problems and determinants underlying late-republican politics is the work of Christian Meier, especially *Res Publica Amissa* (Wiesbaden, Steiner, 1966) and *Caesars Bürgerkrieg* (1964; republished in *Entstehung des Begriffs Demokratie*, Frankfurt am Main, Suhrkamp Verlag, 1970); unfortunately it has not been translated.

Gaston Boissier's *Cicéron et ses amis* (1865; Engl. tr. 1897) can never be superseded as a delightful and sympathetic account of the man and his milieu. Numerous biographies exist in various languages, including M. Gelzer, *Cicero: ein biographischer Versuch* (Wiesbaden, Steiner, 1969); D. Stockton, *Cicero: A Political Biography* (Oxford University Press, 1971); E. Rawson, *Cicero* (Penguin

Books, 1975). My own biography, *Cicero* (Duckworth, 1971), may be regarded as a biographical and historical companion to the correspondence.

G. O. Hutchinson (*Cicero's Correspondence,* Oxford 1998) has compiled a bibliography of some 400 items, most of them issued in the last three decades of this century.

The only modern commentary on the entire correspondence, that of Tyrrell and Purser (=TP: 7 vols., 1904–33), has been described as a mine of honest misinformation.

CICERO'S
LETTERS TO ATTICUS

1 (I.5)

Scr. Romae m. Nov. an. 68

CICERO ATTICO SAL.

1 Quantum dolorem acceperim et quanto fructu sim privatus et forensi et domestico Luci, fratris nostri, morte in primis pro nostra consuetudine tu existimare potes. nam mihi omnia quae iucunda ex humanitate alterius et moribus homini accidere possunt ex illo accidebant. qua re non dubito quin tibi quoque id molestum sit, cum et meo dolore moveare et ipse omni virtute officioque ornatissimum tuique et sua sponte et meo sermone amantem adfinem amicumque amiseris.

2 Quod ad me scribis de sorore tua, testis erit tibi ipsa quantae mihi curae fuerit ut Quinti fratris animus in eam esset is qui esse deberet. quem cum esse offensiorem arbitrarer, eas litteras ad eum misi quibus et placarem ut fratrem et monerem ut minorem et obiurgarem ut errantem. itaque ex iis quae postea saepe ab eo ad me scripta sunt confido ita esse omnia ut et oporteat et velimus.

3 De litterarum missione, sine causa abs te accusor. numquam enim a Pomponia nostra certior sum factus esse cui dare litteras possem; porro autem neque mihi accidit

1 (I.5)

Rome, November 68

CICERO TO ATTICUS

Knowing me as well as you do, you can appreciate better than most how deeply my cousin Lucius' death has grieved me, and what a loss it means to me both in public and in private life. All the pleasure that one human being's kindness and charm can give another I had from him. So I do not doubt that you too are sorry; for you will feel my distress, and you yourself have lost a family connection and a friend, one who possessed every good quality and disposition to serve others, and who loved you both of his own accord and from hearing me speak of you.

You write to me of your sister. She will tell you herself how anxious I have been that my brother Quintus should feel towards her as a husband ought. Thinking that he was rather out of temper I sent him a letter designed to mollify him as a brother, advise him as my junior, and scold him as a man on the wrong track; and from what he has since written to me on a number of occasions I feel confident that all is as it ought to be and as we should wish.

About letter dispatches, you find fault with me unjustly. Pomponia has never told me of any person to whom I could give one, and furthermore I myself as it happens have had

ut haberem qui in Epirum proficisceretur nequedum te Athenis esse audiebamus. 4 de Acutiliano autem negotio, quod mihi mandaras, ut primum a tuo digressu Romam veni, confeceram; sed accidit ut et contentione nihil opus esset et ut ego, qui in te satis consili statuerim esse, mallem Peducaeum tibi consilium per litteras quam me dare. etenim cum multos dies auris meas Acutilio dedissem, cuius sermonis genus tibi notum esse arbitror, non mihi grave duxi scribere ad te de illius querimoniis, cum eas audire, quod erat subodiosum, leve putassem. sed abs te ipso qui me accusas unas mihi scito litteras redditas esse, cum et oti ad scribendum plus et facultatem dandi maiorem habueris.

5 Quod scribis, etiam si cuius animus in te esset offensior, a me recolligi oportere, <teneo>[1] quid dicas neque id neglexi; sed est miro quodam modo adfectus. ego autem quae dicenda fuerunt de te non praeterii; quid autem contendendum esset ex tua putabam voluntate m<e> statuere oportere. quam si ad me perscripseris, intelleges me neque diligentiorem esse voluisse quam tu esses neque neglegentiorem fore quam tu velis.

6 De Tadiana re, mecum Tadius locutus est te ita scripsisse, nihil esse iam quod laboraretur, quoniam hereditas usu capta esset. id mirabamur te ignorare, de tutela legitima, in qua dicitur esse puella, nihil usu capi posse.

7 Epiroticam emptionem gaudeo tibi placere. quae tibi

[1] *add. Orelli*

[1] Known only from the references here and in Letters 4 and 9.
[2] L. Lucceius.

no one going to Epirus and we don't yet hear of you in Athens. Then as to the Acutilius business,[1] I had discharged your commission as soon as I got back to Rome after you left. But, as it turned out, there was no urgency, and reckoning that you were quite capable of making up your own mind I preferred Peducaeus to write and advise you rather than myself. And really, considering I lent my ears day after day to Acutilius, with whose style of conversation I dare say you are well acquainted, I should not have found it too onerous to write to you about his grumbles when I made light of listening to them, which *was* just a little tedious. But let me tell you that only one letter has reached me from *you*, my accuser, though you have more time for writing and more opportunities to send.

You say that even if a certain person[2] were out of humour with you I ought to bring him round. I understand your meaning and have not been remiss, but he is marvellously hipped. I did not fail to say the proper things about you, but I felt I ought to decide how far to press in the light of your wishes. If you will explain them to me you will see that, while I did not want to pay more attention to the matter than you did yourself, I shall pay no less than you desire.

On the Tadius matter, Tadius tells me that he has heard from you to the effect that there is no need to worry any longer as the estate is his by usucapion.[3] We are surprised you don't know that nothing can be alienated by usucapion from a legal tutelage, which is said to be the girl's position.

I am glad you are pleased with your purchase in

[3] Establishment of title by possession. The Tadius matter is very complicated.

mandavi et quae tu intelleges convenire nostro Tusculano velim, ut scribis, cures, quod sine molestia tua facere poteris. nam nos ex omnibus molestiis et laboribus uno illo in loco conquiescimus.

8 Quintum fratrem cottidie exspectamus. Terentia magnos articulorum dolores habet. et te et sororem tuam et matrem maxime diligit salutemque tibi plurimam adscribit et Tulliola, deliciae nostrae. cura ut valeas et nos ames et tibi persuadeas te a me fraterne amari.

2 (I.6)

Scr. Romae paulo post VIII *Kal. Dec. an.* 68 *(§ 2)*

CICERO ATTICO SAL.

1 Non committam posthac ut me accusare de epistularum neglegentia possis; tu modo videto in tanto otio ut par in hoc mihi sis.

Domum Rabirianam Neapoli, quam tu iam dimensam et exaedificatam animo habebas, M. Font‹e›ius emit HS CCCIƆƆƆXXX. id te scire volui, si quid forte ea res ad cogitationes tuas pertineret.

2 Quintus frater, ut mihi videtur, quo volumus animo est in Pomponiam et cum ea nunc in Arpinatibus praediis erat et secum habebat hominem χρηστομαθῆ, D. Turranium.

Pater[1] nobis decessit a. d. VIII Kal. Dec.

Haec habebam fere quae te scire vellem. tu velim, si qua ornamenta γυμνασιώδη reperire poteris quae loci sint

[1] frater *Sternkopf*

---

[4] Atticus had recently bought his estate at Buthrotum.

Epirus.[4] Yes, do please look after my commissions and anything else that may strike you as suitable to my place in Tusculum, so far as you can without putting yourself to too much trouble. It is the one place where I rest from all troubles and toils.

We are expecting Quintus back any day. Terentia has a bad attack of rheumatism. She is very fond of you and of your sister and mother, and sends her best love, as does my darling little Tullia. Take care of yourself and your affection for me; and be sure of my brotherly affection in return.

2 (I.6)

Rome, shortly after 23 November 68

CICERO TO ATTICUS

I shall not give you any further reason to complain of me as a casual correspondent. Mind on your side that with so much time on your hands you keep pace with me in this respect.

The Rabirius house in Naples, which is already laid out and architecturally complete in your mind, has been bought by M. Fonteius for HS 130,000. I wanted you to know this in case it might bear on your plans.

My brother Quintus seems to me to feel towards Pomponia as we wish and is now with her on his estates at Arpinum. He has with him one D. Turranius, a scholarly person.

We lost our father on 23 November.

That is about all I have to tell you. If you succeed in finding any objets d'art suitable for a lecture hall, which

eius quem tu non ignoras, ne praetermittas. nos Tusculano ita delectamur ut nobismet ipsis tum denique cum illo venimus placeamus. quid agas omnibus de rebus et quid acturus sis fac nos quam diligentissime certiores.

3 (I.7)

Scr. Romae ante Id. Febr. an. 67

<CICERO ATTICO SAL.>

Apud matrem recte est eaque nobis curae est. L. Cincio HS $\overline{\text{XX}}$CD constitui me curaturum Id. Febr. tu velim ea quae nobis emisse <te> et parasse scribis des operam ut quam primum habeamus. et velim cogites, id quod mihi pollicitus es, quem ad modum bibliothecam nobis conficere possis. omnem spem delectationis nostrae, quam cum in otium venerimus habere volumus, in tua humanitate positam habemus.

4 (I.8)

Scr. Romae post Id. Febr. an. 67 (§ 1)

CICERO ATTICO SAL.

1 Apud te est ut volumus. mater tua et soror a me Quintoque fratre diligitur. cum Acutilio sum locutus. is sibi negat a suo procuratore quicquam scriptum esse et miratur istam controversiam fuisse, quod ille recusarat satis dare amplius abs te non peti. quod te de Tadiano negotio decidisse[1] scribis,

[1] decepisses *vel* -sset *vel* -sse (*Hervagius*)

would do for you know where,[1] I hope you won't let them slip. I am delighted with my place at Tusculum, so much so that I feel content with myself when, and only when, I get there. Let me know in full detail about everything you are doing and intending to do.

3 (I.7)

Rome, before 13 February 67

CICERO TO ATTICUS

All is in order at your mother's and I am not forgetting her. I have arranged to pay L. Cincius HS 20,400 on the Ides of February. I should be grateful if you would see that I get the articles which you say you have bought and have ready for me as soon as possible. And please give some thought to how you are to procure a library for me as you have promised. All my hopes of enjoying myself as I want to do when I get some leisure depend upon your kindness.

4 (I.8)

Rome, after 13 February 67

CICERO TO ATTICUS

All is as we wish *chez toi*. Quintus and I are taking good care of your mother and sister. I have had a talk with Acutilius. He says that he has heard nothing from his agent and expresses surprise that this dispute should have arisen, because he (the agent) had refused to give security against any further claim on you. So you have reached a settlement

[1] The 'Academy' at Tusculum.

id ego Tadio et gratum esse intellexi et magno opere iucundum. ille noster amicus, vir mehercule optimus et mihi amicissimus, sane tibi iratus est. hoc si quanti tu aestimes sciam, tum quid mihi elaborandum sit scire possim.

2 L. Cincio HS ccIↃↃ ccIↃↃ cccc pro signis Megaricis, ut tu ad me scripseras, curavi. Hermae tui Pentelici cum capitibus aëneis, de quibus ad me scripsisti, iam nunc me admodum delectant. qua re velim et eos et signa et cetera quae tibi eius loci et nostri studi et tuae elegantiae esse videbuntur quam plurima quam primumque mittas, et maxime quae tibi gymnasi xystique videbuntur esse. nam in eo genere sic studio efferimur, ut abs te adiuvandi, ab aliis prope reprehendendi simus. si Lentuli navis non erit, quo tibi placebit imponito.

3 Tulliola, deliciolae nostrae, tuum munusculum flagitat et me ut sponsorem appellat. mihi autem abiurare certius est quam dependere.

5 (I.9)

Scr. Romae m. Mart. aut Apr. an. 67

CICERO ATTICO SAL.

1 Nimium raro nobis abs te litterae adferuntur, cum et multo tu facilius reperias qui Romam proficiscantur quam ego qui Athenas et certius tibi sit me esse Romae quam mihi

---

[1] Lucceius.

[2] Square pedestals or posts surmounted by heads of deities, Heracles in this instance. 'Megarian' and 'Pentelic' mean made of marble from Megara and Mt Pentelicon, near Athens, respectively.

about the Tadius business. I can see that Tadius is grateful and very pleased. That friend of ours,[1] an excellent fellow really and very friendly to me, is much annoyed with you. If I knew how much importance you attach to that, I should then be able to judge how far I ought to exert myself.

I have paid L. Cincius the HS 20,400 for the Megarian statues in accordance with your earlier letter. I am already quite enchanted with your Pentelic herms[2] with the bronze heads, about which you write to me, so please send them and the statues and any other things you think would do credit to the place in question and to my enthusiasm and to your good taste, as many and as soon as possible, especially any you think suitable to a lecture hall and colonnade. I am so carried away by my enthusiasm for this sort of thing that it's your duty to help me—and other people's perhaps to scold me. If a ship of Lentulus'[3] is not available, put them aboard any you think fit.

My darling Tullia is demanding your little present and calling on me as surety. I have made up my mind to repudiate sooner than pay up.

5 (I.9)

Rome, March or April 67

CICERO TO ATTICUS

Letters from you reach me all too seldom, though travellers to Rome are much easier for you to come by than travellers to Athens for me, and you are more sure of my being in Rome than I of your being in Athens. This uncer-

[3] Perhaps Lentulus Spinther (Consul in 57).

te Athenis. itaque propter hanc dubitationem meam brevior haec ipsa epistula est, quod, cum incertus essem ubi esses, nolebam illum nostrum familiarem sermonem in alienas manus devenire.

2 Signa Megarica et Hermas de quibus ad me scripsisti vehementer exspecto. quicquid eiusdem generis habebis dignum Academia tibi quod videbitur, ne dubitaris mittere et arcae nostrae confidito. genus hoc est voluptatis meae. quae *γυμνασιώδη* maxime sunt, ea quaero. Lentulus navis suas pollicetur. peto abs te ut haec cures diligenter.

Thyillus te rogat et ego eius rogatu Εὐμολπιδῶν *πάτρια*.

6 (I.10)

Scr. in Tusculano c. m. Mai. an. 67

(CICERO ATTICO SAL.)

1 Cum essem in Tusculano (erit hoc tibi pro illo tuo 'cum essem in Ceramico'), verum tamen cum ibi essem, Roma puer a sorore tua missus epistulam mihi abs te adlatam dedit nuntiavitque eo ipso die post meridiem iturum eum qui ad te proficisceretur. eo factum est ut epistulae tuae rescriberem aliquid, brevitate temporis tam pauca cogerer scribere.

2 Primum tibi de nostro amico placando aut etiam plane restituendo polliceor. quod ego etsi mea sponte ante faciebam, eo nunc tamen et agam studiosius et contendam

---

[1] The unknown Greek quotation, if quotation it is, refers to the Eleusinian mysteries. Evidently Atticus already knew what kind of information was needed.

tainty makes my present letter shorter than it would have been, for not being sure of your whereabouts I don't want our familiar chat to get into strangers' hands.

I am eagerly expecting the Megarian statues and the herms you wrote to me about. Anything you may have of the same sort which you think suitable for the Academy, don't hesitate to send it and trust my purse. This is how my fancy takes me. Things that are specially suitable for a lecture hall are what I want. Lentulus promises his ships. Please attend to this carefully.

Thyillus requests you, and so at his request do I, for information about 'the rites ancestral of Eumolpus' clan.'[1]

6 (I.10)

Tusculum, ca. May 67

CICERO TO ATTICUS

I was at my place in Tusculum—that will do in return for your 'I was in Ceramicus'—anyhow I was there, when a boy sent from Rome by your sister brought me a letter which had come in from you, and told me that someone was leaving to join you this very afternoon. That is how I come to be writing an answer to your letter and how I am obliged by shortage of time to write such a brief one.

First, I give you my word about appeasing our friend[1] or even bringing him round altogether. I have been doing this already of my own accord, but I shall now set to work more zealously and press him harder because I think I see

[1] Lucceius.

ab illo vehementius quod tantam ex epistula voluntatem eius rei tuam perspicere videor. hoc te intellegere volo, pergraviter illum esse offensum; sed quia nullam video gravem subesse causam, magno opere confido illum fore in officio et in nostra potestate.

3 Signa nostra et Hermeraclas, ut scribis, cum commodissime poteris, velim imponas, et si quid aliud *οἰκεῖον* eius loci quem non ignoras reperies, et maxime quae tibi palaestrae gymnasique videbuntur esse. etenim ibi sedens haec ad te scribebam, ut me locus ipse admoneret. praeterea typos tibi mando quos in tectorio atrioli possim

4 includere et putealia sigillata duo. bibliothecam tuam cave cuiquam despondeas, quamvis acrem amatorem inveneris; nam ego omnis meas vindemiolas eo reservo, ut illud subsidium senectuti parem.

5 De fratre, confido ita esse ut semper volui et elaboravi. multa signa sunt eius rei, non minimum quod soror praegnans est.

6 De comitiis meis, et tibi me permisisse memini et ego iam pridem hoc communibus amicis qui te exspectant praedico, te non modo non arcessi a me sed prohiberi, quod intellegam multo magis interesse tua te agere quod agendum esset hoc tempore quam mea te adesse comitiis. proinde eo animo te velim esse quasi mei negoti causa in ista loca missus esses. me autem eum et offendes erga te et audies quasi mihi si quae parta erunt non modo te praesente sed per te parta sint.

Tulliola tibi diem dat, sponsorem non appellat.

---

[2] Kerbs to surround wells.

[3] To the Praetorship.

from your letter how earnestly you wish it. I do want you to realize that he is very seriously offended. But since, so far as I can see, there is no serious reason behind it, I am full of confidence that he will behave as a friend should and as I tell him.

Yes, I should be grateful if you would ship when you most conveniently can my statues and Heracles herms and anything else you may discover that would be *convenable* you know where, especially things you think suitable to a palaestra and lecture hall. In fact I am sitting there now as I write, so that the place itself is a reminder. Further please get me some bas-reliefs which I can lay in the stucco of the small entrance hall and two figured puteals.[2] Mind you don't engage your library to anyone, no matter how ardent a wooer you may find. I am putting all my little gleanings aside to pay for this standby for my old age.

As to my brother, I feel sure things are as I have always wished and worked for. There are many signs of that, not least the fact that your sister is expecting a baby.

As regards my election,[3] I do not forget that I left it to you, and I have all along been giving out to common friends who expect you back that, far from summoning you, I have told you *not* to come because I realize that it is much more important to you to be doing what you had to do at the present time than to me to have you here for the election. Accordingly I should like you to feel as though you had been sent to Greece on business of mine. My attitude will be just as though you had not only been present but responsible for any success that may come my way. So you will find and so you will hear from others.

Little Tullia is putting you into court, without calling on the surety.

7 (I.11)

Scr. Romae m. Sext. an. 67

CICERO ATTICO SAL.

1 Et mea sponte faciebam antea et post duabus epistulis tuis perdiligenter in eandem rationem scriptis magno opere sum commotus. eo accedebat hortator adsiduus Sallustius, ut agerem quam diligentissime cum Lucceio de vestra vetere gratia reconcilianda. sed cum omnia fecissem, non modo eam voluntatem eius quae fuerat erga te reciperare non potui verum ne causam quidem elicere immutatae voluntatis. tametsi iactat ille quidem illud suum[1] arbitrium et ea quae iam tum cum aderas offendere eius animum intellegebam, tamen habet quiddam profecto quod magis in animo eius insederit, quod neque epistulae tuae neque nostra legatio tam potest facile delere quam tu praesens non modo oratione sed tuo vultu illo familiari tolles, si modo tanti putaris; id quod, si me audies et si humanitati tuae constare voles, certe putabis. ac ne illud mirere, cur, cum ego antea significarim tibi per litteras me sperare illum in nostra potestate fore, nunc idem videar diffidere, incredibile est quanto mihi videatur illius voluntas obstinatior et in hac iracundia obfirmatior. sed haec aut sanabuntur cum veneris aut ei molesta erunt in utro culpa erit.

2 Quod in epistula tua scriptum erat me iam ‹te›[2] arbitrari designatum esse, scito nihil tam exercitum esse nunc Romae quam candidatos omnibus iniquitatibus nec quando futura sint comitia sciri. verum haec audies de Philadelpho.

[1] tuum *Pius* [2] *add. SB* (*ante* iam *Lambinus*)

7 (I.11)

Rome, August 67

CICERO TO ATTICUS

I had been active of my own accord before, but your two very sedulous letters to the same purpose were a powerful stimulus. Add to that constant exhortation from Sallustius to do my utmost with Lucceius for the restoration of your old friendship. But after all I could do I have failed, not only to reestablish his former sentiments towards you but even to get out of him *why* his sentiments have changed. To be sure he flourishes that arbitration business of his and other grievances which I knew existed even before you left, but there must surely be something else which has taken deeper root in his mind, something that cannot so easily be removed either by your letters or by my ambassadorial effort as by yourself in person—not only what you say but your old familiar face; that is, if you think it worth the trouble, as you certainly will if you take my advice and don't wish to belie your own good heart. You may think it odd that I seem so pessimistic now after writing to you earlier that I expected him to do as I told him. The fact is, you can hardly believe how much stiffer I find his attitude and more obstinate in this dudgeon. But your return will cure it, or else whichever is to blame will be the sufferer.

When you wrote in one of your letters that you supposed I was already elected you little knew the worries of a candidate in Rome at the present time, with all kinds of injustices to plague him. No one knows when the elections will take place. But you'll hear all this from Philadelphus.

3 Tu velim quae nostrae Academiae parasti quam primum mittas. mire quam illius loci non modo usus sed etiam cogitatio delectat. libros vero tuos cave cuiquam tradas; nobis eos, quem ad modum scribis, conserva. summum me eorum studium tenet, sicut odium iam ceterarum rerum; quas tu incredibile est quam brevi tempore quanto deteriores offensurus sis quam reliquisti.

8 (I.3)

Scr. Romae ex. an. 67 (§ 2)

‹CICERO ATTICO SAL.›

1 Aviam tuam scito desiderio tui mortuam esse, et simul quod verita sit ne Latinae in officio non manerent et in montem Albanum hostias non adducerent. eius rei consolationem ad te L. Saufeium missurum esse arbitror.

2 Nos hic te ad mensem Ianuarium exspectamus ex quodam rumore an ex litteris tuis ad alios missis; nam ad me de eo nihil scripsisti.

Signa quae nobis curasti, ea sunt ad Caietam exposita. nos ea non vidimus; neque enim exeundi Roma potestas nobis fuit. misimus qui pro vectura solveret. te multum amamus quod ea abs te diligenter parvoque curata sunt.

3 Quod ad me saepe scripsisti de nostro amico placando, feci, et expertus sum omnia, sed mirandum in modum est animo abalienato; quibus de suspicionibus, etsi audisse te arbitror, tamen ex me cum veneris cognosces. Sallustium

[1] There seems to be some private allusion. 'Animals' = sacrificial victims.

Please send the things you have got for my Academy as soon as possible. The very thought of the place, let alone the actual use of it, gives me enormous pleasure. Mind you don't hand over your books to anybody. Keep them for me, as you say you will. I am consumed with enthusiasm for them, as with disgust for all things else. It's unbelievable in how short a time how much worse you will find them than you left them.

8 (I.3)

Rome, end of 67

CICERO TO ATTICUS

I have to tell you that your grandmother has died of missing you, and also because she was afraid the Latin Festival might not come up to scratch and bring the animals to Mt Albanus.[1] I expect L. Saufeius will be sending you an essay of condolence.

I am expecting you back by January, from a current rumour or it may be from letters of yours to other people—you have written nothing on the subject to me.

The statues you acquired for me have been disembarked at Caieta. I have not seen them, not having had an opportunity of leaving Rome. I have sent a man to pay the freight. I am most grateful to you for taking so much trouble and getting them cheaply.

You often write to me about mollifying our friend. I have made the attempt and tried all I know, but he is amazingly estranged. The suspicions which have made him so you shall learn from me when you get back, though I expect you have heard what they are. I could not induce

praesentem restituere in eius veterem gratiam non potui. hoc eo ad te scripsi quod is me accusare de te solebat. in se expertus est illum esse minus exorabilem, meum studium nec tibi defuisse.

Tulliolam C. Pisoni L. f. Frugi despondimus.

9 (I.4)

Scr. Romae an. 66 parte priore

CICERO ATTICO SAL.

1 Crebras exspectationes nobis tui commoves. nuper quidem, cum te iam adventare arbitraremur, repente abs te in mensem Quintilem reiecti sumus. nunc vero censeo,[1] quod commodo tuo facere poteris, venias ad id tempus quod scribis. obieris Quinti fratris comitia, nos longo intervallo viseris, Acutilianam controversiam transegeris. hoc me etiam Peducaeus ut ad te scriberem admonuit. putamus enim utile esse te aliquando iam rem transigere. mea intercessio parata et est et fuit.

2 Nos hic incredibili ac singulari populi voluntate de C. Macro transegimus. cui cum aequi fuissemus, tamen multo maiorem fructum ex populi existimatione illo damnato cepimus quam ex ipsius, si absolutus esset, gratia cepissemus.

3 Quod ad me de Hermathena scribis per mihi gratum

[1] sentio (*Hervagius*)

---

[1] For the Plebeian Aedileship.

[2] C. Licinius Macer, historian, antisenatorial politician, and father of the orator Calvus, had been on trial for extortion. Cicero as Praetor was president of the court.

him to get back to his old friendly footing with Sallustius, though *he* is on the spot. I tell you this because Sallustius used to tax me with failing *you*. He has found in his own case that our friend is not so easily placated, and that my efforts have not been wanting on your behalf any more than on his.

Tullia is engaged to C. Piso Frugi, son of Lucius.

9 (I.4)

Rome, first half of 66

CICERO TO ATTICUS

You keep on raising our hopes of your return. Recently we thought you were on your way, only to be suddenly put off until July. As things are, I think you should come back by the time you say, if you can do so conveniently. You will then be here for Quintus' elections,[1] you will see me after a long break, and you will settle your dispute with Acutilius. Peducaeus too has asked me to say this. We think it would be desirable for you to settle the business at long last. I am and have been at your disposal as intermediary.

Here in Rome my handling of C. Macer's[2] case has won popular approval to a really quite extraordinary degree. Though I was favourably disposed to him, I gained far more from popular sentiment by his conviction than I should have gained from *his* gratitude if he had been acquitted.

I am very grateful for what you say about the Her-

est. est ornamentum Academiae proprium meae, quod et Hermes commune est omnium et Minerva singulare est insigne eius gymnasi. qua re velim, ut scribis, ceteris quoque rebus quam plurimis eum locum ornes. quae mihi antea signa misisti, ea nondum vidi; in Formiano sunt, quo ego nunc proficisci cogitabam. illa omnia in Tusculanum deportabo. Caietam, si quando abundare coepero, ornabo. libros tuos conserva et noli desperare eos <me> meos facere posse. quod si adsequor, supero Crassum divitiis atque omnium vicos et prata contemno.

10 (I.1)

Scr. Romae paulo ante XVI *Kal. Sext. an. 65 (§ 1)*

CICERO ATTICO SAL.

1 Petitionis nostrae, quam tibi summae curae esse scio, huius modi ratio est, quod adhuc coniectura provideri possit. prensat unus P. Galba. sine fuco ac fallaciis more maiorum negatur. ut opinio est hominum, non aliena rationi nostrae fuit illius haec praepropera prensatio. nam illi ita negant vulgo ut mihi se debere dicant. ita quiddam spero nobis profici, cum hoc percrebrescit, plurimos nostros amicos inveniri. nos autem initium prensandi facere cogitabamus eo ipso <tempo>re quo tuum puerum cum his litteris proficisci Cincius dicebat, in campo comitiis tribuniciis a.

[3] A herm (see Letter 4, note 2) with head of Athena (Minerva), goddess of wisdom and wit.

[4] I.e. the villa, which lay between Caieta and Formiae.

[5] Probably proverbial, referring to a third-century Crassus

mathena.[3] It's an appropriate ornament for my Academy, since Hermes is the common emblem of all such places and Minerva special to that one. So please beautify it with other pieces, as you promise, as many as possible. I have not yet seen the statues you sent me earlier. They are in my house at Formiae, which I am now preparing to visit. I shall take them all up to Tusculum, and decorate Caieta[4] if and when I begin to have a surplus. Hold on to your books and don't despair of my being able to make them mine. If I manage that, I am richer than Crassus[5] and can afford to despise any man's manors and meadows.

10 (I.1)

Rome, shortly before 17 July 65

CICERO TO ATTICUS

The position as regards my candidature,[1] in which I know you are deeply interested, is as follows, so far as can be foreseen up to date: Only P. Galba is canvassing, and he is getting for answer a good old Roman 'No,' plain and unvarnished. It's generally thought that this premature canvass of his has rather helped my prospects, for people are commonly refusing him on the ground that they are obligated to me. So I hope to draw some advantage when the word goes round that a great many friends of mine are coming to light. I was thinking of starting my canvass just when Cincius says your boy is leaving with this letter, i.e.

who acquired the additional cognomen Dives ('Rich') for himself and his descendants.

[1] For the Consulship of 63.

d. XVI Kal. Sext. competitores, qui certi esse videbantur, Galba et Antonius et Q. Cornificius. puto te in hoc aut risisse aut ingemuisse. ut frontem ferias, sunt qui etiam Caesonium putent. nam Aquillium[1] non arbitramur, qui et negavit et iuravit morbum et illud suum regnum iudiciale opposuit. Catilina, si iudicatum erit meridie non lucere, certus erit competitor. de Aufidio et de Palicano non puto te exspectare dum scribam.

2 De his qui nunc petunt Caesar certus putatur. Thermus cum Silano contendere existimatur. qui sic inopes et ab amicis et existimatione sunt ut mihi videatur non esse ἀδύνατον Turium obducere; sed hoc praeter me nemini videtur. nostris rationibus maxime conducere videtur Thermum fieri cum Caesare. nemo est enim ex his qui nunc petunt qui, si in nostrum annum reciderit, firmior candidatus fore videatur, propterea quod curator est viae Flaminiae, quae tum erit absoluta sane facile. eum libenter nunc Caesari[2] consuli accuderim.[3] petitorum haec est informata adhuc cogitatio. nos in omni munere candidatorio fungendo summam adhibebimus diligentiam; et fortasse, quoniam videtur in suffragiis multum posse Gallia, cum Romae a iudiciis forum refrixerit, excurremus mense Sep-

[1] putent nam qui illum *al.* (*SB* : putent. Aquilium *edd.*)
[2] nunciteri *al.* (*Manutius*) [3] acciderim (*Bosius*)

---

[2] These phrases are ironical.

[3] Catiline was facing trial for extortion in Africa. He was acquitted.

[4] For the Consulship of 64.

[5] L. Julius Caesar. He was elected.

[6] Almost certainly identical with C. Marcius Figulus, the man

17 July, at the tribunician elections in the Campus. As apparently certain rivals I have Galba, Antonius, and Q. Cornificius. When you read this last I fancy you will either laugh or cry. Now get ready to slap your forehead: some folk think Caesonius may stand too! As for Aquillius, I don't expect he will. He has both said he won't and entered a plea of ill health and alleged his monarchy over the law courts in excuse.[2] If Catiline's jury finds that the sun doesn't shine at midday,[3] he will certainly be a candidate. I don't think you will be waiting for me to write about Aufidius and Palicanus.

Of the present candidates[4] Caesar[5] is regarded as a certainty. The other place is thought to lie between Thermus[6] and Silanus. They are so poorly off for friends and reputation that it doesn't seem to me an absolute impossibility to put Turius in their light, but I am alone in thinking so. From my point of view the best result would seem to be for Thermus to get in with Caesar, since he looks like being as strong a candidate as any of the present lot if he is left over to my year; the reason being that he is Curator of the Flaminian Way,[7] which will easily be finished by then. I should be happy to tack him on to Consul Caesar now. Such in outline is my present idea of the position as to candidatures. For my part I shall spare no pains in faithfully fulfilling the whole duty of a candidate, and perhaps, as Gaul looks like counting heavily in the voting, I shall run

actually elected, who will have been a Minucius Thermus before adoption. D. Junius Silanus (stepfather of M. Brutus) was elected the following year.

[7] The great north road of Italy, from Rome to Ariminum (Rimini). It was apparently under repair or improvement.

tembri legati ad Pisonem, ut Ianuario revertamur. cum perspexero voluntates nobilium, scribam ad te. cetera spero prolixa esse, his dumtaxat urbanis competitoribus. illam manum tu mihi cura ut praestes, quoniam propius abes, Pompei, nostri amici. nega me ei iratum fore si ad mea comitia non venerit. atque haec huius modi sunt.

3 Sed est quod abs te mihi ignosci pervelim. Caecilius, avunculus tuus, a P. Vario cum magna pecunia fraudaretur, agere coepit cum eius fratre Caninio Satyro de iis rebus quas eum dolo malo mancipio accepisse de Vario diceret. una agebant ceteri creditores, in quibus erat ‹L.›[4] Lucullus et P. Scipio et is quem putabant magistrum fore si bona venirent, L. Pontius — verum hoc ridiculum est de magistro. nunc cognosce rem. rogavit me Caecilius ut adessem contra Satyrum. dies fere nullus est quin hic Satyrus domum meam ventitet. observat L. Domitium maxime, me habet proximum. fuit et mihi et Quinto fratri magno 4 usui in nostris petitionibus. sane sum perturbatus, cum ipsius Satyri familiaritate tum Domiti, in quo uno maxime ambitio nostra nititur. demonstravi haec Caecilio, simul et illud ostendi, si ipse unus cum illo uno contenderet, me ei satis facturum fuisse; nunc, in causa universorum creditorum, hominum praesertim amplissimorum, qui sine eo quem Caecilius suo nomine perhiberet facile causam com-

[4] *add. Baiter*

---

[8] C. Calpurnius Piso (Consul in 67) was governor of Transalpine and Cisalpine Gaul.

[9] Cicero was afraid that Pompey might put up a candidate of his own.

down to join Piso's[8] staff in September, in the dead period after the courts have closed, returning in January. When I have made out the attitudes of the nobles I shall write to you. I hope the rest is plain sailing, at any rate as far as these local competitors are concerned. *You* must answer for the other phalanx, since you are not so far away, I mean our friend Pompey's. Tell him I shall not be offended if he doesn't turn up for my election![9]

Well, that's how it all stands. But I have something to tell you for which I very much hope you will forgive me. Your uncle Caecilius, having been defrauded by P. Varius of a large sum of money, has taken proceedings against Varius' cousin, Caninius Satyrus, for articles alleged to have been fraudulently conveyed to him by Varius. The other creditors are joined with him, including L. Lucullus, P. Scipio, and L. Pontius, who they expect will be receiver if it comes to a distraint. But this talk of a receiver is ridiculous. Now for the point. Caecilius asked me to appear against Satyrus. Well, hardly a day passes without this Satyrus calling on me. L. Domitius comes first in his attentions, I next. He made himself most useful both to me and to my brother Quintus when we were candidates. I was naturally most embarrassed in view of my friendship not only with Satyrus but with Domitius, on whom my hopes of success depend beyond any other man. I explained all this to Caecilius, making it clear at the same time that had the dispute been solely between himself and Satyrus I should have met his wishes. As it was, seeing that the whole group of creditors was involved, men moreover of the highest station who would easily maintain their common cause without help from anyone Caecilius might bring in on his own account, I suggested that it would be reasonable for him to make

munem sustinerent, aequum esse eum et officio meo consulere et tempori. durius accipere hoc mihi visus est quam vellem et quam homines belli solent, et postea prorsus ab instituta nostra paucorum dierum consuetudine longe refugit.

Abs te peto ut mihi hoc ignoscas et me existimes humanitate esse prohibitum ne contra amici summam existimationem miserrimo eius tempore venirem, cum is omnia sua studia et officia in me contulisset. quod si voles in me esse durior, ambitionem putabis mihi obstitisse. ego autem arbitror, etiam si id sit, mihi ignoscendum esse, 'ἐπεὶ οὐχ ἱερήιον οὐδὲ βοείην.' vides enim in quo cursu simus et quam omnis gratias non modo retinendas verum etiam acquirendas putemus. spero tibi me causam probasse, cupio quidem certe.

5 Hermathena tua valde me delectat et posita ita belle est ut totum gymnasium †eliu ἀνάθημα†[5] esse videatur. multum te amamus.

11 (I.2)

Scr. Romae paulo post superiorem

<CICERO ATTICO SAL.>

1 L. Iulio Caesare C. Marcio Figulo consulibus filiolo me auctum scito, salva Terentia.

[5] *varia codd.* : eius ἀν- *coni. Schütz*

---

[10] *Iliad*, 22.159: 'Since for no beast for sacrifice or ox hide were the twain striving . . . but they ran for the life of god-like Hector.'

[1] I.e., just elected. The mock-pompous opening travesties the ordinary dating of a year by its Consuls; not, however, to fix a day,

allowance for my obligations and my present position. I had the impression that he took this less kindly than I should have wished or than is usual among gentlemen, and from that time on he entirely dropped our friendly contacts which had begun only a few days previously.

May I ask you to forgive me over this, and to believe that it was good feeling that prevented me from appearing against a friend in great trouble, who had given me every support and service in his power, in a matter most gravely affecting his good name? If however you like to take a less charitable view, you may assume that the exigencies of my candidature made the stumbling block. *I* consider that even if it were so I might be pardoned, 'since for no hide of bull nor slaughtered beast . . . .'[10] You know the game I am playing and how vital I think it not only to keep old friends but to gain new ones. I hope you now see my point of view in the matter—I am certainly anxious that you should.

I am quite delighted with your Hermathena. It's so judiciously placed that the whole hall is like an offering at its feet(?). Many thanks.

11 (I.2)

Rome, shortly after 10 (I.1)

CICERO TO ATTICUS

I have the honour to inform you that I have become the father of a little son, L. Julius Caesar and C. Marcius Figulus being Consuls.[1] Terentia is well.

but to announce the result of the elections. Some editors omit the words as spurious.

Abs te iam[1] diu nihil litterarum. ego de meis ad te rationibus scripsi antea diligenter. hoc tempore Catilinam, competitorem nostrum, defendere cogitamus. iudices habemus quos volumus, summa accusatoris voluntate. spero, si absolutus erit, coniunctiorem illum nobis fore in ratione petitionis; sin aliter acciderit, humaniter feremus.

2 Tuo adventu nobis opus est maturo. nam prorsus summa hominum est opinio tuos familiaris, nobilis homines, adversarios honori nostro fore. ad eorum voluntatem mihi conciliandam maximo te mihi usui fore video. qua re Ianuario ineunte, ut constituisti, cura ut Romae sis.

12 (I.12)

Scr. Romae Kal. Ian. an. 61 (§ 4)

<CICERO ATTICO SAL.>

1 Teucris illa lentum sane negotium, neque Cornelius ad Tere<ntia>m postea rediit. opinor, ad Considium, Axium, Selicium confugiendum est; nam a Caecilio propinqui minore centesimis nummum movere non possunt. sed ut ad prima illa redeam, nihil ego illa impudentius, astutius, lentius vidi. 'libertum mitto.' 'Tito mandavi.' *σκήψεις* atque *ἀναβολαί*. sed nescio an *ταὐτόματον ἡμῶν*. nam mihi Pompeiani prodromi nuntiant aperte Pompeium acturum Antonio succedi oportere, eodemque tempore aget prae-

[1] etiam (*Boot*)

[2] See Letter 10, note 3. For some reason Cicero changed his mind. [3] I.e., the prosecutor (Cicero's future enemy P. Clodius) was in collusion with the defence.

It's a long time since I had a line from you. I have already written to you in detail about my prospects. At the moment I am proposing to defend my fellow candidate Catiline.[2] We have the jury we want, with full cooperation from the prosecution.[3] If he is acquitted I hope he will be more inclined to work with me in the campaign. But should it go otherwise, I shall bear it philosophically.

I need you home pretty soon. There is a decidedly strong belief abroad that your noble friends are going to oppose my election. Clearly you will be invaluable to me in gaining them over. So mind you are in Rome by the beginning of January as you arranged.

12 (I.12)

Rome, 1 January 61

CICERO TO ATTICUS

That Teucris[1] is an infernal slow coach, and Cornelius has not been back to Terentia since. I suppose I must resort to Considius or Axius or Selicius—as for Caecilius, his own blood relations can't prise a sesterce out of him at less than one percent per month. But to go back to what I was saying, for impudence, trickiness, and stickiness I have never met her like. 'I am sending a freedman,' 'I have sent word to Titus.'[2] Nothing but excuses and put-offs. But maybe there is a silver lining. Members of Pompey's advance guard tell me openly that Pompey is going to move for Antonius'

[1] C. Antonius, Cicero's colleague as Consul and now governor of Macedonia, had promised him a loan. Teucris seems to have been an intermediary, but the name (= 'woman of Troy') may be fictitious. [2] Presumably Atticus.

tor ad populum. res eius modi est ut ego nec per bonorum nec per popularem existimationem honeste possim hominem defendere, nec mihi libeat, quod vel maximum est.

2 etenim accedit[1] hoc, quod totum cuius modi sit mando tibi ut perspicias. libertum ego habeo, sane nequam hominem, Hilarum dico, ratiocinatorem et clientem tuum. de eo mihi Valerius interpres nuntiat Thyillusque se audisse scribit haec: esse hominem cum Antonio; Antonium porro in cogendis pecuniis dictitare partem mihi quaeri et a me custodem communis quaestus libertum esse missum. non sum mediocriter commotus, neque tamen credidi; sed certe aliquid sermonis fuit. totum investiga, cognosce, perspice et nebulonem illum, si quo pacto potes, ex istis locis amove. huius sermonis Valerius auctorem Cn. Plancium nominabat. mando tibi plane totum ut videas cuius modi sit.

3 Pompeium nobis amicissimum constat esse. divortium Muciae vehementer probatur. P. Clodium Appi f. credo te audisse cum veste muliebri deprehensum domi C. Caesaris cum sacrificium pro populo fieret, eumque per manus servulae servatum et eductum; rem esse insigni infamia. quod te moleste ferre certo scio.

4 Quid praeterea ad te scribam non habeo, et mehercule eram in scribendo conturbatior. nam puer festivus, anagnostes noster Sositheus, decesserat meque plus quam servi mors debere videbatur commoverat. tu velim saepe ad nos scribas. si rem nullam habebis, quod in buccam venerit scribito.

[1] accidit (*Otto*)

---

[3] Actually Cicero did defend him, in 59, but lost the case.

[4] The festival of the Good Goddess (see Glossary).

supersession, and a Praetor will simultaneously make a proposal to the Assembly. The case is such that I cannot defend the fellow without loss of credit;[3] public opinion, better-class and popular alike, would not stand it. Nor should I care to, which is the main thing. And there is something else—I must ask you to look into it for me thoroughly. I have a freedman, a thorough scoundrel—I refer to your accountant and client Hilarus. Valerius the interpreter sends me word of him, and Thyillus too writes that he has heard, as follows: that the fellow is with Antonius; and that Antonius, when levying money, is in the habit of saying that part of it is for me and that I have sent my freedman to keep an eye on our joint profits. I was a good deal disturbed, though I didn't believe it. But there has certainly been some talk. Investigate the whole thing and find out just what has been going on; and if you can manage it, get that scamp out of the country. Valerius gives Cn. Plancius as his authority for the talk. I leave the whole thing entirely in your hands. See what's in it.

It's generally agreed that Pompey is very much my friend. His divorcing Mucia is warmly approved. I imagine you will have heard that P. Clodius, son of Appius, was caught dressed up as a woman in C. Caesar's house at the national sacrifice,[4] and that he owed his escape alive to the hands of a servant girl—a spectacular scandal. I am sure it distresses you.

I have nothing else to tell you. As a matter of fact I am writing in some distress of mind. My *lecteur* Sositheus, a charming lad, has died, and it has affected me more than the death of a slave perhaps ought to do. I hope you will write to me often. If you lack a topic, just put down whatever comes into your head.

Kal. Ian. M. Messalla M. Pisone coss.

13 (I.13)

Scr. Romae VI *Kal. Febr. an. 61 (§ 6)*

CICERO ATTICO SAL.

1 Accepi tuas tris iam epistulas: unam a M. Cornelio quam a Tribus ei Tabernis, ut opinor, dedisti, alteram quam mihi Canusinus tuus hospes reddidit, tertiam quam, ut scribis, iam ora[1] soluta de phaselo dedisti; quae fuerunt omnes, ‹ut› rhetorum pueri[2] loquuntur, cum humanitatis sparsae sale tum insignes amoris notis. quibus epistulis sum equidem abs te lacessitus ad rescribendum, sed idcirco sum tardior quod non invenio fidelem tabellarium. quotus enim quisque est qui epistulam paulo graviorem ferre possit nisi eam perlectione relevarit? accedit eo quod mihi non, ut quisque in Epirum proficiscitur, ‹ita ad te proficisci videtur›.[3] ego enim te arbitror caesis apud Amaltheam tuam victimis statim esse ad Sicyonem oppugnandum profectum, neque tamen id ipsum certum habeo, quando ad Antonium proficiscare aut quid in Epiro temporis ponas. ita neque Achaicis hominibus neque Epiroticis paulo liberiores litteras committere audeo.

2 Sunt autem post discessum a me tuum res dignae lit-

[1] anc(h)ora (*Dahlman, duce Casaubon*)
[2] rhetorum pure (*Madvig*). [3] *add. SB*

---

[1] Like a general before a campaign.

[2] A nymph, nurse of Zeus. There was a chapel dedicated to her on Atticus' Buthrotian estate.

Kalends of January, M. Messalla and M. Piso being Consuls.

13 (I.13)

Rome, 25 January 61

CICERO TO ATTICUS

Three letters from you have now come to hand, the first by M. Cornelius, given him I think at Tres Tabernae, the second forwarded to me by your host at Canusium, the third dispatched from the boat 'as they loosed the cable': all of them, to speak euphuistically, not only sprinkled with the salt of courtesy but also distinguished by tokens of affection. In them you challenged a reply, but I have been rather slow in making one because I can't find a trustworthy carrier. There are so few who can carry a letter of any substance without lightening the weight by perusal. And then, I don't feel sure that any and every traveller to Epirus is on his way to you. For I imagine that no sooner had you sacrificed[1] at the altar of your Amalthea[2] than you set off for the siege of Sicyon,[3] though even that I am not sure about, I mean when you are going to join Antonius or how much time you are spending in Epirus. Accordingly I dare not trust letters of a more or less confidential sort to either Achaeans[4] or Epirotes.

Since you left me there are things that well deserve a

[3] I.e., 'You left Buthrotum almost immediately in order to visit C. Antonius and ask him to put pressure on the town of Sicyon'—which owed Atticus money.

[4] Inhabitants of Greece proper.

teris nostris, sed non committendae eius modi periculo ut aut interire aut aperiri aut intercipi possint. primum igitur scito primum me non esse rogatum sententiam praepositumque esse nobis pacificatorem Allobrogum, idque admurmurante senatu neque me invito esse factum. sum enim et ab observando homine perverso liber et ad dignitatem in re publica retinendam contra illius voluntatem solutus, et ille secundus in dicendo locus habet auctoritatem paene principis, voluntatem non nimis devinctam beneficio consulis. tertius est Catulus, quartus, si etiam hoc quaeris, Hortensius. consul autem ipse parvo animo et pravo tamen, cavillator genere illo moroso quod etiam sine dicacitate ridetur, facie magis quam facetiis ridiculus, nihil agens in[4] re publica, seiunctus ab optimatibus, a quo nihil speres boni rei publicae quia non vult, nihil metuas mali quia non audet. eius autem collega et in me perhonorificus
3 et partium studiosus ac defensor bonarum. qui nunc leviter inter se dissident, sed vereor ne hoc quod infectum est serpat longius. credo enim te audisse, cum apud Caesarem pro populo fieret, venisse eo muliebri vestitu virum, idque sacrificium cum virgines instaurassent, mentionem a Q. Cornificio in senatu factam (is fuit princeps, ne tu forte aliquem nostrum putes); postea rem ex senatus consulto

[4] cum (ς)

---

[5] The Consulars spoke each year in an order predetermined by the Consul presiding at the first meeting. The Allobroges, the principal tribe of Narbonese Gaul, being in revolt, C. Piso, Consul in 67, may be called their 'pacifier' in irony, as having oppressed them during his governorship (Cicero had defended him in 63 on

letter of mine, but I must not expose such to the risk of getting lost or opened or intercepted. First then you may care to know that I have *not* been given first voice in the Senate, the peacemaker[5] of the Allobroges being put in front of me—at which the House murmured but I myself was not sorry. I am thereby relieved of any obligation to be civil to a cross-grained individual and left free to maintain my political standing in opposition to his wishes. Moreover the second place carries almost as much prestige as the first, while one's inclinations are not too much fettered by one's sense of the consular favour. Catulus comes third, Hortensius, if you are still interested, fourth. The Consul[6] himself is of petty but perverse mentality, given to the sort of peevish sneer that raises a laugh even in the absence of any wit. His *moue* is funnier than his *mot*. He is politically inactive and stands aloof from the optimates, having neither will to make him politically useful nor courage to make him dangerous. His colleague however is most complimentary to me personally and a zealous champion of the right side. At present their differences are slight enough, but I am afraid that a certain infected spot may spread. I expect you have heard that at the national sacrifice in Caesar's residence a *man* in woman's clothes got in, and that after the Vestals had repeated the ceremony Q. Cornificius (he took the lead, in case you think it was one of us[7]) raised the matter in the Senate. It was then referred back by

a charge of wrongfully executing a provincial). But the word used normally means 'peacemaker,' and may possibly refer to otherwise unrecorded diplomatic activity on Piso's part.

[6] M. Pupius Piso.

[7] I.e., a Consular.

ad virgines atque ad pontifices relatam idque ab iis nefas esse decretum; deinde ex senatus consulto consules rogationem promulgasse; uxori Caesarem nuntium remisisse. in hac causa Piso amicitia P. Clodi ductus operam dat ut ea rogatio quam ipse fert, et fert ex senatus consulto et de religione, antiquetur. Messalla vehementer adhuc agit <et> severe. boni viri precibus Clodi removentur a causa, operae comparantur. nosmet ipsi, qui Lycurgei a principio fuissemus, cottidie demitigamur. instat et urget Cato. quid multa? vereor ne haec †iniecta† a bonis, defensa ab improbis magnorum rei publicae malorum causa sit.

4 Tuus autem ille amicus (scin quem dicam? de quo tu ad me scripsisti, postea quam non auderet reprehendere laudare coepisse) nos, ut ostendit, admodum diligit, amplecitur, amat, aperte laudat, occulte, sed ita ut perspicuum sit, invidet. nihil come, nihil simplex, nihil *ἐν τοῖς πολιτικοῖς* illustre, nihil honestum, nihil forte, nihil liberum. sed haec ad te scribam alias subtilius. nam neque adhuc mihi satis nota sunt et huic terrae filio nescio cui committere epistulam tantis de rebus non audeo.

5 Provincias praetores nondum sortiti sunt. res eodem est loci quo reliquisti. *τοποθεσίαν* quam postulas Miseni et

---

[8] Pompeia, with whom Clodius was supposed to be having an affair. Hence Caesar's explanation: 'Caesar's wife must be above suspicion.'

[9] I.e., all for stern measures, probably with reference to an Athenian orator who made a hobby of prosecutions rather than the Spartan lawgiver.

[10] Pompey.

[11] Including Q. Cicero.

senatorial decree to the Vestals and College of Pontiffs, who pronounced that the occurrence constituted a sacrilege. Then by senatorial decree the Consuls promulgated a bill. And Caesar sent his wife[8] notice of divorce. Such being the position, Piso out of friendship for P. Clodius is working for the rejection of the bill which he is himself proposing, and proposing moreover under a senatorial decree on a matter of religion. Messalla is so far taking a strong and stringent line. The honest men are yielding to Clodius' pleas and dropping out. Gangs of roughs are in formation. I myself, though I was quite a Lycurgus[9] to start with, am softening every day. Cato presses and prods. All in all, I am afraid that what with neglect (?) by the honest men and resistance by the rascals these proceedings may be productive of great mischief in the body politic.

As to that friend of yours[10] (you know whom I mean? The person of whom you write to me that he began to praise when he no longer dared to criticize), he professes the highest regard for me and makes a parade of warm affection, praising on the surface while below it, but not so far below that it's difficult to see, he's jealous. Awkward, tortuous, politically paltry, shabby, timid, disingenuous—but I shall go more into detail on another occasion. As yet I am not sufficiently *au fait* with the topic, and I dare not entrust a letter on such high matters to this who knows what of a messenger.

The Praetors[11] have not yet drawn lots for their provinces. The matter stands where it stood when you left. I shall put in my speech[12] the topographical description of

[12] Probably a speech of 62 in reply to Q. Metellus Nepos which Cicero was now editing.

Puteolorum includam orationi meae. 'a. d. III Non. Dec.' mendose fuisse animadverteram. quae laudas ex orationibus, mihi crede, valde mihi placebant, sed non audebam antea dicere. nunc vero, quod a te probata sunt, multo mi Ἀττικώτερα videntur, in illam orationem Metellinam addidi quaedam. liber tibi mittetur, quoniam te amor nostri φιλορήτορα reddidit.

6 Novi tibi quidnam scribam? quid? etiam. Messalla consul Autronianam domum emit HS ⌈CXXXIIII⌉.[5] 'quid id ad me?' inquis. tantum, quod ea emptione et nos bene emisse iudicati sumus et homines intellegere coeperunt licere amicorum facultatibus in emendo ad dignitatem aliquam pervenire. Teucris illa lentum negotium est, sed tamen est in spe. tu ista confice. a nobis liberiorem epistulam exspecta.

VI Kal. Febr. M. Messalla M. Pisone coss.

14 (I.14)

Scr. Romae Id. Febr. an. 61 (§ 7)

‹CICERO ATTICO SAL.›

1 Vereor ne putidum sit scribere ad te quam sim occupatus, sed tamen ita distinebar ut vix huic tantulae epistulae tempus habuerim atque id ereptum e summis occupationibus.

Prima contio Pompei qualis fuisset scripsi ad te antea: non iucunda miseris, inanis improbis, beatis non grata, bonis non gravis. itaque frigebat. tum Pisonis consulis im-

[5] *varia codd.* : ⌈XXXIII⌉ *Constans*

Misenum and Puteoli which you ask for. I had noticed that '3 December' was an error. Of the things you praise in the speeches I had, let me tell you, a pretty good opinion, though I did not dare to say so before; now I assure you they look to me far more Attic than ever in the light of your approbation. I have made some additions to the Metellus one, and shall send you the volume, since affection for me has made you an amateur of oratory.

What news have I to tell you? Why yes, Consul Messalla has bought Autronius' house for HS 13,400,000. You wonder what concern it is of yours. Only that after this transaction I am considered to have made a good bargain, and folk have begun to realize that it's legitimate to make a respectable show in the world with purchases financed by one's friends. That Teucris is an infernal slow coach, but I have hopes of her. Please settle things over there. Expect a less guarded letter from me by and by.

25 January, M. Messalla and M. Piso being Consuls.

14 (I.14)

Rome, 13 February 61

CICERO TO ATTICUS

I am afraid it's not in the best of taste to tell you how busy I am, but in fact I am so harassed that I have hardly found time even for these few lines, and stolen at that from most pressing business.

I have already given you a description of Pompey's first public speech—of no comfort to the poor or interest to the rascals; on the other hand the rich were not pleased and the honest men were not impressed. So—a frost. Then an

pulsu levissimus tribunus pl. Fufius in contionem producit Pompeium. res agebatur in circo Flaminio, et erat in eo ipso loco illo die nundinarum πανήγυρις. quaesivit ex eo placeretne ei iudices a praetore legi, quo consilio idem

2 praetor uteretur. id autem erat de Clodiana religione ab senatu constitutum. tum Pompeius μάλ' ἀριστοκρατικῶς locutus est senatusque auctoritatem sibi omnibus in rebus maximi videri semperque visam esse respondit, et id multis verbis.

Postea Messalla consul in senatu de Pompeio quaesivit quid de religione et de promulgata rogatione sentiret. locutus ita est [in senatu][1] ut omnia illius ordinis consulta γενικῶς laudaret, mihique, ut adsedit, dixit se putare satis

3 ab se [et]iam[2] de istis rebus esse responsum. Crassus, postea quam vidit illum excepisse laudem ex eo quod [hi] suspicarentur homines ei consulatum meum placere, surrexit ornatissimeque de meo consulatu locutus est, ut ita diceret, se quod esset senator, quod civis, quod liber, quod viveret, mihi acceptum referre; quotiens coniugem, quotiens domum, quotiens patriam videret, totiens se beneficium meum videre. quid multa? totum hunc locum, quem ego varie meis orationibus, quarum tu Aristarchus es, soleo pingere, de flamma, de ferro (nosti illas ληκύθους), valde graviter pertexuit. proxime Pompeium sedebam. intellexi hominem moveri, utrum Crassum inire eam gratiam quam ipse praetermisisset an esse tantas res nostras quae tam libenti senatu laudarentur, ab eo praesertim

[1] *secl. SB**
[2] etiam (*SB*)

---

[1] In the Campus Martius.

irresponsible Tribune, Fufius, egged on by Consul Piso, called Pompey out to address the Assembly. This took place in the Flaminian Circus,[1] on market day just where the holiday crowd was gathered. Fufius asked him whether he thought it right for a jury to be selected by a Praetor to serve under the same Praetor's presidency, that being the procedure determined by the Senate in the Clodius sacrilege case. Pompey then replied, very much *en bon aristocrate*, that in all matters he held and had always held the Senate's authority in the highest respect—at considerable length too.

Subsequently Consul Messalla asked Pompey in the Senate for his views about the sacrilege and the promulgated bill. He then made a speech commending in general terms all decrees of that body, and remarked to me as he sat down beside me that he hoped he had now replied sufficiently to questioning on these matters. When Crassus saw that Pompey had netted some credit from the general impression that he approved of my Consulship, he got to his feet and held forth on the subject in most encomiastic terms, going so far as to say that it was to me he owed his status as a Senator and a citizen, his freedom, and his very life. Whenever he saw his wife or his house or the city of his birth, he saw a gift of mine. In short, he worked up the whole theme which I am in the habit of embroidering in my speeches one way and another, all about fire, sword, etc. (you are their Aristarchus and know my colour box), really most impressively. I was sitting next to Pompey and I could see he was put out, whether at Crassus gaining the credit which might have been his or to realize that my achievements are of sufficient consequence to make the Senate so willing to hear them praised—praised too by a

qui mihi laudem illam eo minus deberet quod meis omnibus litteris in Pompeiana laude perstrictus esset. hic dies me valde Crasso adiunxit, et tamen ab illo aperte tecte quicquid est datum libenter accepi.

4 Ego autem ipse, di boni! quo modo ἐνεπερπερευσάμην novo auditori Pompeio! si umquam mihi περίοδοι ἢ καμπαὶ ἢ ἐνθυμήματα ἢ κατασκευαὶ suppeditaverunt, illo tempore. quid multa? clamores. etenim haec erat ὑπόθεσις, de gravitate ordinis, de equestri concordia, de consensione Italiae, de in<ter>mortuis reliquiis coniurationis, de vilitate,[3] de otio. nosti iam in hac materia sonitus nostros. tanti fuerunt ut ego eo brevior sim quod eos usque istinc exauditos putem.

5 Romanae autem se res sic habent. senatus Ἄρειος πάγος. nihil constantius, nihil severius, nihil fortius. nam cum dies venisset rogationi ex senatus consulto ferendae, concursabant barbatuli iuvenes, totus ille grex Catilinae duce filiola Curionis, et populum ut antiquaret rogabant. Piso autem consul, lator rogationis, idem erat dissuasor. operae Clodianae pontis occuparant, tabellae ministrabantur ita ut nulla daretur 'uti rogas.' hic tibi <in> rostra Cato advolat, commulcium Pisoni consuli mirificum facit, si id est commulcium, vox plena gravitatis, plena auctoritatis, plena denique salutis. accedit eodem etiam noster Hortensius, multi praeterea boni; insignis vero opera <F>avoni fuit. hoc

[3] utilitate (*Manutius*)

---

[2] Four Greek rhetorical terms are only approximately rendered.

[3] Curio the younger. Velleius the historian calls him 'a spendthrift of money and chastity—his own and other people's.'

man who had all the less reason to offer me such incense in that everything I have written glorifies Pompey at his expense. This day's work has brought me very close to Crassus, not but what I was glad enough to take whatever tribute Pompey more or less obliquely vouchsafed.

As for myself—ye gods, how I spread my tail in front of my new audience, Pompey! If ever periods and *clausulae* and enthymemes and *raisonnements*[2] came to my call, they did on that occasion. In a word, I brought the house down. And why not, on such a theme—the dignity of our order, concord between Senate and Knights, unison of Italy, remnants of the conspiracy in their death throes, reduced price of grain, internal peace? You should know by now how I can boom away on such topics. I think you must have caught the reverberations in Epirus, and for that reason I won't dwell on the subject.

Affairs in Rome stand thus: The Senate is quite an Areopagus, thoroughly resolute, strict, and courageous. When the day came for the bill to be put to the Assembly under the terms of the senatorial decree, there was a flocking together of our goateed young bloods, the whole Catilinarian gang with little Miss Curio[3] at their head, to plead for its rejection. Consul Piso, the proposer of the bill, spoke against it. Clodius' roughs had taken possession of the gangways. The voting papers were distributed without any 'ayes.' Suddenly up springs Cato to the platform and gives Consul Piso a spectacular dressing down, if one can apply such a term to a most impressive, powerful, in fact wholesome speech. He was joined by our friend Hortensius and many honest men besides, Favonius' contribution being

concursu optimatium comitia dimittuntur; senatus vocatur. cum decerneretur frequenti senatu, contra pugnante Pisone, ad pedes omnium singillatim accidente Clodio, ut consules populum cohortarentur ad rogationem accipiendam, homines ad quindecim Curioni nullum senatus consultum facienti adsenserunt; facile ex altera parte CCCC fuerunt. acta res est. Fufius intercessit.[4] Clodius contiones miseras habebat, in quibus Lucullum, Hortensium, C. Pisonem, Messallam consulem contumeliose laedebat; me tantum comperisse omnia criminabatur. senatus et de provinciis praetorum et de legationibus et de ceteris rebus decernebat ut ante quam rogatio lata esset ne quid ageretur.

6 Habes res Romanas. sed tamen etiam illud, quod non speraram, audi. Messalla consul est egregius; fortis, constans, diligens, nostri laudator, amator, imitator. ille alter uno vitio minus vitiosus quod iners, quod somni plenus, quod imperitus, quod *ἀπρακτότατος*; sed voluntate ita *καχέκτης* ut Pompeium post illam contionem in qua ab eo senatus laudatus est odisse coeperit. itaque mirum in modum omnis a se bonos alienavit. neque id magis amicitia Clodi adductus fecit quam studio perditarum rerum atque partium. sed habet sui similem in magistratibus praeter Fufium neminem. bonis utimur tribunis pl., Cornuto vero Pseudocatone. quid quaeris? * * *.[5]

7 Nunc ut ad privata redeam, *Τεῦκρις* promissa patravit. tu mandata effice quae recepisti. Quintus frater, qui Argile-

[4] tertium concessit (*SB* : trib. pl. i- *Pantagathus*)
[5] *lacunam ind. Casaubon*

---

[4] Cicero's enemies used to twit him with this phrase in allusion to his underground activities in collecting information about Catiline's plot.

especially notable. At this rally of optimates the Assembly was dismissed, and the Senate summoned. A full house voted a decree instructing the Consuls to urge the people to accept the bill. Piso fought against it, and Clodius went on his knees to every member individually, but Curio, who moved the rejection of the decree, only got about 15 votes against a good 400 on the other side. So that was that. Fufius then vetoed the decree. Clodius is making pathetic speeches, full of abusive attacks on Lucullus, Hortensius, C. Piso, and Consul Messalla. Me he simply accuses of having 'fully informed myself.'[4] The Senate is resolving to take no action on praetorian provinces, embassies or other business until the bill has been put to the Assembly.

So much then for affairs in Rome—though there is one thing more I may mention, which has come to me as a surprise. Messalla is an excellent Consul, courageous, steady, conscientious; I am the object of his praise, regard, and imitation. The other has just one redeeming vice; he is lazy—somnolent, ignorant, a complete *fainéant*, but in disposition so *méchant* that he has turned against Pompey ever since that public speech in which he eulogized the Senate. Naturally he has become extremely unpopular with all the honest men. His behaviour is prompted quite as much by sympathy with subversion and subversive movements as by his friendship with Clodius. But he has no kindred spirit among the magistrates except Fufius. We have a good lot of Tribunes. Cornutus in particular is a mock-Cato. In a word, * * *.

Now to return to private matters. Teucris has carried out her promise. On your side please discharge the commission you undertook. My brother Quintus, having

tani aedifici reliquum dodrantem emit HS $\overline{\text{DCCXXV}}$, Tusculanum venditat ut, si possit, emat Pacilianam domum. cum Lucceio in gratiam redi‹i›. video hominem valde petiturire. navabo operam. tu quid agas, ubi sis, cuius modi istae res sint, fac me quam diligentissime certiorem.

Id. Febr.

15 (I.15)

Scr. Romae Id. Mart. an. 61 (§ 2)

CICERO ATTICO SAL.

1 Asiam Quinto, suavissimo fratri, obtigisse audisti; non enim dubito quin celerius tibi hoc rumor quam ullius nostrum litterae nuntiarint. nunc, quoniam et laudis avidissimi semper fuimus et praeter ceteros φιλέλληνες et sumus et habemur et multorum odia atque inimicitias rei publicae causa suscepimus, ʽπαντοίης ἀρετῆς μιμνήσκεο,ʼ curaque ‹et› effice ut ab omnibus et laudemur et amemur. his de rebus plura ad te in ea epistula scribam quam ipsi Quinto dabo.

2 Tu me velim certiorem facias quid de meis mandatis egeris, atque etiam quid de tuo negotio; nam ut Brundisio profectus es, nullae mihi abs te sunt redditae litterae. valde aveo scire quid agas.

Id. Mart.

[5] Apparently Cicero too had fallen out with him. He became a candidate for the Consulship of 59.

[1] I.e., the Roman province. Quintus governed it for three years. Cicero hoped that Atticus would take a position on his staff.

bought the remaining three quarters of the building in Argiletum for HS 725,000, is trying to sell his place at Tusculum in order, if possible, to buy the Pacilius house in Rome. I have made my peace with Lucceius.[5] He's clearly a bad case of candidate fever. I shall put my shoulder to the wheel. Let me have an account as full as you can make it of your doings and whereabouts and the shape of things over there.

Ides of February.

15 (I.15)

Rome, 15 March 61

CICERO TO ATTICUS

You will have heard that Asia[1] has fallen to my dearest of brothers—I don't doubt that rumour brought you the news faster than any of us could do by letter. So now bear in mind that we have always been eager to shine, that we both are and are generally reputed outstanding philhellenes, and that we have incurred unpopularity and enmity in many quarters for our country's sake. Gird up your loins then! Do your best to make us universally both lauded and loved. I shall write more to you about this in a letter which I shall send by Quintus himself.

Please let me know what you have done about my commission and about your own affair[2] too. Since you left Brundisium I have not had a single letter from you. I am very anxious to know how you are getting on.

Ides of March.

[2] The Sicyonian debt.

16 (I.16)

Scr. Romae in. m. Quint. an. 61

CICERO ATTICO SAL.

1 Quaeris ex me quid acciderit de iudicio quod tam praeter opinionem omnium factum sit, et simul vis scire quo modo ego minus quam soleam proeliatus sim. respondebo tibi ὕστερο<ν> πρότερον, Ὁμηρικῶς.

Ego enim, quam diu senatus auctoritas mihi defendenda fuit, sic acriter et vehementer proeliatus sum ut clamor concursusque maxima cum mea laude fierent. quod si tibi umquam sum visus in re publica fortis, certe me in illa causa admiratus esses. cum enim ille ad contiones confugisset in iisque meo nomine ad invidiam uteretur, di immortales! quas ego pugnas et quantas strages edidi! quos impetus in Pisonem, in Curionem, in totam illam manum feci! quo modo sum insectatus levitatem senum, libidinem iuventutis! saepe, ita me di iuvent, te non solum auctorem consiliorum meorum verum etiam spectatorem pugnarum 2 mirificarum desideravi. postea vero quam Hortensius excogitavit ut legem de religione Fufius tribunus pl. ferret, in qua nihil aliud a consulari rogatione differebat nisi iudicum genus (in eo autem erant omnia), pugnavitque ut id ita fieret, quod et sibi et aliis persuaserat nullis illum iudicibus effugere posse, contraxi vela perspiciens inopiam iudicum neque dixi quicquam pro testimonio nisi quod erat ita notum atque testatum ut non possem praeterire.

Itaque si causam quaeris absolutionis, ut iam πρὸς τὸ

---

[1] Perhaps an allusion to the *Odyssey*, in which Odysseus' earlier adventures occupy the middle of the poem.

16 (I.16)

Rome, beginning of July 61

CICERO TO ATTICUS

You ask me what happened over the trial for it to turn out so contrary to everybody's expectations, and you also want to know how it was that I took less than my usual part in the fray. I shall answer you Homerically,[1] cart before horse.

Well then, so long as I had the Senate's authority to defend, I took so brisk and vigorous a 'part in the fray' that crowds flocked around me shouting enthusiastic applause. If ever you gave me credit for courage in public life, you would surely have admired me in that affair. When Clodius had betaken himself to speech-making at meetings and used my name to stir up ill feeling, ye gods, what battles, what havoc I made! The onslaughts on Piso, Curio, the whole bunch! How I pilloried irresponsible age and licentious youth! Upon my sacred word, I often longed to have you by, not only as an adviser to follow but as a spectator of those memorable bouts. But then Hortensius conceived the idea of getting Tribune Fufius to propose a law on the sacrilege differing from the consular bill only in respect of the constitution of the jury, on which however everything turned, and worked hard for its acceptance because he had persuaded himself and others that no jury on earth could acquit Clodius. I saw we had got a jury of paupers, and drew in my horns, saying nothing in evidence but what was so generally known and attested that I could not leave it out.

If therefore you want to know the reason for the verdict of not guilty (to come back from cart to horse), it was

πρότερον revertar, egestas iudicum fuit et turpitudo. id autem ut accideret commissum est Hortensi consilio, qui, dum veritus est ne Fufius ei legi intercederet quae ex senatus consulto ferebatur, non vidit illud, satius esse illum in infamia relinqui ac sordibus quam infirmo iudicio committi, sed ductus odio properavit rem deducere in iudicium, cum illum plumbeo gladio iugulatum iri tamen diceret.

3 Sed iudicium si quaeris quale fuerit, incredibili exitu, sic uti nunc ex eventu ab aliis, a me tamen ex ipso initio consilium Hortensi reprehendatur. nam ut reiectio facta est clamoribus maximis, cum accusator tamquam censor bonus homines nequissimos reiceret, reus tamquam clemens lanista frugalissimum quemque secerneret, ut primum iudices consederunt, valde diffidere boni coeperunt. non enim umquam turpior in ludo talario consessus fuit: maculosi senatores, nudi equites, tribuni non tam aerati quam, ut appellantur, aerarii. pauci tamen boni inerant, quos reiectione fugare ille non potuerat, qui maesti inter sui dissimilis et †maerentes†[1] sedebant et contagione turpitudinis vehementer permovebantur. 4 hic, ut quaeque res ad consilium primis postulationibus referebatur, incredibilis erat severitas nulla varietate sententiarum. nihil impetrabat reus, plus accusatori dabatur quam postulabat. quid quaeris?[2] triumphabat Hortensius se vidisse tantum, nemo erat qui illum reum ac non miliens condemnatum arbi-

[1] verentes *coni. SB* [2] quid quaeris? *post* triumph- (*Pius*)

---

[2] Of gladiators. Apparently the better sort of these were sometimes kept out of specially dangerous fights.

the needy and disreputable quality of the jury, and *that* was due to Hortensius' miscalculation. Afraid that Fufius might veto the law proposed under the senatorial decree, he failed to see how much better it would have been to leave Clodius under the stigma of an impending trial than to commit him to an unreliable tribunal. His hatred made him impatient to bring the case to court. He said that a sword of lead would be sharp enough to cut Clodius' throat.

But if you want to know what sort of a trial it was, it was a trial with an incredible outcome; so that others beside myself (who did so from the very first) are now criticizing Hortensius' tactics after the event. The challenging of the jury took place amid uproar, with the prosecutor throwing out the most unsavoury characters like an honest Censor, while the defendant put all the more respectable elements on one side like a soft-hearted trainer.[2] As soon as the jury took their seats, honest men began to fear the worst. A more raffish assemblage never sat down in a low-grade music hall. Flyblown Senators, beggar Knights, and Paymaster Tribunes who might better have been called 'Paytakers.' Even so there were a few honest men whom the accused had not been able to drive off at the challenge. There they sat, gloomy and shamefaced (?) in this incongruous company, sadly uncomfortable to feel themselves exposed to the miasma of disreputability. In these circumstances the strictness and unanimity of the court as various matters were referred to it during the preliminaries was quite astounding. The defendant met with nothing but rebuffs, the prosecutor was repeatedly given more than he asked. In short Hortensius triumphed in his perspicacity, and everybody looked on Clodius, not as a man standing

traretur. me vero teste producto credo te ex acclamatione Clodi advocatorum audisse quae consurrectio iudicum facta sit, ut me circumsteterint, ut aperta iugula sua pro meo capite P. Clodio ostentarint. quae mihi res multo honorificentior visa est quam aut illa, cum iurare tui cives Xenocratem testimonium dicentem prohibuerunt, aut cum tabulas Metelli Numidici, cum eae, ut mos est, circumferrentur, nostri iudices aspicere noluerunt; multo haec, inquam, nostra res maior. itaque iudicum vocibus,
5 cum ego sic ab iis ut salus patriae defenderer, fractus reus et una patroni omnes conciderunt. ad me autem eadem frequentia postridie convenit quacum abiens consulatu sum domum reductus. clamare praeclari Ariopagitae se non esse venturos nisi praesidio constituto. refertur ad consilium. una sola sententia praesidium non desideravit. defertur res ad senatum. gravissime ornatissimeque decernitur, laudantur iudices, datur negotium magistratibus. responsurum hominem nemo arbitrabatur.

'Ἔσπετε νῦν μοι, Μοῦσαι . . . ὅππως δὴ πρῶτον πῦρ ἔμπεσε.' Nosti Calvum ex Nanneianis illum, illum laudatorem meum, de cuius oratione erga me honorifica ad te scripseram. biduo per unum servum, et eum ex ludo gladiatorio, confecit totum negotium. arcessivit ad se, promisit, intercessit, dedit. iam vero (o di boni, rem perditam!) etiam noctes certarum mulierum atque adulescentulorum nobilium introductiones non nullis iudicibus pro

[3] At his trial for extortion.

[4] I.e., the jury.

[5] *Iliad,* 16.112.

[6] I.e., Crassus.

his trial, but as one convicted twenty times over. When I myself was called as a witness, you must have heard from the shouts of Clodius' supporters how the jury rose in a body and surrounded me, pointing to their bare throats as if offering their lives to P. Clodius in exchange for mine. I felt the incident as a much finer tribute than the action of your compatriots in not letting Xenocrates take the oath when he gave evidence, or of our Roman jurymen who refused to look at Metellus Numidicus' accounts[3] when they were taken round in the usual way—yes indeed, this was a far grander gesture. Accordingly, when they heard the jury clamouring in my defence as though I were the salvation of Rome, the accused and all his counsel collapsed in despair. Next morning a crowd gathered at my house as large as took me home the day I laid down the Consulship. Our splendid Areopagites[4] loudly declared that they would not come unless they were given a guard. This being put to the court, there was only one vote against asking for a guard. The matter was brought before the Senate, which passed a solemn, elaborate decree, commending the jury and instructing the magistrates to take the necessary steps. Nobody thought the fellow would reply to the indictment.

'Now tell me, Muses nine . . . how first the fire did fall.'[5] You know Baldhead,[6] him of the Nanneius sale (?), my encomiast, of whose complimentary speech I wrote to you. Inside a couple of days, with a single slave (an ex-gladiator at that) for go-between, he settled the whole business—called them to his house, made promises, backed bills, or paid cash down. On top of that (it's really too abominable!) some jurors actually received a bonus in the form of assignations with certain ladies or introductions to

mercedis cumulo fuerunt. ita summo discessu bonorum, pleno foro servorum, XXV iudices ita fortes tamen fuerunt ut summo proposito periculo vel perire maluerint quam perdere omnia; XXXI fuerunt quos fames magis quam fama commoverit. quorum Catulus cum vidisset quendam, 6 'quid vos' inquit 'praesidium a nobis postulabatis? an ne nummi vobis eriperentur timebatis?' habes, ut brevissime potui, genus iudici et causam absolutionis.

Quaeris deinceps qui nunc sit status rerum et qui meus. rei publicae statum illum quem tu meo consilio, ego divino confirmatum putabam, qui bonorum omnium coniunctione et auctoritate consulatus mei fixus et fundatus videbatur, nisi quis nos deus respexerit, elapsum scito esse de manibus uno hoc iudicio, si iudicium est triginta homines populi Romani levissimos ac nequissimos nummulis acceptis ius ac fas omne delere et, quod omnes non modo homines verum etiam pecudes factum esse sciant, id Talnam et Plautum et Spongiam et ceteras huius modi quisquilias statuere numquam esse factum. 7 sed tamen, ut te de re publica consoler, non ita ut sperarunt mali tanto imposito rei publicae vulnere alacris exsultat improbitas in victoria. nam plane ita putaverunt, cum religio, cum pudicitia, cum iudiciorum fides, cum senatus auctoritas concidisset, fore ut aperte victrix nequitia ac libido poenas ab optimo quoque peteret sui doloris, quem improbissimo cuique 8 inusserat severitas consulatus mei. idem ego ille (non enim

youths of noble family. Yet even so, with the honest men making themselves very scarce and the Forum crowded with slaves, 25 jurors had the courage to take the risk, no small one, preferring to sacrifice their lives rather than the whole community. To 31 on the other hand light purses mattered more than light reputations. Meeting one of them afterwards, Catulus asked him why they had wanted us to provide them with a guard—or was it that they were afraid of having their pockets picked? There then, as briefly as I can give it, you have the quality of the trial and the explanation of the acquittal.

You go on to ask about the general situation now and my own in particular. I can only answer that, unless some god or other takes pity on us, the settlement of the Republic which you attribute to my policy and I to divine providence, and which seemed unshakably established upon the unity of all honest men and the prestige of my Consulship, has slipped through our fingers in this one trial, if one can call it a trial in which thirty of the most irresponsible rascals in Rome pocket their bribes and play ducks and drakes with religion and morality, in which Talna and Plautus and Spongia and the other riffraff find that an offence was not committed when every man and beast too knows it was. And yet, to offer you some comfort on public affairs, rascality does not exult so merrily in victory as bad men had expected after the infliction of so grave an injury upon the body politic. They quite supposed that with the collapse of religion and good morals, of the integrity of the courts and the authority of the Senate openly triumphant villainy and vice would wreak vengeance on the best in our society for the pain branded by the severity of my Consulship upon the worst. Yet once again it was I—I don't feel that I am

mihi videor insolenter gloriari cum de me apud te loquor, in ea praesertim epistula quam nolo aliis legi), idem, inquam, ego recreavi adflictos animos bonorum, unumquemque confirmans, excitans; insectandis vero exagitandisque nummariis iudicibus omnem omnibus studiosis ac fautoribus illius victoriae παρρησίαν eripui; Pisonem consulem nulla in re consistere umquam sum passus, desponsam homini iam Syriam ademi; senatum ad pristinam suam severitatem revocavi atque abiectum excitavi; Clodium praesentem fregi in senatu cum oratione perpetua plenissima gravitatis tum altercatione eius modi (ex qua licet pauca degustes; nam cetera non possunt habere eandem neque vim neque venustatem remoto illo studio contentionis quem ἀγῶνα vos appellatis):

9 Nam ut Id. Mai. in senatum convenimus, rogatus ego sententiam multa dixi de summa re publica, atque ille locus inductus a me est divinitus, ne una plaga accepta patres conscripti conciderent, ne deficerent; vulnus esse eius modi quod mihi nec dissimulandum nec pertimescendum videretur, ne aut ignorando stultissimi ‹aut metuendo ignavissimi›[3] iudicaremur; bis absolutum esse Lentulum, bis Catilinam, hunc tertium iam esse a iudicibus in rem publicam immissum. 'erras, Clodi. non te iudices urbi sed carceri reservarunt neque te retinere in civitate sed exsilio privare voluerunt. quam ob rem, patres conscripti, erigite animos, retinete vestram dignitatem. manet illa in re publica bonorum consensio; dolor accessit bonis viris, virtus

[3] *add. anon. ap. Victorium*

---

[7] I.e. Athenians, with reference to Atticus' cognomen.

[8] P. Cornelius Lentulus Sura, Catiline's principal lieutenant.

bragging offensively when I talk about myself in your hearing, especially in a letter which I don't wish to be read to other people—well, as I say, it was I yet again who revived the drooping courage of the honest men, fortifying and rousing them one by one. Then by denouncing and harassing the venal jurors I effectively stopped the mouths of all sympathizers and backers of the winning side. I drove Consul Piso from pillar to post, and deprived him of Syria, which had already been pledged to him. I recalled the Senate to its earlier strict temper and roused it from despondency. Clodius I quashed face to face in the Senate in a set speech of impressive solemnity and also in an exchange which went somewhat as follows—you can sample it here and there, but the rest cannot retain its force and piquancy without the thrill of battle which you folks[7] call *le feu de l'action*:

When we met in the Senate on the Ides of May and my turn came, I spoke at length about the political situation on the highest level, bringing in with happiest effect that stock piece urging members not to collapse or flag because of a single blow. I said that I did not think the reverse was such as to call either for disguise or undue alarm. We should be judged arrant fools if we ignored it and arrant cowards if we let it frighten us. Lentulus[8] had been twice acquitted, Catiline twice also, and now a jury had let loose a third enemy upon the state. 'Clodius, you are mistaken. The jury has not preserved you for the streets of Rome, but for the death chamber. Their object was not to keep you in the community but to deprive you of the chance of exile. And so, gentlemen, take heart and maintain your dignity. The political consensus of honest men still holds. They have gained the spur of indignation, but lost nothing of

non est imminuta; nihil est damni factum novi, sed quod erat inventum est. in unius hominis perditi iudicio plures
10 similes reperti sunt.' sed quid ago? paene orationem in epistulam inclusi. redeo ad altercationem.

Surgit pulchellus puer, obicit mihi me ad Baias fuisse. falsum, sed tamen. 'quid? hoc simile est' inquam 'quasi in operto dicas fuisse?' 'quid' inquit 'homini Arpinati cum aquis calidis?' 'narra' inquam 'patrono tuo, qui Arpinatis aquas concupivit' (nosti enim Mari<a>nas). 'quousque' inquit 'hunc regem feremus?' 'regem appellas' inquam, 'cum Rex tui mentionem nullam fecerit?' — ille autem Regis hereditatem spe devorarat. 'domum' inquit 'emisti.' 'putes' inquam 'dicere "iudices emisti."' 'iuranti' inquit 'tibi non crediderunt.' 'mihi vero' inquam 'XXV iudices crediderunt, XXXI, quoniam nummos ante acceperunt, tibi nihil crediderunt.' magnis clamoribus adflictus conticuit et concidit.

11 Noster autem status est hic: apud bonos idem sumus quos reliquisti, apud sordem urbis et faecem multo melius quam reliquisti. nam et illud nobis non obest, videri nostrum testimonium non valuisse; missus est sanguis invidiae sine dolore, atque etiam hoc magis quod omnes illi fautores illius flagiti rem manifestam illam redemptam esse a iudicibus confitentur. accedit illud, quod illa con-

---

[9] Or 'Pretty Boy.' Cicero uses the diminutive of Pulcher ('handsome'), Clodius' cognomen. Elsewhere he says it was a misnomer. [10] Literally 'was in a secret place,' alluding to Clodius' intrusion on the Good Goddess' festival. [11] I.e., the elder Curio, who had acquired Marius' villa near Baiae in Sulla's Proscriptions.

[12] Q. Marcius Rex, Consul in 68, was Clodius' brother-in-law, recently deceased. Clodius did not benefit under his will.

their manly spirit. No fresh harm has been done, but harm already there has come to light. The trial of a single wretch has unmasked more like him.' But what am I thinking of? I have nearly put my speech into my letter. To come back to our exchange:

Our little Beauty[9] gets on his feet and accuses me of having been at Baiae—not true, but anyhow, 'Well,' I reply, 'is that like saying I intruded on the Mysteries?'[10] 'What business has an Arpinum man with the warm springs?' 'Tell that to your counsel,'[11] I retorted; 'he was keen enough to get certain of them that belonged to an Arpinum man' (you know Marius' place of course). 'How long,' cried he, 'are we going to put up with this king?' 'You talk about kings,' I answered, 'when Rex[12] didn't have a word to say about you?' (he had hoped to have the squandering of Rex's money). 'So you've bought a house,' said he. I rejoined, 'One might think he was saying that I had bought a jury.' 'They didn't credit you on oath.' 'On the contrary, 25 jurymen gave *me* credit and 31 gave *you* none—they got their money in advance!' The roars of applause were too much for him and he collapsed into silence.

As for my personal position, it is as follows: With the honest men I stand as I did when you left, with the dregs of the city populace much better than you left me. It does me no harm that my evidence apparently failed to carry weight. My unpopularity has been reduced by a sort of painless bloodletting, especially as all who sympathize with the outrage acknowledge that a perfectly clear case was bought off from the jury. There is a further point: this wretched starveling rabble that comes to meetings and

tionalis hirudo aerari, misera ac ieiuna plebecula, me ab hoc Magno unice diligi putat; et hercule multa et iucunda consuetudine coniuncti inter nos sumus, usque eo ut nostri isti comissatores coniurationis, barbatuli iuvenes, illum in sermonibus Cn. Ciceronem appellent. itaque et ludis et gladiatoribus mirandas ἐπισημασίας sine ulla pastoricia fistula auferebamus.

12 Nunc est exspectatio comitiorum; in quae omnibus invitis trudit noster Magnus Auli filium, atque in eo neque auctoritate neque gratia pugnat sed quibus Philippus omnia castella expugnari posse dicebat in quae modo asellus onustus auro posset ascendere. consul autem ille δευτερεύοντος[4] histrionis similis suscepisse negotium dicitur et domi divisores habere. quod ego non credo, sed senatus consulta duo iam facta sunt odiosa quae in consulem facta putantur, Catone et Domitio postulante, unum, ut apud magistratus inquiri liceret, alterum, cuius domi divisores 13 habitarent, adversus rem publicam. Lurco autem tribunus pl., †qui magistratum simul cum lege alia†[5] iniit, solutus est et Aelia et Fufia ut legem de ambitu ferret quam ille bono auspicio claudus homo promulgavit. ita comitia in a. d. VI Kal. Sext. dilata sunt. novi est in lege hoc, ut qui

[4] deterioris (*Seyffert*) [5] qui magistratus simultatem cum lege Aelia *SB olim, ducibus aliis*

---

[13] Magnus, the honorific cognomen received by Pompey from Sulla. Cicero seems never to use it simply as a name except in formal letter headings.

[14] I.e., as elsewhere, L. Afranius, whose father's *praenomen* was Aulus. But the point of so referring to him is uncertain (possibly from the first two letters of the name; *A.f.* = *Auli filius*).

sucks the treasury dry imagines that I have no rival in the good graces of our Great One.[13] And it is a fact that we have been brought together by a good deal of pleasant personal contact, so much so that those conspirators of the wine table, our goateed young bloods, have nicknamed him Cn. Cicero. Accordingly I get wonderful ovations at the games and the gladiators, without a single shepherd's whistle.

Now we are waiting for the elections, into which, to everybody's disgust, our Great Man has pushed Aulus' son,[14] using neither prestige nor personal influence to get him in, but those engines with which Philip[15] said any fortress could be stormed provided there was a way up for a donkey with a load of gold on its back. That second fiddle of a Consul is said to have undertaken the business, and to be keeping distributing agents at his house. *I* don't believe that, but two vexatious decrees, which are thought to be aimed at the Consul, have now been passed at the instance of Cato and Domitius, one permitting magistrates' houses to be searched, the other declaring it an offence against the state to harbour distributing agents in one's house. Moreover Lurco the Tribune, an office at declared enmity with the Lex Aelia(?), has been dispensed from its provisions and those of the Lex Fufia[16] too, to enable him to propose a law on bribery which he has promulgated—his lameness makes a fine omen! So the elections have been put off till 27 July. The novel feature in his law is that any

[15] Philip II of Macedon.

[16] These two laws, sometimes mentioned as one, restricted the legislative powers of Tribunes.

nummos in tribu pronuntiarit, si non dederit, impune sit, sin dederit, ut quoad vivat singulis tribubus HS CIↃ CIↃ CIↃ debeat. dixi hanc legem P. Clodium iam ante servasse; pronuntiare enim solitum esse et non dare. sed heus tu, videsne consulatum illum nostrum, quem Curio antea *ἀποθέωσιν* vocabat, si hic factus erit, fabam mimum futurum? qua re, ut opinor, *φιλοσοφητέον*, id quod tu facis, et istos consulatus non flocci facteon.

14 Quod ad me scribis te in Asiam statuisse non ire, equidem mallem ut ires, ac vereor ne quid in ista re minus commode fiat; sed tamen non possum reprehendere consilium tuum, praesertim cum egomet in provinciam non sim profectus.

15 Epigrammatis tuis, quae in Amaltheo posuisti, contenti erimus, praesertim cum et Thyillus nos reliquerit et Archias nihil de me scripserit; ac vereor ne, Lucullis quoniam Graecum poëma condidit, nunc ad Caecilianam fabulam spectet.

16 Antonio tuo nomine gratias egi eamque epistulam Mallio dedi — ad te ideo antea rarius scripsi quod non habebam idoneum cui darem nec satis sciebam quo darem. valde te venditavi.

17 Cincius si quid ad me tui negoti detulerit, suscipiam. sed nunc magis in suo est occupatus, in quo ego ei non desum. tu, si uno in loco es futurus, crebras a nobis litteras

18 exspecta; sed[6] pluris etiam ipse mittito. velim ad me scribas cuius modi sit Ἀμαλθεῖον tuum, quo ornatu, qua *τοπο-*

[6] ast (*Madvig*)

---

[17] See Letter 15.

[18] I.e., Archias might write a poem in praise of one of the

person promising money in a tribe shall not be punishable provided he does not pay it; but if he does, he shall be liable for HS 3000 to every tribe for life. I said that P. Clodius had already complied with this law, being in the habit of promising and then not paying. But note! That consular office of mine, which Curio once used to call an apotheosis, will be worth no more than a rat's tail if this fellow is elected. Therefore I suppose one must take to letters, as you do, and not care a button for their Consulships.

You say you have decided not to go to Asia.[17] For my part I would rather you had been going, and I have some fear of awkwardness arising over it. Still I can't blame your decision, especially as I have not gone out to a province myself.

I shall make do with the mottoes that you have put in your Shrine of Amalthea, especially as Thyillus has forsaken me and Archias has written nothing *à mon sujet*. I'm afraid that having composed a Greek poem for the Luculli he may now be thinking in terms of Caecilian drama.[18]

I have thanked Antonius on your behalf, and have given the letter to Mallius. The reason why I have not written to you more often in the past is that I had no suitable bearer and was not sufficiently sure of your address. I have given you a fine write-up.

If Cincius brings me any affair of yours, I shall see to it; but at present he is more concerned with one of his own, in which I am doing what I can for him. If you are going to be in one place, you may expect plenty of letters from me. But send even more yourself. I should be grateful for a

Caecilii Metelli instead of writing about Cicero. 'Caecilian drama' plays on the name of the early comic dramatist Caecilius Statius.

ϑεσίᾳ, et, quae poëmata quasque historias de Ἀμαλϑείᾳ habes, ad me mittas. libet mihi facere in Arpinati. ego tibi aliquid de meis scriptis mittam. nihil erat absoluti.

17 (I.17)

Scr. Romae Non. Dec. an. 61 (§ 11)

CICERO ATTICO SAL.

1 Magna mihi varietas voluntatis et dissimilitudo opinionis ac iudici Quinti, fratris mei, demonstrata est ex litteris tuis in quibus ad me epistularum illius exempla misisti. qua ex re et molestia sum tanta adfectus quantam mihi meus amor summus erga utrumque vestrum adferre debuit et admiratione quidnam accidisset quod adferret Quinto, fratri meo, aut offensionem tam gravem aut commutationem tantam voluntatis. atque illud a me iam ante intellegebatur, quod te quoque ipsum discedentem a nobis suspicari videbam, subesse nescio quid opinionis incommodae sauciumque esse animum et insedisse quasdam odiosas suspiciones. quibus ego mederi cum cuperem et antea saepe et vehementius etiam post sortitionem provinciae, nec tantum intellegebam esse offensionis quantum litterae tuae 2 declarant nec tantum proficiebam quantum volebam. sed tamen hoc me ipse consolabar quod non dubitabam quin te ille aut Dyrrachi aut in istis locis uspiam visurus esset. quod cum accidisset, confidebam ac mihi persuaseram fore ut omnia placarentur inter vos non modo sermone ac disputatione sed conspectu ipso congressuque vestro. nam quanta sit in Quinto, fratre meo, comitas, quanta iucundi-

description of your Shrine of Amalthea, its furnishings and layout; and would you send me any poems or narratives you have about her? I have a fancy to make one on my place at Arpinum. I shall be sending you a sample of my writings. I have nothing quite finished.

17 (I.17)

Rome, 5 December 61

CICERO TO ATTICUS

Your letter in which you enclose copies of my brother Quintus' letters argues, I agree, a remarkable change of feeling and inconsistency of judgement and opinion on his part. Naturally, in view of my deep affection for you both, I am very much distressed, and also puzzled to imagine what can have happened to offend my brother so seriously as to bring about such a revulsion of sentiment. I had indeed already perceived, and saw that you too suspected at the time you left us, an undercurrent of grievance; evidently his feelings had been hurt, and some disagreeable suspicions had sunk into his mind. I tried to counteract them on many occasions, more especially after the allotment of his province, but I did not realize he had taken umbrage to the extent revealed by your letter, nor did I make as much headway as I wished. However, I took comfort in the assurance that he would be seeing you at Dyrrachium or somewhere else over there. I trusted, and indeed convinced myself, that once this happened a frank talk or even the mere meeting and sight of one another would set all to rights between you. I need not tell you, for you already know, what a kindly, amiable fellow my brother

tas, quam mollis animus et ad accipiendam et ad deponendam offensionem, nihil attinet me ad te, qui ea nosti, scribere. sed accidit perincommode quod eum nusquam vidisti. valuit enim plus quod erat illi non nullorum artibus inculcatum quam aut officium aut necessitudo aut amor 3 vester ille pristinus, qui plurimum valere debuit. atque huius incommodi culpa ubi resideat facilius possum existimare quam scribere; vereor enim ne, dum defendam meos, non parcam tuis. nam sic intellego, ut nihil a domesticis vulneris factum sit, illud quidem quod erat eos certe sanare potuisse. sed huiusce rei totius vitium, quod aliquanto etiam latius patet quam videtur, praesenti tibi commodius exponam.

4 De iis litteris quas ad te Thessalonica misit et de sermonibus quos ab illo et Romae apud amicos tuos et in itinere habitos putas, ecquid tant‹ul›um[1] causae sit ignoro; sed omnis in tua posita est humanitate mihi spes huius levandae molestiae. nam si ita statueris, et irritabilis animos esse optimorum saepe hominum et eosdem placabilis, et esse hanc agilitatem, ut ita dicam, mollitiamque naturae plerumque bonitatis, et, id quod caput est, nobis inter nos nostra sive incommoda sive vitia sive iniurias esse tolerandas, facile haec, quem ad modum spero, mitigabuntur; quod ego ut facias te oro. nam ad me, qui te unice diligo, maxime pertinet neminem esse meorum qui aut te non amet aut abs te non ametur.

5 Illa pars epistulae tuae minime fuit necessaria, in qua exponis quas facultates aut provincialium aut urbanorum

[1] *add. SB*

is, how impressionable he is both in taking offence and in laying it aside. But most unfortunately you did not see him at all. The notions implanted by certain designing persons had more influence upon him than his sense of family and friendship or your former affection for one another, which ought to have been paramount. Where the blame for this unhappy rift may lie is easier for me to judge than to put into writing. I am afraid that in defending my own relations I might have hard things to say of yours. For it is plain to me that even if his domestic circle did nothing to cause the damage, they could at least have counteracted it when they found it. But it will be better for me to explain the whole thing when I can talk to you—it's a malaise which goes rather further even than appears on the surface.

With regard to the letter he sent you from Thessalonica and the things you believe he said in Rome in the hearing of friends of yours and en route, whether or not some grain of reason for them may exist is outside my knowledge; but my hopes of alleviating this unpleasantness lie entirely in your good nature. If you take the view that the best people are apt to be easily provoked and also easily appeased, that this mobility, so to speak, and impressionability of temperament is usually the sign of a good heart, and above all that we ought to bear with one another's drawbacks, shall I say, or faults, or injuries, then all this will I hope be easily assuaged. Let me beg you so to do. So particularly fond of you as I am, I feel more concerned than anyone that none of those near to me should lack affection towards you or fail of its return.

One part of your letter was quite unnecessary, that in which you point out the various advantageous opportunities both in Rome and in the provinces that you have let

commodorum et aliis temporibus et me ipso consule praetermiseris. mihi enim perspecta est et ingenuitas et magnitudo animi tui, neque ego inter me atque te quicquam interesse umquam duxi praeter voluntatem institutae vitae, quod me ambitio quaedam ad honorum studium, te autem alia minime reprehendenda ratio ad honestum otium duxit. vera quidem laude probitatis, integritatis, diligentiae, religionis neque me tibi neque quemquam antepono, amoris vero erga me, cum a fraterno ‹a›more do-

6 mesticoque discessi, tibi primas defero. vidi enim, vidi penitusque perspexi in meis variis temporibus et sollicitudines et laetitias tuas. fuit mihi saepe et laudis nostrae gratulatio tua iucunda et timoris consolatio grata. quin mihi nunc te absente non solum consilium, quo tu excellis, sed etiam sermonis communicatio, quae mihi suavissima tecum solet esse, maxime deest—quid dicam? in publicane re, quo in genere mihi neglegenti esse non licet, an in forensi labore, quem antea propter ambitionem sustinebam, nunc ut dignitatem tueri gratia possim, an in ipsis domesticis negotiis, in quibus ego cum antea tum vero post discessum fratris te sermonesque nostros desidero? postremo non labor meus non requies, non negotium non otium, non forenses res non domesticae, ‹non publicae› non privatae carere diutius tuo suavissimo atque amantissimo consilio ac sermone possunt.

7 Atque harum rerum commemorationem verecundia saepe impedivit utriusque nostrum; nunc autem ea fuit

go by during my Consulship and at other times. I am perfectly aware of your large-minded indifference to personal profit, and I have never felt any difference between us except in the modes of life we have chosen. What may be called ambition has led me to seek political advancement, while another and entirely justifiable way of thinking has led you to an honourable independence. In the things that really matter—uprightness, integrity, conscientiousness, fidelity to obligation—I put you second neither to myself nor to any other man, while as to affection towards me, leaving aside my brother and my own home circle, I give you first prize. I have seen with my own eyes and very thoroughly noted your anxieties and your joys in the ups and downs of my career. Your congratulation has often given me pleasure in success and your comfort consoled my apprehensions. Indeed at the present time I badly miss in your absence not only your excellent advice but also our habitual exchange of talk, which is such a delight to me. I don't know whether I miss it more in public affairs, which I am in duty bound not to neglect, or in my court work, which I formerly undertook for advancement's sake and still keep up in order to maintain my position by the personal influence so acquired, or in my own private concerns, in which I have felt the want of you and of our talks together more especially since my brother's departure. In short, whether working or resting, in business or in leisure, in professional or domestic affairs, in public life or private, I cannot for any length of time do without your affectionate advice and the delight of your conversation.

Delicacy has often kept both you and me from putting these things into words, as it has now been necessary to do because of the passage in your letter in which you have set

necessaria propter eam partem epistulae tuae per quam te ac mores tuos mihi purgatos ac probatos esse voluisti. atque in ista incommoditate alienati illius animi et offensi illud inest tamen commodi, quod et mihi et ceteris amicis nota fuit et abs te aliquanto ante testificata tua voluntas omittendae provinciae, ut, quod una non estis, non dissensione ac discidio vestro sed voluntate ac iudicio tuo factum esse videatur. qua re et illa quae violata expiabuntur et haec nostra, quae sunt sanctissime conservata, suam religionem obtinebunt.

8 Nos hic in re publica infirma, misera commutabilique versamur. credo enim te audisse nostros equites paene a senatu esse diiunctos; qui primum illud valde graviter tulerunt, promulgatum ex senatus consulto fuisse ut de eis qui ob iudicandum accepissent quaereretur. qua in re decernenda cum ego casu non adfuissem sensissemque id equestrem ordinem ferre moleste neque aperte dicere, obiurgavi senatum, ut mihi visus sum, summa cum auctoritate et in causa non verecunda admodum gravis et copio-

9 sus fui. ecce aliae deliciae equitum vix ferendae! quas ego non solum tuli sed etiam ornavi. Asiam qui de censoribus conduxerunt questi sunt in senatu se cupiditate prolapsos nimium magno conduxisse; ut induceretur locatio postulaverunt. ego princeps in adiutoribus atque adeo secundus; nam ut illi auderent hoc postulare, Crassus eos impulit. invidiosa res, turpis postulatio et confessio temeritatis.

---

[1] Knights (unlike Senators) enjoyed legal immunity from prosecutions for judicial corruption.

out to justify yourself and your manner of life to me. There is at any rate one good thing in this bad business of Quintus' estrangement and dudgeon, I mean that I and your other friends know from statements of your own made some time beforehand of your inclination to say no to the province, so that your not being together won't be attributed to any difference or rift between you but to your own inclination and decision. Well then, so far as you and Quintus are concerned, trespasses shall be made good; while *our* friendship has been preserved inviolate and shall remain as sacred as ever.

The state of the commonwealth in which we live here is weak and sad and unstable. I suppose you have heard that our friends the Knights have pretty well broken with the Senate. To begin with they were greatly annoyed by the promulgation under a senatorial decree of a bill providing for an investigation into the conduct of jurors guilty of taking bribes.[1] I happened to be absent when the decree was voted. Aware that the equestrian order took it amiss, though they said nothing in public, I administered what I felt to be a highly impressive rebuke to the Senate, speaking with no little weight and fluency in a not very respectable cause. Now along come the Knights with another fancy, really almost insupportable—and I have not only borne with it but lent it my eloquence. The farmers who bought the Asiatic taxes from the Censors complained in the Senate that they had been led by overeagerness into making too high an offer and asked for the cancellation of their contract. I was their foremost supporter, or rather foremost but one, for it was Crassus who egged them on to make such an audacious demand. An invidious business! The demand was disgraceful, a confession of recklessness.

summum erat periculum ne, si nihil impetrassent, plane alienarentur a senatu. huic quoque rei subventum est maxime a nobis perfectumque ut frequentissimo senatu et liberalissimo uterentur, multaque a me de ordinum dignitate et concordia dicta sunt Kal. Dec. et postridie. neque adhuc res confecta est, sed voluntas senatus perspecta. unus enim contra dixerat Metellus consul designatus; [qui][2] erat dicturus, ad quem propter diei brevitatem perventum non est, heros ille noster Cato.

10 Sic ego conservans rationem institutionemque nostram tueor, ut possum, illam a me conglutinatam concordiam. sed tamen, quoniam ista sunt tam infirma, munitur quaedam nobis ad retinendas opes nostras tuta, ut spero, via, quam tibi litteris satis explicare non possum, significatione parva ostendam tamen: utor Pompeio familiarissime. video quid dicas. cavebo quae sunt cavenda, ac scribam alias ad te de meis consiliis capessendae rei publicae plura.

11 Lucceium scito consulatum habere in animo statim petere. duo enim soli dicuntur petituri, Caesar (cum eo coire per Arrium cogitat) et Bibulus (cum hoc se putat per C. Pisonem posse coniungi). rides? non sunt haec ridicula, mihi crede. quid aliud scribam ad te? quid? multa sunt, sed in aliud tempus. ‹Tu fac ut nos quod ad tempus›[3] te exspectare velis cures ut sciam. iam illud modeste rogo, quod maxime cupio, ut quam primum venias.

Non. Dec.

[2] *secl. SB* [3] *add. coni. Sjögren*

---

[2] In fact, however, Cato did succeed in obstructing the demand. The tax farmers finally won their point through Caesar in 59.

But there was the gravest danger of a complete break between Senate and Knights if it had been turned down altogether. Here again it was I principally who stepped into the breach. Through my efforts they found the Senate in full attendance and in generous mood, and on the Kalends of December and the day following I discoursed at length upon the dignity and harmony of the two orders. The matter has not yet been settled, but the Senate's attitude was made clear, the only opposing voice being Consul-Designate Metellus. Our doughty champion Cato was to have been another, but darkness fell before his turn came.[2]

Thus, in maintenance of my settled policy, I am defending as best I can the alliance I myself cemented. But as this is all so unreliable, I am building another road, a safe one I hope, to protect my position. I can't very well explain what I mean in a letter, but a small hint will show: I am on the friendliest terms with Pompey. Yes, I know what you will say. I shall watch the dangers; and later on I shall write to you more at length concerning my political plans.

You may be interested to learn that Lucceius has it in mind to stand for the Consulship straight away. Only two prospective candidates are talked of, Caesar (he plans to make a pact with him through Arrius) and Bibulus (he thinks he might join forces with *him* through C. Piso). That makes you laugh? These are no laughing matters, believe me. What else can I tell you, I wonder? There are lots of things, but another time. Please see that I get word when to expect you. I now ask of you with all diffidence what I desire very much indeed—come home as soon as you can.

Nones of December.

18 (I.18)

Scr. Romae XI *Kal. Febr. an. 60 (§ 8)*

CICERO ATTICO SAL.

1 Nihil mihi nunc scito tam deesse quam hominem eum quocum omnia quae me cura aliqua adficiunt una communicem, qui me amet, qui sapiat, quicum ego cum loquar nihil fingam, nihil dissimulem, nihil obtegam. abest enim frater *ἀφελέστατος* et amantissimus. †Metellus† non homo sed 'litus atque aër' et 'solitudo me<r>a.' tu autem qui saepissime curam et angorem animi mei sermone et consilio levasti tuo, qui mihi et in publica re socius et in privatis omnibus conscius et omnium meorum sermonum et consiliorum particeps esse soles, ubinam es? ita sum ab omnibus destitutus ut tantum requietis habeam quantum cum uxore et filiola et mellito Cicerone consumitur. nam illae ambitiosae nostrae fucosaeque amicitiae sunt in quodam splendore forensi, fructum domesticum non habent. itaque cum bene completa domus est tempore matutino, cum ad forum stipati gregibus amicorum descendimus, reperire ex magna turba neminem possumus quocum aut iocari libere aut suspirare familiariter possimus. qua re te exspectamus, te desideramus, te iam etiam arcessimus. multa sunt enim quae me sollicitant anguntque, quae mihi videor auris nactus tuas unius ambulationis sermone exhaurire posse.

2 Ac domesticarum quidem sollicitudinum aculeos omnis et scrupulos occultabo neque ego huic epistulae atque ig-

[1] The manuscripts have 'Metellus,' which seems to be a mis-

18 (I.18)

Rome, 20 January 60

CICERO TO ATTICUS

I must tell you that what I most badly need at the present time is a confidant—someone with whom I could share all that gives me any anxiety, a wise, affectionate friend to whom I could talk without pretence or evasion or concealment. My brother, the soul of candour and affection, is away. *[1] is not a person at all—only 'seashore and air' and 'mere solitude.' And you whose talk and advice has so often lightened my worry and vexation of spirit, the partner in my public life and intimate of all my private concerns, the sharer of all my talk and plans, where are you? I am so utterly forsaken that my only moments of relaxation are those I spend with my wife, my little daughter, and my darling Marcus. My worldly, meretricious friendships may make a fine show in public, but at home they are barren things. My house is crammed of a morning, I go down to the Forum surrounded by droves of friends, but in all the multitude I cannot find one with whom I can pass an unguarded joke or fetch a private sigh. That is why I am waiting and longing for you, why I now fairly summon you home. There are many things to worry and vex me, but once I have you here to listen I feel I can pour them all away in a single walk and talk.

Of family worries with all their pricks and pains I shall say nothing. I won't commit them to this letter and an

take for some other name, though it is conceivable that Cicero is replying to a reference by Atticus to the Consul Metellus Celer. The quoted words will come from a Latin play.

noto tabellario committam. atque hi (nolo enim te permoveri) non sunt permolesti, sed tamen insident et urgent et nullius amantis consilio aut sermone requiescunt; in re publica vero, quamquam animus est praesens, tamen vulnus[1] etiam atque etiam ipsa medicina efficit. nam ut ea breviter quae post tuum discessum acta sunt colligam, iam exclames necesse est res Romanas diutius stare non posse. etenim post profectionem tuam primus, ut opinor, introitus fuit fabulae Clodianae, in qua ego nactus, ut mihi videbar, locum resecandae libidinis et coërcendae iuventutis vehemens flavi et omnis profudi viris animi atque ingeni mei, non odio adductus alicuius sed spe non corrigendae sed sanandae civitatis.

3 Adflicta res publica est empto constupratoque iudicio. vide quae sint postea consecuta. consul est impositus is nobis quem nemo praeter nos philosophos aspicere sine suspiritu posset. quantum hoc vulnus! facto senatus consulto de ambitu, de iudiciis, nulla lex perlata; exagitatus senatus, alienati equites Romani quod erat 'qui ob rem iudicandam.' sic ille annus duo firmamenta rei publicae per me unum constituta evertit; nam et senatus auctoritatem abiecit et ordinum concordiam diiunxit. instat hic nunc annus egregius. eius initium eius modi fuit ut anniversaria sacra Iuventatis[2] non committerentur; nam M. Luculli uxorem Memmius suis sacris initiavit. Menelaus aegre id passus divortium fecit. quamquam ille pastor Idaeus Menelaum solum contempserat, hic noster Paris tam

[1] voluntas (*Sternkopf*)
[2] iuventutis (*Lambinus*)

unknown courier. They are not *very* distressing (I don't want to upset you), but still they are on my mind, nagging away, with no friendly talk and advice to set them at rest. As for the state, I am ready enough to do my part, but time and again the medicine itself injures the patient. I need only summarize what has taken place since your departure for you to cry out perforce that Rome is doomed. I believe it was after you left that the Clodian drama came on to the stage. I thought I saw there a chance to cut back licence and teach the young folk a lesson. So I played fortissimo, put my whole heart and brain into the effort, not from any personal animus but in the hope, I won't say of reforming our society, but at least of healing its wounds.

Then came the calamity of a bought, debauched trial. Mark what followed. A Consul[2] was thrust upon us whom only philosophers like you and me could look at without a sigh. There was a blow! The Senate passed a decree on electoral bribery and another on the courts, but no law was carried through. The Senate was abused, the Knights estranged because of the provision 'whoever as juror . . .' Thus the year saw the overthrow of the two foundations of the constitution which I (and I alone) had established. The authority of the Senate was thrown to the winds and the harmony of the orders dissolved. Now this fine new year is upon us. It has begun with failure to perform the annual rites of the Goddess of Youth, Memmius having initiated M. Lucullus' wife into rites of his own. Menelaus took this hard and divorced the lady—but the shepherd of Ida in olden days only flouted Menelaus, whereas our modern

[2] Afranius.

Menelaum quam Agamemnonem liberum non putavit.

4 Est autem C. Herennius quidam, tribunus pl., quem tu fortasse ne nosti quidem; tametsi potes nosse, tribulis enim tuus est et Sextus, pater eius, nummos vobis dividere solebat. is ad plebem P. Clodium traducit idemque fert ut universus populus in campo Martio suffragium de re Clodi ferat. hunc ego accepi in senatu ut soleo, sed nihil est illo homine lentius.

5 Metellus est consul egregius et nos amat, sed imminuit auctoritatem suam quod habet dicis causa promulgatum illud idem de Clodio. Auli autem filius, o di immortales! quam ignavus ac sine animo miles! quam dignus qui Palicano, sicut facit, os ad male audiendum cottidie praebeat!

6 agraria autem promulgata est a Flavio, sane levis, eadem fere quae fuit Plotia. sed interea *πολιτικὸς ἀνὴρ οὐδ' ὄναρ* quisquam inveniri potest. qui poterat, familiaris noster (sic est enim, volo te hoc scire) Pompeius, togulam illam pictam silentio tuetur suam. Crassus verbum nullum contra gratiam. ceteros iam nosti; qui ita sunt stulti ut amissa re publica piscinas suas fore salvas sperare videantur.

7 unus est qui curet, constantia magis et integritate quam, ut mihi videtur, consilio aut ingenio, Cato; qui miseros publicanos, quos habuit amantissimos sui, tertium iam mensem vexat neque iis a senatu responsum dari patitur.

---

[3] The rites of the goddess Juventas (Youth) were in the charge of the Lucullus family. It is implied that Memmius (Paris) had been involved with the wives of both M. Lucullus (Menelaus) and his elder brother Lucius (Agamemnon).

[4] In order to qualify for office as Tribune, Clodius (a patrician) had to become a plebian (this was finally arranged by means of an adoption). [5] Nothing is known of this law.

Paris has wiped his boots on Agamemnon as well.[3]

There is a Tribune called C. Herennius, whom perhaps you don't even know, though you *may* know him because he belongs to your tribe and his father Sextus used to disburse your gratuities. He is trying to make a plebeian out of P. Clodius and proposing that the assembly of the whole people should vote on Clodius' matter in the Campus Martius.[4] I gave him my usual warm reception in the Senate, but he is a complete pachyderm.

Metellus is an excellent Consul and a good friend of mine, but he has lost face by having promulgated the same proposal about Clodius, as a matter of form. As for Aulus' son, gods above, what a lazy, poor-spirited warrior! All he is fit for is to offer himself as a daily butt for Palicanus' abuse, which is what he does. An agrarian law has been promulgated by Flavius, an irresponsible affair, pretty much the same as the Plotia.[5] But all the while, not so much as the shadow of a statesman is to be found. The man who might have been one, my friend—for so he is, let me tell you—Pompey, lives up to that lovely embroidered toga[6] of his by holding his tongue. From Crassus not a word that might lose him popularity. The others you know. They seem fools enough to expect to keep their fish ponds after losing constitutional freedom. The one man who cares for that, with more resolution and integrity, it seems to me, than judgement or intelligence, is Cato. He has now been over two months tormenting the unfortunate tax farmers, who were his devoted friends, and won't let the Senate give them an

[6] At Caesar's instance Pompey had been authorized to wear triumphal insignia, including the special embroidered gown, at public shows.

ita nos cogimur reliquis de rebus nihil decernere ante quam publicanis responsum sit. qua re etiam legationes reiectum iri puto.

8 Nunc vides quibus fluctibus iactemur; et si ex iis quae scripsi multa[3] etiam a me non scripta perspicis, revise nos aliquando, et, quamquam sunt haec fugienda quo te voco, tamen fac ut amorem nostrum tanti aestimes ut eo vel cum his molestiis pervenire[4] velis. nam ne absens censeare curabo edicendum et proponendum locis omnibus; sub lustrum autem censeri germani negotiatoris est. qua re cura ut te quam primum videamus.

XI Kal. Febr. Q. Metello L. Afranio coss.

19 (I.19)

Scr. Romae Id. Mart. an. 60 (§ 11)

CICERO ATTICO SAL.

1 Non modo si mihi tantum esset oti quantum est tibi, verum etiam si tam brevis epistulas vellem[1] mittere quam tu soles, facile te superarem et in scribendo[2] multo essem crebrior quam tu. sed ad summas atque incredibilis occupationes meas accedit quod nullam a me volo[3] epistulam ad te sine aliquo[4] argumento ac sententia pervenire. et primum tibi, ut aequum est civi amanti patriam, quae sint in re publica exponam; deinde, quoniam nos amore tibi proximi sumus, scribemus etiam de nobis ea quae scire te non nolle arbitramur.

[3] scripsimus tanta (*Watt*) [4] perfrui *Bosius*

[1] velim (*Ernesti*) [2] facere . . . scripto (*Manutius*)

[3] sol(e)o (*Baiter*) [4] absque (*Lehmann*)

answer. So we are unable to pass any decrees on other matters until the tax farmers are given their answer, which I suppose will mean that the deputations will be put off.

You see now what heavy seas we are in, and if between these lines you read much else which I leave unwritten, rejoin us at long last. The conditions here to which I am asking you to return are such that anyone might wish to run away from them, but I hope you value my affection enough to want to get back to *that*, even with all the accompanying disagreeables. As to being registered in your absence, I shall see that a notice is published and displayed everywhere. But registration at the very end of the census period is real businessman's style. So let us see you as soon as may be. Keep well.

20 January, Q. Metellus and L. Afranius being Consuls.

19 (I.19)

Rome, 15 March 60

CICERO TO ATTICUS

If I had as much time as you, or even if I were willing to send letters as short as yours generally are, I should get the better of you easily enough and be far the more assiduous correspondent. But besides being excessively and incredibly busy, I don't choose that any letter should reach you from me without some content and purpose in it. And first, as is right and proper in writing to a patriotic citizen like yourself, I shall give you an account of public affairs; then, since I take next place in your affections, pass on to my own, so far as I think they may be of interest to you.

2 Atque in re publica nunc quidem maxime Gallici belli versatur metus. nam Haedui, fratres nostri, pugnam[5] nuper malam[6] pugnarunt et ‹Helvetii› sine dubio sunt in armis excursionesque in provinciam faciunt. senatus decrevit ut consules duas Gallias sortirentur, dilectus haberetur, vacationes ne valerent, legati cum auctoritate mitterentur qui adirent Galliae civitates darentque operam ne eae se cum Helvetiis coniungerent. legati sunt Q. Metellus Creticus et L. Flaccus et, *τὸ ἐπὶ τῇ φακῇ μύρον*, Lentu-
3 lus, Clodiani filius. atque hoc loco illud non queo praeterire, quod, cum de consularibus mea prima sors exisset, una voce senatus frequens retinendum me in urbe censuit. hoc idem post me Pompeio accidit, ut nos duo quasi pignora rei publicae retineri videremur. quid enim ego aliorum in me *ἐπιφωνήματα* exspectem cum haec domi nascantur?

4 Urbanae autem res se sic habent. agraria lex a Flavio tribuno pl. vehementer agitabatur auctore Pompeio, quae nihil populare habebat praeter actorem.[7] ex hac ego lege secunda contionis voluntate omnia illa tollebam quae ad privatorum incommodum pertinebant; liberabam agrum eum qui P. Mucio L. Calpurnio consulibus publicus fuisset; Sullanorum hominum possessiones confirmabam; Volater-

[5] pugnant (*Koch*) [6] puer(i) malam *al.* (*Allen*)
[7] auctorem (*SB**)

[1] The Gallic tribe of the Aedui (Haedui) had been given the title of 'brothers of the Roman people.' They had just been defeated by a German chieftain, Ariovistus. The (Celtic) Helvetii were about to invade Gaul from the area of Lake Geneva.

[2] The Cisalpine and Narbonese provinces.

In public life the great thing just now is the Gallic war scare. Our Haeduan brothers[1] have recently taken a beating, and there is no doubt that the Helvetii are up in arms and raiding the Province. The Senate has decreed that the Consuls should cast lots for the two Gauls,[2] that a levy should be held with all exemptions cancelled, and ambassadors with full powers sent to visit the Gallic communities and try to stop them making common cause with the Helvetii. The ambassadors are Q. Metellus Creticus, L. Flaccus, and ('perfume on lentils'[3]) Lentulus son of Clodianus. While on the subject I cannot help mentioning that when I drew the first lot among the Consulars a full House unanimously declared that I must be kept in Rome. The same thing happened to Pompey after me, so it looked as if we two were being kept as gages one might say for the Republic. Why after all should I wait for other people's *applaudissements* when I am so good a hand at the game myself?

Home affairs stand thus: Tribune Flavius is vigorously pushing his agrarian law, with Pompey's backing. There is nothing *popular* about it except the mover. With the approval of an assembly I advocated the deletion from the bill of all provisions detrimental to private interest. I was for releasing from its operation such land as was in state ownership in the Consulship of P. Mucius and L. Calpurnius,[4] for confirming the Sullan settlers in their holdings, and for leaving the people of Volaterrae and Ar-

[3] A Greek saying. The implication seems to be that this Lentulus, who was Praetor in 59 and son of Cn. Lentulus Clodianus, Consul in 72, was an inadequate choice. There is a pun on his name. [4] I.e., 133.

ranos et Arretinos, quorum agrum Sulla publicarat neque diviserat, in sua possessione retinebam; unam rationem non reiciebam, ut ager hac adventicia pecunia emeretur quae ex novis vectigalibus per quinquennium reciperetur. huic toti rationi agrariae senatus adversabatur, suspicans Pompeio novam quandam potentiam quaeri; Pompeius vero ad voluntatem perferendae legis incubuerat. ego autem magna cum agrariorum gratia confirmabam omnium privatorum possessiones; is enim est noster exercitus, hominum, ut tute scis, locupletium. populo autem Pompeioque (nam id quoque volebam) satis faciebam emptione, qua constituta diligenter et sentinam urbis exhauriri et Italiae solitudinem frequentari posse arbitrabar. sed haec tota res interpellata bello refrixerat. Metellus est consul sane bonus et nos admodum diligit. ille alter nihil ita est ut plane quid emerit nesciat.

5 Haec sunt in re publica, nisi etiam illud ad rem publicam putas pertinere, Herennium quendam, tribunum pl., tribulem tuum, sane hominem nequam atque egentem, saepe iam de P. Clodio ad plebem traducendo agere coepisse. huic frequenter interceditur. haec sunt, ut opinor, in re publica.

6 Ego autem, ut semel Nonarum illarum Decembrium iunctam invidia ac multorum inimicitiis eximiam quandam atque immortalem gloriam consecutus sum, non destiti eadem animi magnitudine in re publica versari et illam institutam ac susceptam dignitatem tueri; sed postea quam primum Clodi absolutione levitatem infirmitatemque iudi-

[5] From Pompey's eastern conquests. [6] The day on which the Catilinarian conspirators were executed.

retium, whose land Sulla confiscated but did not distribute, in possession. One proposal I did not reject, that land should be purchased out of the additional funds accruing during a period of five years from the new tributary revenues.[5] The Senate is opposing the whole scheme for land distribution, suspecting that some new powers for Pompey are in view. Pompey himself has set his heart on the bill going through. I, with the cordial gratitude of the prospective grantees, am standing for the confirmation of all private persons in their holdings; for this, as you know, is my army—the well-to-do. As for the populace and Pompey, I am meeting them (as I also want to do) by way of purchase. If that is properly organized I believe the dregs of the urban population can be cleared out and Italy repeopled. But the war has supervened and the whole issue faded into the background. Metellus makes a very good Consul and is a firm friend of mine. His colleague is such a ninny that he just doesn't know what he's bought.

That is all in the way of public affairs, unless you think it a public affair that a Tribune called Herennius, a fellow tribesman of yours and a thoroughly worthless, penniless fellow, has started making repeated attempts to have P. Clodius transferred to the plebs. He gets a collection of vetoes. That is all, I think, in the way of public affairs.

As for me, ever since the immortal Nones of December[6] when I rose to what I may call a pinnacle of immortal glory, combined with unpopularity and many enmities, I continue to play my part in politics with the same disregard of self and to maintain the position and responsibilities I then assumed. But when I perceived the levity and weakness of the courts, demonstrated by Clodius' acquit-

ciorum perspexi, deinde vidi nostros publicanos facile a senatu diiungi, quamquam a me ipso non divellerentur, tum autem beatos homines, hos piscinarios dico, amicos tuos, non obscure nobis invidere, putavi mihi maiores
7 quasdam opes et firmiora praesidia esse quaerenda. itaque primum eum qui nimium diu de rebus nostris tacuerat, Pompeium, adduxi in eam voluntatem ut in senatu non semel sed saepe multisque verbis huius[8] mihi salutem imperi atque orbis terrarum adiudicarit. quod non tam interfuit mea (neque enim illae res aut ita sunt obscurae ut testimonium aut ita dubiae[9] ut laudationem desiderent) quam rei publicae, quod erant quidam improbi qui contentionem fore aliquam mihi cum Pompeio ex rerum illarum dissensione arbitrarentur. cum hoc ego me tanta familiaritate coniunxi ut uterque nostrum in sua ratione munitior et in re publica firmior hac coniunctione esse
8 possit. odia autem illa libidinosae ac delicatae iuventutis quae erant in me incitata sic mitigata sunt comitate quadam mea me unum ut omnes illi colant. nihil iam denique a me asperum in quemquam fit, nec tamen quicquam populare ac dissolutum, sed ita temperata tota ratio est ut rei publicae constantiam praestem, privatis meis rebus propter infirmitatem bonorum, iniquitatem malevolorum, odium in me improborum adhibeam quandam cautionem et diligentiam; atque ita tamen [si][10] his novis amicitiis implicati sumus ut crebro mihi vafer ille Siculus

[8] suis (*Manutius*)
[9] dubiae . . . obscurae *coni. SB*
[10] *del. Lambinus*

tal, and then saw how readily our friends the tax farmers were estranged from the Senate, though not detached from me personally, and furthermore how certain affluent gentlemen, I mean your friends the fish fanciers,[7] hardly concealed their jealousy of me, why, I felt I must add to my resources and look for more reliable support. To begin with, I brought Pompey, who had kept his own counsel about my achievements too long, into such a frame of mind that he assigned to me in the Senate, not once but often and at length, the credit of having saved our empire and the world. That was not so valuable to *me* (for what I did is neither so little known as to need witnesses nor so questionable as to need encomiasts) as to the state, since certain rascals thought that differences arising out of these matters would set Pompey and myself at loggerheads. With him I have entered into so close a friendship that both of us can feel safer as individuals and politically stronger by our coalition. The hostility excited against me in the minds of our spoiled and licentious young men has been so mitigated by what I may call my affability that they all make me the object of their special attention. In fact I now avoid treading on anybody's toes, though without currying popularity or sacrificing principle. My whole line of conduct is nicely balanced. I am as steadfast as patriotism requires, but as a private individual I exercise a certain amount of care and circumspection on account of the weakness of the honest men, the unfairness of the ill-disposed, and the hostility of the rascals. But I am not so deeply involved in these new friendships but that crafty old Sicilian Epicharmus often

[7] Cicero's term for aristocrats like Hortensius and Lucullus who were proud of the rare fish in their private pools.

insusurret Epicharmus cantilenam illam suam, 'νᾶφε καὶ μέμνασ' ἀπιστεῖν. ἄρθρα ταῦτα τᾶν φρενῶν.' ac nostrae quidem rationis ac vitae quasi quandam formam, ut opinor, vides.

9 De tuo autem negotio saepe ad me scribis; cui mederi nunc non possumus. est enim illud senatus consultum summa pedariorum voluntate, nullius nostrum auctoritate factum. nam quod me esse ad scribendum vides, ex ipso senatus consulto intellegere potes aliam rem tum relatam, hoc autem de populis liberis sine causa additum. et ita factum est a P. Servilio filio, qui in postremis sententiam dixit; sed immutari hoc tempore non potest. itaque conventus, qui initio celebrabantur, iam diu fieri desierunt. tu si tuis blanditiis tamen a Sicyoniis nummulorum aliquid expresseris, velim me facias certiorem.

10 Commentarium consulatus mei Graece compositum misi ad te. in quo si quid erit quod homini Attico minus Graecum eruditumque videatur, non dicam quod tibi, ut opinor, Panhormi Lucullus de suis historiis dixerat, se, quo facilius illas probaret Romani hominis esse, idcirco barbara quaedam et soloeca dispersisse; apud me si quid erit eius modi, me imprudente erit et invito. Latinum si perfecero, ad te mittam. tertium poëma exspectato, ne quod genus a me ipso laudis meae praetermittatur. hic tu cave dicas, 'τίς πατέρ' αἰνήσει;'; si est enim apud homines quicquam quod potius [si] laudetur, nos vituperemur qui non potius

---

[8] Its purport is unknown, but the 'irrelevant' additional clause seems to have invalidated debts incurred by 'free' communities such as Sicyon.

[9] Cicero liked to pretend that Atticus was really an Athenian.

whispers his old song into my ears: 'Don't get drunk or trust your neighbour; there's the kernel of good sense.' I think you now see a kind of outline of my way of life and behaviour.

You often write to me about your affair, in which I can now do nothing to help. That decree[8] was passed with great enthusiasm on the part of the rank and file, but with no countenance from any of us Consulars. True, you find my name attached, but you can see from the text of the decree that the proposal then put to the House was separate and that this clause about free communities was an irrelevant addition; and so it was, by P. Servilius junior, who was among the last to speak. But it can't be changed at present. Accordingly the meetings which were largely attended to begin with were dropped some time ago. If you still manage to coax a sesterce or two out of the Sicyonians I shall be glad to hear of it.

I am sending you the sketch of my Consulship in Greek. If there is anything in it that may appear un-Greek or unscholarly to a man of Attica,[9] I shan't say what Lucullus said to you, at Panhormus I think, about his history, that he had sprinkled a few barbarisms and solecisms to make his readers more willing to believe that it was written by a Roman. Anything of that sort in *my* work will be unintended and regretted. As soon as I finish a Latin version, I shall send it to you. As a third item you may expect a poem, not to leave any form of singing my own praises unattempted. Now don't say, 'Who shall applaud his sire?'[10] If there is anything in the world better worth praising, I may fairly

[10] Part of a Greek proverb: 'It's a sorry child that brags about his father.' Cicero misapplies it to self-praise in general.

alia laudemus; quamquam non ἐγκωμιαστικὰ sunt haec sed ἱστορικὰ quae scribimus.

11 Quintus frater purgat se mihi per litteras et adfirmat nihil a se cuiquam de te secus esse dictum. verum haec nobis coram summa cura et diligentia sunt agenda. tu modo nos revise aliquando. Cossinius hic, cui dedi litteras, valde mihi bonus homo et non levis et amans tui visus est et talis qualem esse eum tuae mihi litterae nuntiarant.

Id. Mart.

20 (I.20)

Scr. Romae post IV *Id. Mai. an. 60 (§ 1)*

CICERO ATTICO SAL.

1 Cum e Pompeiano me Romam recepissem a. d. IIII Id. Mai, Cincius noster eam mihi abs te epistulam reddidit quam tu Id. Febr. dederas. ei nunc epistulae litteris his respondebo.

Ac primum tibi perspectum esse iudicium de te meum laetor; deinde te in iis rebus quae tibi[1] asperius a nobis atque ‹adeo a›[2] nostris et iniucundius actae videbantur moderatissimum fuisse vehementissime gaudeo idque neque amoris mediocris et ingeni summi ac sapientiae iudico. qua de re cum ad me ita suaviter, diligenter, officiose, humaniter scripseris ut non modo te hortari amplius non debeam sed ne exspectare quidem abs te aut ab ullo homine tantum facilitatis ac mansuetudinis potuerim, nihil duco esse commodius quam de his rebus nihil iam amplius scribere. cum erimus congressi, tum, si quid res feret, coram inter nos conferemus.

[1] mihi (*TP*) [2] *add. Wesenberg*

be censured for not preferring other subjects for panegyric—though these compositions of mine are historical rather than encomiastic.

My brother Quintus writes to me exculpating himself and affirming that he has never said anything amiss about you to anyone. But we must handle this together, very, very carefully. Only do come back to us at long last. The bearer of this, Cossinius, seemed to me a thoroughly good fellow, responsible and fond of you—just what your letter to me had represented him.

Ides of March.

20 (I.20)

Rome, after 12 May 60

CICERO TO ATTICUS

On my return from Pompeii on 12 May our friend Cincius gave me your letter dated the Ides of February. That is the letter to which I shall now reply.

To begin with, I am glad to know that you are well aware of what I think of you. Next, it gives me the warmest pleasure that you have taken so temperate an attitude over what you felt to be wounding and disagreeable behaviour on our part, or I ought rather to say on the part of those near to me; and I think this says a good deal for your affection and much more for your character and wisdom. Your letter is so charming, considerate, loyal, and kind, that, far from feeling it right to urge you any further, I could never have expected such placability and forbearance from you or any man. So I think the best thing we can do is to say no more on this subject in writing. When we meet we can discuss it together if desirable.

2 Quod ad me de re publica scribis, disputas tu quidem et amanter et prudenter, et a meis consiliis ratio tua non abhorret; nam neque de statu nobis nostrae dignitatis est recedendum neque sine nostris copiis intra alterius praesidia veniendum et is de quo scribis nihil habet amplum, nihil excelsum, nihil non submissum atque populare. verum tamen fuit ratio mihi fortasse ad tranquillitatem meorum temporum non inutilis sed mehercule rei publicae multo etiam utilior quam mihi, civium improborum impetus in me reprimi cum hominis amplissima fortuna, auctoritate, gratia fluctuantem sententiam confirmassem et a spe malorum ad mearum rerum laudem convertissem. quod si cum aliqua levitate mihi faciendum fuisset, nullam rem tanti aestimassem; sed a me ita sunt acta omnia non ut ego illi adsentiens levior sed ut ille me probans gravior

3 videretur. reliqua sic a me aguntur et agentur ut non committamus ut ea quae gessimus fortuito gessisse videamur. meos bonos illos viros quos significas et eam quam mihi dicis obtigisse *Σπάρταν* non modo numquam deseram sed, etiam si ego ab illa deserar, tamen in mea pristina sententia permanebo. illud tamen velim existimes, me hanc viam optimatem post Catuli mortem nec praesidio ullo nec comitatu tenere. nam ut ait Rhinton,[3] ut opinor, '*οἱ μὲν παρ' οὐδέν εἰσι, τοῖς δ' οὐδὲν μέλει*.' mihi vero ut invideant piscinarii nostri aut scribam ad te alias aut in congressum nostrum reservabo. a curia autem nulla me res

[3] phi(n)ton (ς)

---

[1] Pompey. [2] Atticus had quoted a Greek saying: 'Sparta is your portion, make the most of it.' Here Sparta symbolizes the cause of the optimates.

In the political part of your letter there is both affection and wisdom in what you say, and your argument squares pretty well with my own ideas. Clearly I must not retreat from the high position I have taken up, nor must I enter somebody else's lines without support, and the person of whom you write[1] *is* without largeness and loftiness of view, entirely given over to a mean pursuit of popularity. All the same I had my policy—a policy not perhaps without its advantages for me personally, as tending to give me a quiet life, but I really believe far more advantageous to the state than to myself; namely, to check the onslaughts of rascally citizens upon myself by strengthening the mind of one who stands preeminent in fortune, prestige, and influence, and turning him away from the hopes of wicked men to become an encomiast of my record. If that had involved any sacrifice of principle, I should not have thought anything worth such a price; but I have so managed throughout that instead of *my* losing respect by appearing to flatter him *he* has gained it by approving me. As for the future, I am so acting and shall continue so to act as to run no risk of having my achievements attributed to chance. Far from deserting those honest men of mine to whom you refer and the Sparta[2] which you say has fallen to my lot, I shall stay loyal to my old views even if Sparta deserts *me*. But I should like you to realize that since Catulus died I have been holding to this optimate road without supporters or companions. As Rhinton (I think) has it, 'Some count for nothing, others nothing care.' I shall write to you some other time about the jealousy towards me of our fish fancying friends, or reserve it for our meeting. But nothing shall separate me from the House, because that is the right

divellet, vel quod ita rectum est vel quod rebus meis maxime consentaneum vel quod a senatu quanti fiam minime me paenitet.

4 De Sicyoniis, ut scripsi ad te antea, non multum spei est in senatu; nemo est enim iam qui queratur. qua re si id exspectas, longum est. alia via, si qua potes, pugna. cum est actum, neque animadversum est ad quos pertineret et raptim in eam sententiam pedarii cucurrerunt. inducendi senatus consulti maturitas nondum est, quod neque sunt qui querantur et multi, partim malevolentia partim opinione aequitatis, delectantur.

5 Metellus tuus est egregius consul; unum reprehendo, quod otium <e> Gallia nuntiari non magno opere gaudet. cupit, credo, triumphare. hoc vellem mediocrius, cetera egregia. Auli filius vero ita se gerit ut eius consulatus non consulatus sit sed Magni nostri *ὑπώπιον*.

6 De meis scriptis misi ad te Graece perfectum consulatum meum. eum librum L. Cossinio dedi. puto te Latinis meis delectari, huic autem Graeco Graecum invidere. alii si scripserint, mittemus ad te; sed, mihi crede, simul atque hoc nostrum legerunt, nescio quo pacto retardantur.

7 Nunc ut ad rem meam redeam, L. Papirius Paetus, vir bonus amatorque noster, mihi libros eos quos Ser. Claudius reliquit donavit. cum mihi per legem Cinciam licere capere Cincius amicus tuus diceret, libenter dixi me accepturum si attulisset. nunc si me amas, si te a me amari scis, enitere per amicos, clientis, hospites, libertos denique ac

[3] This law, of 204 (lex Cincia), forbade advocates to accept fees for their services. Possibly Paetus or Claudius had at some time been a client of Cicero's.

path and the path most consistent with my record and because I have no reason to complain of any lack of appreciation on the Senate's part.

As for Sicyon, as I wrote to you earlier, there is not much to be hoped for from the Senate. Nobody is protesting any longer. So if you wait for that, you will wait a long time. Find some other way to fight, if you can. When the thing was being done, no one noticed whom it affected and the rank and file stampeded to vote for the motion. It would be premature to try to cancel the decree since no one is protesting and many people are pleased, partly from malice, partly from a notion of equity.

Your friend Metellus is an excellent Consul. I have only one criticism, he is not overhappy at the news of peace in Gaul. He wants a triumph, I suppose. I could wish he was not so set on it, but in all other respects he's excellent. The way Aulus' son is behaving is making his Consulship not so much a Consulship as a blot in our Great Man's copybook.

With regard to my writings, I have sent you my 'Consulship' in Greek, finished. I gave the book to L. Cossinius. I fancy you like my Latin stuff, but as a Greek yourself may look askance at this Greek performance. If others write, I'll send you copies, but upon my word, once they've read this thing of mine, somehow or other they slow down.

To come now to my own interests, L. Papirius Paetus, an honest man and an admirer of mine, offered me as a present the books left by Ser. Claudius. As your friend Cincius told me that there was nothing in his namesake's law[3] to stop me taking them, I said I would accept with pleasure if he brought them over. Now if you love me and know that I love you, do make every possible effort, through your friends, clients, guests, even your freedmen

servos tuos, ut scida ne qua depereat. nam et Graecis iis libris quos suspicor et Latinis quos scio illum reliquisse mihi vehementer opus est. ego autem cottidie magis quod mihi de forensi labore temporis datur in iis studiis conquiesco. per mihi, per, inquam, gratum feceris si in hoc tam diligens fueris quam soles in iis rebus quas me valde velle arbitraris, ipsiusque Paeti tibi negotia commendo, de quibus tibi ille agit maximas gratias, et ut iam invisas nos non solum rogo sed etiam suadeo.

21 (II.1)

Scr. Antii, ut vid., fort. III Non. Iun. an. 60

CICERO ATTICO SAL.

1 Kal. Iun. eunti mihi Antium et gladiatores M. Metelli cupide relinquenti venit obviam tuus puer. is mihi litteras abs te et commentarium consulatus mei Graece scriptum reddidit. in quo laetatus sum me aliquanto ante de isdem rebus Graece item scriptum librum L. Cossinio ad te perferendum dedisse; nam si ego tuum ante legissem, furatum me abs te esse diceres. quamquam tua illa (legi enim libenter) horridula mihi atque incompta visa sunt, sed tamen erant ornata hoc ipso quod ornamenta neglexerant, et, ut mulieres, ideo bene olere quia nihil olebant videbantur. meus autem liber totum Isocrati myrothecium atque omnis eius discipulorum arculas ac non nihil etiam Aristotelia pigmenta consumpsit. quem tu Corcyrae, ut mihi aliis litteris significas, strictim attigisti, post autem, ut arbitror, a Cossinio accepisti. quem tibi ego non essem ausus mittere

and slaves, to see that not a page goes astray. I badly need both the Greek books and the Latin—I know he left the latter and suspect the former. More and more the longer I live I find relaxation in these studies in whatever time I have to spare from my legal work. I shall be most, *most* grateful if you will take the trouble over this you always do take when you think I really care about something. Also I commend to you Paetus' own affairs, concerning which he says he is extremely grateful to you; and I not only ask but counsel you to pay us a visit now.

21 (II.1)

Antium(?), ca. June 3(?) 60

CICERO TO ATTICUS

As I was on my way to Antium on the Kalends of June, eager to leave M. Metellus' gladiator show behind me, your boy met me with a letter from you and a sketch of my Consulship in Greek. I was glad when I got it that I had given L. Cossinius a piece on the same topic, likewise in Greek, to take to you some time before. Otherwise, if I had read yours first, you would be accusing me of plagiary. Actually though, your piece, which I have read with pleasure, struck me as a trifle rough and unkempt, but it was embellished by its very neglect of ornament and seemed fragrant because odourless, as with the ladies. Now *my* book has used up Isocrates' entire perfume cabinet along with all the little scent boxes of his pupils, and some of Aristotle's rouge as well. You intimate in another letter that you gave it a cursory inspection at Corcyra, and later I suppose you received it from Cossinius. I shouldn't have

2 nisi eum lente ac fastidiose probavissem. quamquam ad me rescripsit iam Rhodo Posidonius se, nostrum illud ὑπόμνημα <cum> legere<t>, quod ego ad eum ut ornatius de isdem rebus scriberet miseram, non modo non excitatum esse ad scribendum sed etiam plane deterritum.[1] quid quaeris? conturbavi Graecam nationem. ita vulgo qui instabant ut darem sibi quod ornarent iam exhibere mihi molestiam destiterunt. tu, si tibi placuerit liber, curabis ut et Athenis sit et in ceteris oppidis Graeciae. videtur enim posse aliquid nostris rebus lucis adferre.

3 Oratiunculas autem et quas postulas et pluris etiam mittam, quoniam quidem ea quae nos scribimus adulescentulorum studiis excitati te etiam delectant. fuit enim mihi commodum, quod in eis orationibus quae Philippicae nominantur enituerat tuus ille civis Demosthenes et quod se ab hoc refractariolo iudiciali dicendi genere abiunxerat ut σεμνότερός τις et πολιτικώτερος videretur, curare ut meae quoque essent orationes quae consulares nominarentur. quarum una est in senatu Kalendis Ianuariis, altera ad populum de lege agraria, tertia de Othone, quarta pro Rabirio, quinta de proscriptorum filiis, sexta cum provinciam in contione deposui, septima qua Catilinam emisi, octava quam habui ad populum postridie quam Catilina profugit, nona in contione quo die Allobroges indicarunt,[2] decima in senatu Nonis Decembribus. sunt praeterea duae breves, quasi ἀποσπασμάτια legis agrariae. hoc totum σῶμα curabo ut habeas. et quoniam te cum scripta tum

[1] perterritum (*Lambinus*) [2] invocarunt (*Manutius*)

---

[1] Of the following list nos. 1, 2, 4, and 7–10 survive in whole or part as well as one of the two 'chips.'

dared send it to you except after leisurely and fastidious revision. However, Posidonius has already written to me from Rhodes that when he read this *ébauche* of mine, which I had sent him with the idea that he might compose something more elaborate on the same theme, so far from being stimulated to composition he was effectively frightened away. The fact is, I have dumbfounded the whole Greek community, so that the folk who were pressing me on all sides to give them something to dress up are pestering me no longer. If you like the book, please see that it is made available at Athens and the other Greek towns. I think it may add some shine to my achievements.

I'll send my little speeches, both those you ask for and some more besides, since it appears that you too find pleasure in these performances which the enthusiasm of my young admirers prompts me to put on paper. Remembering what a brilliant show your countryman Demosthenes made in his so-called *Philippics* and how he turned away from this argumentative, forensic type of oratory to appear in the more elevated role of statesman, I thought it would be a good thing for me too to have some speeches to my name which might be called 'Consular.' They are:[1] (1) delivered in the Senate on the Kalends of January; (2) to the Assembly, on the agrarian law; (3) on Otho; (4) in defence of Rabirius; (5) on the children of persons proscribed; (6) delivered when I publicly resigned my province; (7) when I sent Catiline out of Rome; (8) to the Assembly the day following Catiline's flight; (9) at a public meeting the day the Allobroges turned informers; (10) in the Senate on the Nones of December. There are two further short pieces, chips, one might say, from the agrarian law. I shall see that you get the whole corpus, and since you like my writings

res meae delectant, isdem ex libris perspicies et quae gesserim et quae dixerim; aut ne poposcisses. ego enim tibi me non offerebam.

4 Quod quaeris quid sit quod te arcessam ac simul impeditum te negotiis esse significas, neque recusas quin, non modo si opus sit sed etiam si velim, accurras, nihil sane est necesse, verum tamen videbare mihi tempora peregrinationis commodius posse discribere. nimis abes diu, praesertim cum sis in propinquis locis; neque nos te fruimur et tu nobis cares. ac nunc quidem otium est, sed si paulo plus furor Pulchelli progredi posset, valde ego te istinc excitarem. verum praeclare Metellus impedit et impediet. quid quaeris? est consul φιλόπατρις et, ut semper iudicavi, natura bonus.

5 Ille autem non simulat, sed plane tribunus pl. fieri cupit. qua <de> re cum in senatu ageretur, fregi hominem et inconstantiam eius reprehendi qui Romae tribunatum pl. peteret cum in Sicilia hereditatem[3] se petere dictitasset,[4] neque magno opere dixi <e>sse nobis laborandum, quod nihilo magis ei liciturum esset plebeio rem publicam perdere quam similibus eius me consule patriciis esset licitum. iam cum se ille septimo die venisse a freto neque sibi obviam quemquam prodire potuisse et noctu se introisse dixisset in eoque se in contione iactasset, nihil ei novi dixi accidisse. ex Sicilia septimo die Romam: at[5] tribus horis Roma Interamnam. noctu introisse: idem ante. 'non est

[3] edilitatem *vel* haeredil- *al.*
[4] s(a)epe hereditasset *al.* (*Manutius*) [5] a (*Lambinus*)

[2] An allusion to Clodius' alibi in the Bona Dea trial, which had been exploded by Cicero's evidence.

as well as my doings, the same compositions will show you both what I did and what I said. Otherwise you shouldn't have asked—I was not forcing myself upon you.

You ask why I call you home and at the same time intimate that you are involved in business; though you add that this doesn't mean you wouldn't hurry back at need, or even at my wish. Well, there is no real necessity, but I did think you might arrange your periods abroad more conveniently. You are away too long at a time, especially as you are quite close. I can't enjoy your company and you have to do without mine. At present things are quiet, but if our little Beauty were able to push his folly a bit further I should be calling you out of your retreat in no uncertain voice. But Metellus is stopping him in fine style and will so continue. He is in fact a patriotic Consul and, as I have always believed him, honest at heart.

As for Clodius, he is not pretending; he is really set upon becoming Tribune. When the subject was raised in the Senate I knocked the stuffing out of him. I took him to task for inconsistency in wanting to contest elections in Rome when in Sicily he had talked all the time of contesting a will. But I said we need not worry overmuch, because he would have no more chance of destroying the state as a plebeian than his kindred spirits among the patricians had had when I was Consul. Then, recalling his statements that he had made the journey from the Straits in a week, and that no one had had the opportunity to come out and welcome him, and that he had entered Rome after dark, points with which he had made great play in a public speech, I remarked that all this was nothing new for Clodius. 'From Sicily to Rome in a week: but from Rome to Interamna in three hours.[2] Entry after dark: just as before. Nobody came

itum obviam: ne tum quidem cum iri maxime debuit.' quid quaeris? hominem petulantem modestum reddo non solum perpetua gravitate orationis sed etiam hoc genere dictorum. itaque iam familiariter cum ipso etiam cavillor ac iocor. quin etiam cum candidatum deduceremus, quaerit ex me num consuessem Siculis locum gladiatoribus dare. negavi. 'at ego' inquit 'novus patronus instituam. sed soror, quae tantum habeat consularis loci, unum mihi solum pedem dat.' 'noli' inquam 'de uno pede sororis queri; licet etiam alterum tollas.' 'non consulare' inquies, 'dictum.' fateor; sed ego illam odi male consularem: 'ea est enim seditiosa, ea cum viro bellum gerit,' neque solum cum Metello sed etiam cum Fabio, quod eos nihil<i>[6] esse moleste fert.

6 Quod de agraria lege scribis, sane iam videtur refrixisse. quod me quodam modo molli bracchio de Pompei familiaritate obiurgas, nolim ita existimes, me mei praesidi causa cum illo coniunctum esse; sed ita res erat instituta ut, si inter nos esset aliqua forte dissensio, maximas in re publica discordias versari esset necesse. quod a me ita praecautum atque provisum est, non ut ego de optima illa mea ratione decederem, sed ut ille esset melior et aliquid de populari levitate deponeret. quem de meis rebus, in

[6] ni(c)hil *al.* (*SB*)

---

[3] Cicero as formerly Quaestor in Sicily and prosecutor of Verres was patron of the island.

[4] Clodia, later called 'Ox Eyes' and probably the Lesbia to whom Catullus wrote his love poems, was married to the Consul Metellus Celer. Clodius was supposed to have incestuous relations with her and his two other sisters.

in your way: no more they did that other time, when it was much to be wished that someone had *got* in your way.' All in all, I am teaching the ruffian manners, by quips of this sort as well as by sustained serious oratory. So nowadays I actually jeer and joke with him familiarly in person. Why, when we were both taking down a candidate to the Forum, he asked me whether I had been in the habit of giving Sicilians[3] places at the gladiators. I said not. 'Ah,' said he, 'but I'm their new patron and I'm going to institute the practice. But my sister[4] with all that consular space at her disposal gives me one wretched foot.' 'Oh,' I said, 'don't grumble about one foot in your sister's case. You can always hoist the other.' Not a very consular sort of joke, you may think. I admit it, but I can't abide that consular lady. 'For she's a shrew, she battles with her man'[5]—and not only with Metellus but with Fabius too because he objects to their rascally goings-on.

You mention the agrarian law. It seems to have become quite *vieux jeu*. And in a mild sort of way you take me to task for my friendly relations with Pompey. I should not wish you to think that I have drawn close to him for my own protection. The position however was that any dissension that might arise between us would inevitably bring major political conflicts in its train. If I have foreseen and provided against this danger, that does not mean that I have abandoned my own constitutionalist policy, but that he has become more constitutionally minded and less inclined to court popularity with the masses at the expense of

[5] From some Latin comedy. Fabius (possibly Q. Fabius Maximus Sanga) must have been Clodia's lover, who like her husband disapproved of her relations with Clodius.

quas eum multi incitarant, multo scito gloriosius quam de suis praedicare; sibi enim bene gestae, mihi conservatae rei publicae dat testimonium. hoc facere illum mihi quam prosit nescio; rei publicae certe prodest. quid si etiam Caesarem, cuius nunc venti valde sunt secundi, reddo meliorem? num tantum obsum rei publicae? quin etiam si mihi nemo invideret, si omnes, ut erat aequum, faverent, tamen non minus esset probanda medicina quae sanaret vitiosas partis rei publicae quam quae exsecaret. nunc vero, cum equitatus ille quem ego in clivo Capitolino te signifero ac principe collocaram senatum deseruerit, nostri autem principes digito se caelum putent attingere si mulli barbati in piscinis sint qui ad manum accedant, alia autem neglegant, nonne tibi satis prodesse videor si perficio ut ii nolint obesse qui possunt?

7

8 Nam Catonem nostrum non tu amas plus quam ego; sed tamen ille optimo animo utens et summa fide nocet interdum rei publicae; dicit enim tamquam in Platonis *πολιτείᾳ*, non tamquam in Romuli faece, sententiam. quid verius quam in iudicium venire qui ob rem iudicandam pecuniam acceperit? censuit hoc Cato et adsensit senatus: equites curiae bellum—non mihi, nam ego dissensi. quid impudentius publicanis renuntiantibus? fuit tamen retinendi ordinis causa facienda iactura. restitit et pervicit Cato. itaque nunc, consule in carcere incluso, saepe item

[6] Caesar was about to return from a successful term as governor in Spain to stand for the Consulship.

[7] The road from the Forum up to the Capitol on which the Knights stationed themselves in support of the Senate on 4–5 December 63.

principle. You may be interested to learn that he eulogizes my achievements, which many persons had prompted him to attack, in far more glowing terms than his own, acknowledging himself as a good servant of the state but me as its saviour. How much *I* gain by his doing so I hardly know, but there is certainly a gain to the commonwealth. I will go even further. Supposing I manage to make even Caesar, who is riding on the crest of the wave just now,[6] a better citizen, am I harming the state so very much? Why, even if I had no ill-wishers, even if I had everyone's good will, as I ought to have, there would still be as much to be said for healing the unsound members of the body politic as for amputating them. But look at the facts. The Senate has been deserted by the Knights, whom I once stationed on Capitol Rise[7] with you as their leader and standard bearer. Our leading men think they have transcended the summit of human ambition if the bearded mullet in their fish ponds feed out of their hands, and let all else go hang. Don't you think I do service enough if I succeed in removing the desire to do harm from those who have the power?

As for our friend Cato, I have as warm a regard for him as you. The fact remains that with all his patriotism and integrity he is sometimes a political liability. He speaks in the Senate as though he were living in Plato's Republic instead of Romulus' cesspool. What could be fairer than that jurors who take bribes should be brought to trial? Cato moved accordingly and the Senate agreed. Result, the Knights declare war upon the House—not upon me, for I was against it. Could anything be more shameless than tax farmers repudiating their contract? All the same the loss was worth standing to keep the Order on our side. Cato opposed, and carried his point. So now we see a Consul

seditione commota, aspiravit nemo eorum quorum ego concursu itemque ii consules qui post me fuerunt rem publicam defendere solebant. 'quid ergo? istos' inquies 'mercede conductos habebimus?' quid faciemus si aliter non possumus? an libertinis atque etiam servis serviamus? sed, ut tu ais, ἅλις σπουδῆς.

9 Favonius meam tribum tulit honestius quam suam, Luccei perdidit. accusavit Nasicam inhoneste, ac moleste[7] tamen; dixit ita ut Rhodi videretur molis potius quam Moloni operam dedisse. mihi quod defendissem leviter suscensuit. nunc tamen petit iterum rei publicae causa. Lucceius quid agat scribam ad te cum Caesarem videro, qui aderit biduo.

10 Quod Sicyonii te laedunt, Catoni et eius aemulatori attribues[8] Servilio. quid? ea plaga nonne ad multos bonos viros pertinet? sed si ita placuit, laudemus, deinde in dissensionibus soli relinquamur.

11 Amalthea mea te exspectat et indiget tui. Tusculanum et Pompeianum valde me delectant, nisi quod me, illum ipsum vindicem aeris alieni, aere non Corinthio sed hoc circumforaneo obruerunt. in Gallia speramus esse otium. Prognostica mea cum oratiunculis prope diem exspecta, et

[7] modeste (ς*) [8] attribuis (*Wesenberg*)

---

[8] Metellus Celer had been taken to prison by the Tribune Flavius for obstructing his agrarian bill.

[9] I.e., Q. Metellus Scipio. The office for which he and Favonius were rival candidates is uncertain. Lucceius probably supported the latter. Apollonius Molo(n) taught rhetoric in Rhodes.

[10] See Letter 13 note 2.

shut up in gaol[8] and one riot following another, while not one of the men who used to rally round me and the Consuls my successors for the defence of the state lifts a finger. Are we then to keep these fellows as mercenaries? What else, if we can't keep them on any other terms? Or should we take orders from our freedmen, even our slaves? But, as you would say, *trêve de sérieux*.

Favonius carried my tribe with greater credit than his own, but lost Lucceius'. He has prosecuted Nasica[9] with venom but with no credit at all. From the way he spoke you might think he had spent his time at Rhodes grinding corn at the mill, not rhetoric with Molo. He was a trifle out of humour with me because I appeared for the defence. However, he is now going to stand again, for patriotic reasons. I shall let you know what Lucceius is up to when I have seen Caesar, who will be here in two days' time.

You must put down your ill usage by the Sicyonians to Cato and his emulator Servilius. After all many honest men are hit. However, since they wanted it so, let us clap our hands—and then when it comes to a tussle find ourselves left to fight our own battles!

My Amalthea[10] awaits you and needs you. I am very pleased with my properties at Tusculum and Pompeii except that they have loaded me, the Creditors' Friend, with debt—just plain ordinary *aes alienum*, not Corinthian.[11] We hope it is peace in Gaul. You can expect my *Prognostica*[12] along with the speeches any day, but write to me all

[11] Corinthian bronzes (*aes Corinthium*) were prized objets d'art. *Aes alienum*, literally 'other people's bronze (money),' = debt. [12] Cicero's youthful version of a Greek poem by Aratus on weather signs.

tamen quid cogites de adventu tuo scribe ad nos. nam mihi Pomponia nuntiari iussit te mense Quintili Romae fore. id a tuis litteris quas ad me de censu tuo miseras discrepabat.

12 Paetus, ut antea ad te scripsi, omnis libros quos frater suus reliquisset mihi donavit. hoc illius munus in tua diligentia positum est. si me amas, cura ut conserventur et ad me perferantur. hoc mihi nihil potest esse gratius. et cum Graecos tum vero Latinos diligenter ut conserves velim. tuum esse hoc munusculum putabo.

Ad Octavium dedi litteras. cum ipso nihil eram locutus; neque enim ista tua negotia provincialia esse putabam neque te in tocullionibus habebam. sed scripsi, ut debui, diligenter.

22 (II.2)

Scr. Antii (?), med. vel ex. m. Dec. an. 60

CICERO ATTICO SAL.

1 Cura, amabo te, Ciceronem nostrum. ei nos *θεῖοι*[1] videmur.

2 ‘*Πελληναίων*’ in manibus tenebam et hercule magnum acervum Dicaearchi mihi ante pedes exstruxeram. o magnum hominem, et unde multo plura didiceris quam de Procilio! ‘*Κορινθίων*’ et ‘*Αθηναίων*’ puto me Romae habere. mihi crede (sed ego[2] te hoc doceo?), mirabilis vir est.

[1] cinos —ΘΕΟΙ (ς) : *συννοσεῖν Watt, ducibus aliis*
[2] credes lege (*SB*)

---

[1] Young Quintus, now six or seven years old.
[2] If the reading is correct, Cicero uses a Greek word which means both ‘divine’ and ‘uncles.’

the same about your plans for coming home. Pomponia sent me word that you would be in Rome in July. That doesn't agree with the letter you sent me about your census returns.

Paetus, as I told you in my last letter, has presented me with his late cousin's entire library. His generosity now depends on your cooperation. I do beg of you to see that the books are kept intact and sent to me. You could not do me a greater kindness. And please be particularly careful to conserve the Latin ones as well as the Greek. I shall then feel that I owe this little present to you.

I have written to Octavius. I had not spoken to him personally, for I didn't suppose that these business affairs of yours were province matters and I had not reckoned you as one of *MM. les petits usuriers*. However, I have written with all proper care.

22 (II.2)

Antium (?), mid- or late December 60

CICERO TO ATTICUS

Do, I beg you, take good care of our young Cicero.[1] To him we uncles seem godlike creatures (?).[2]

I have the 'Pellene' in my hand and a goodly heap of Dicaearchus piled up in front of me. What a great man! There's a deal more to be learned from him than from Procilius. I think I have the 'Corinth' and the 'Athens' in Rome.[3] Believe me (but am *I* telling *you*?), he's a wonder-

[3] The works mentioned dealt with the political constitutions of certain Greek cities. Procilius wrote on Roman topography and antiquities.

Ἡρώδης, si homo esset, eum potius legeret quam unam litteram scriberet; qui me epistula petivit, ad te, ut video, comminus accessit. coniurasse mallem quam restitisse

3 coniurationi si illum mihi audiendum putassem. de lolio, sanus non es; de vino, laudo.

Sed heus tu, ecquid vides Kalendas venire, Antonium non venire? iudices cogi? nam ita ad me mittunt, Nigidium minari in contione se iudicem qui non adfuerit compellaturum. velim tamen si quid est de Antoni adventu quod audieris scribas ad me et, quoniam huc non venis, cenes apud nos utique prid. Kal. cave aliter facias. cura ut valeas.

23 (II.3)

Scr. Romae, ut vid., paulo post superiorem

CICERO ATTICO SAL.

1 Primum, ut opinor, εὐαγγέλια. Valerius absolutus est Hortensio defendente. id iudicium Auli filio[1] condonatum putabatur; et Epicratem[2] suspicor, ut scribis, lascivum fuisse. etenim mihi caligae eius et[3] fasciae cretatae non placebant. quid sit, sciemus cum veneris.

2 Fenestrarum angustias quod reprehendis, scito te Κύρου παιδείαν reprehendere. nam cum ego idem istuc

[1] at(t)ilio *al.* (*Tunstall*) [2] Iphicratem *Tyrrell*
[3] ut (*Orelli*)

---

[4] Probably as medicine for young Quintus.

[1] Probably Cicero's friend M. Valerius Messalla Rufus, Consul in 53 and Hortensius' nephew. I suspect that the references to Afranius and Pompey (Epicrates = 'powerful') are ironic, i.e., they were *against* Valerius.

ful man. If Herodes had any sense he would be reading him instead of writing a single line himself. He has attacked me with a letter and met you, I see, hand to hand. I'd rather have joined the conspiracy than opposed it if I had thought I should have to listen to him. You are out of your mind about the darnel.[4] As to the wine, I approve.

Now then, do you notice that the Kalends are coming and that Antonius cometh not? And that the jury is being empanelled? They send me word that Nigidius has been threatening at a public meeting to prosecute any juror who is not in his place. Still, if you get any news about Antonius' arrival I should be obliged if you would write to me; and as you are not coming here, don't fail to dine with us on the 29th. Mind you do, and take good care of yourself.

23 (II.3)

Rome (?), shortly after 22 (II. 2)

CICERO TO ATTICUS

First, as I imagine, good news! Valerius[1] has been acquitted, Hortensius defending. The verdict is thought to have been a sop for Aulus' son. I suspect that Epicrates too has been, as you say, cutting a dash. At any rate I don't care for his pipe-clayed boots and spats.[2] We shall know the truth when you return.

You find fault with the narrowness of my windows. Let me tell you that you are censuring the Education of Cyrus.[3]

[2] Apparently worn by Pompey for reasons of health, but gibed at as a foppish affectation.

[3] Title of Xenophon's pseudobiography of the first Persian king. His namesake was a contemporary architect.

dicerem, Cyrus aiebat virid<ar>iorum[4] *διαφάσεις* latis luminibus non tam esse suavis. etenim *ἔστω ὄψις μὲν ἡ* Α, *τὸ δὲ ὁρώμενον <τὸ>*[5] ΒΓ, *ἀκτῖνες δὲ* †ΑΙΤΑ†[6] — vides enim cetera. nam si *κατ᾽ εἰδώλων ἐμπτώσεις* videremus, valde laborarent *εἴδωλα* in angustiis; nunc fit lepide illa *ἔκχυσις* radiorum. cetera si reprehenderis, non feres tacitum, nisi si quid erit eius modi quod sine sumptu corrigi possit.

3 Venio nunc ad mensem Ianuarium et ad *ὑπόστασιν* nostram ac *πολιτείαν*, in qua *Σωκρατικῶς εἰς ἑκάτερον*, sed tamen ad extremum, ut illi solebant, *τὴν ἀρέσκουσαν*. est res sane magni consili. nam aut fortiter resistendum est legi agrariae, in quo est quaedam dimicatio sed plena laudis, aut quiescendum, quod est non dissimile atque ire in Solonium aut Antium, aut etiam adiuvandum, quod a me aiunt Caesarem sic exspectare ut non dubitet. nam fuit apud me Cornelius, hunc dico Balbum, Caesaris familiarem. is adfirmabat illum omnibus in rebus meo et Pompei consilio usurum daturumque operam ut cum 4 Pompeio Crassum coniungeret. hic sunt haec: coniunctio mihi summa cum Pompeio, si placet, etiam cum Caesare, reditus in gratiam cum inimicis, pax cum multitudine, senectutis otium. sed me *κατακλεὶς*[7] mea illa commovet quae est in libro tertio:

[4] *add. Lambinus* [5] *add. SB*
[6] *vide CLA* [7] *κατακρεσις vel sim.* (*Turnebus*)

---

[4] I.e., on the eye. This was the Epicurean theory, in which Cicero, of course, did not believe.

[5] The Academy, founded by Socrates' pupil Plato.

When I said precisely the same thing, Cyrus told me that views of greenery through wide apertures are not so agreeable. For let vision be *A*, the object perceived *BC*, the rays, etc. (?)—you see the rest. Of course, if sight were due to the incidence of images,[4] the images would have a hard time of it in the narrow spaces, but as things are the emission of rays operates very nicely. If you find fault with the other features, I'll have an answer for you, unless it's something that can be put right without expense.

I come now to the month of January and *la base de ma politique*. I shall argue thereupon *in utramque partem à la Socrate*, but in the end, according to the practice of the school,[5] shall declare my preference. It is certainly a matter for careful consideration. Either I put up a stout resistance to the agrarian law,[6] which means something of a struggle but an honourable one, or I lie low, which is nearly tantamount to retiring to Antium or Solonium, or I actually lend it my assistance as they say that Caesar confidently expects me to do. I have had a visit from Cornelius, Balbus I mean, Caesar's intimate. He assured me that Caesar will follow my and Pompey's advice in all things and will try to bring Pompey and Crassus together. This course presents the following advantages: intimate association with Pompey, with Caesar too if I want it, reconciliation with my enemies, peace with the populace, tranquillity in my old age. But I can't forget my finale in Book III:

[6] Caesar's first agrarian bill, which he put to the Senate early in his Consulship, mainly to find land for Pompey's veterans. It proved inadequate, and had to be supplemented by a second bill in April.

interea cursus, quos prima a parte iuventae
quosque adeo consul virtute animoque petisti,
hos retine atque auge famam laudesque bonorum.

haec mihi cum in eo libro in quo multa sunt scripta ἀριστοκρατικῶς Calliope ipsa praescripserit, non opinor esse dubitandum quin semper nobis videatur 'εἷς οἰωνὸς ἄριστος ἀμύνασθαι περὶ πάτρης.'

Sed haec ambulationibus Compitaliciis reservemus. tu prid. Compitalia memento. balineum calfieri iubebo. et Pomponiam Terentia rogat; matrem adiungemus. Θεοφράστου 'περὶ Φιλοτιμίας' adfer mihi de libris Quinti fratris.

24 (II.4)

Scr. Antii in. m. Apr. an. 59

CICERO ATTICO SAL.

1 Fecisti mihi pergratum quod Serapionis librum ad me misisti; ex quo quidem ego, quod inter nos liceat dicere, millesimam partem vix intellego. pro eo tibi praesentem pecuniam solvi imperavi, ne tu expensum muneribus ferres. sed[1] quoniam nummorum mentio facta est, amabo te, cura ut cum Titinio, quoquo modo poteris, transigas. si in eo quod ostenderat non stat, mihi maxime placet ea quae male empta sunt reddi, si voluntate Pomponiae fieri po-

[1] a(s)t (*Lambinus*)

---

[7] The Muse, in the poem he wrote on his Consulship. Cicero, like Propertius after him, put a speech into her mouth addressed to himself. [8] Hector's famous saying in *Iliad,* 12.243.

Meantime the paths which you from earliest days
didst seek,
Ay, and when Consul too, as mood and virtue bade,
These hold, and foster still your fame and good men's
praise.

Such was Calliope's[7] own lesson to me in a book which contains many aristocratic sentiments. So I don't think I can hesitate. I must always find 'one omen best: to fight for fatherland.'[8]

But let us keep all this for our strolls together at the Compitalia. Remember the day before. I shall have the bath heated. Terentia invites Pomponia as well and we shall have your mother over too. Please bring me Theophrastus on Ambition from Quintus' library.

24 (II.4)

Antium, early April 59

CICERO TO ATTICUS

I am very much obliged to you for sending me Serapion's book,[1] of which, between ourselves, I hardly understand one line in a thousand. I have given instructions for you to be paid for it in cash so that you won't have to put it down under the heading of 'presents.' But since I have mentioned money, do please get things settled with Titinius[2] any way you can. If he doesn't keep his word, the best thing in my opinion is to return the bad bargain, if Pomponia can

[1] On mathematical geography. [2] Possibly the Senator of that name. He may have bought some article for Cicero on behalf of his brother Quintus, now absent in Asia.

terit; si ne id quidem, nummi potius reddantur quam ullus sit scrupulus. valde hoc velim ante quam proficiscare amanter, ut soles, diligenterque conficias.

2 Clodius ergo, ut ais, ad Tigranem! velim †sirpie†[2] condicione; sed facile patior. accommodatius enim nobis est ad liberam legationem tempus illud, cum et Quintus noster iam, ut speramus, in otio consederit et iste sacerdos Bonae Deae cuius modi futurus sit sci<em>us.[3] interea quidem cum Musis nos delectabimus animo aequo, immo vero etiam gaudenti ac libenti, neque mihi umquam veniet in mentem Crasso invidere neque paenitere quod a me ipso non desciverim.

3 De geographia, dabo operam ut tibi satis faciam; sed nihil certi polliceor. magnum opus est. sed tamen, ut iubes, 4 curabo ut huius peregrinationis aliquod tibi opus exstet. Tu quicquid indagaris de re publica, et maxime quos consules futuros putes, facito ut sciam. tametsi nimis sum curiosus; statui enim nihil iam de re publica cogitare.

5 Terentiae saltum perspeximus. quid quaeris? praeter quercum Dodonaeam nihil desideramus quo minus Epi- 6 rum ipsam possidere videamur. nos circiter Kalendas aut in Formiano erimus aut in Pompeiano. tu, si in Formiano non erimus, si nos amas, in Pompeianum venito. id et nobis erit periucundum et tibi non sane devium.

7 De muro, imperavi Philotimo ne impediret quo minus id fieret quod tibi videretur. tu censeo tamen adhibeas

[2] ipse pari *Lehmann*
[3] -rus scius sit *vel sim.* (*Ernesti*)

---

[3] The reason for this proposed embassy to Armenia is unknown. [4] Clodius.

be brought to agree. If even that won't do, better pay the money than have any awkwardness. I should be most grateful if you would clear this up before you go away in your usual kind and businesslike way.

So Clodius, you say, is going to Tigranes.[3] I should be glad to go myself on the same terms (?), but never mind. It will be a more convenient time for me to take a Free Commission when Quintus has, as I hope, settled down in peace and we see how that Priest[4] of Bona Dea is going to turn out. Meanwhile I shall amuse myself with the Muses in equanimity, indeed cheerfully and gladly, and it will never enter my head to envy Crassus or to regret that I have remained true to myself.

I shall try to meet your wishes about the Geography but I don't promise anything for certain. It's a big undertaking. However, I shall take care, following your admonition, to have some work to show you for this spell away from home. On your side let me know anything you ferret out about public affairs, in particular whom you expect to be the next Consuls—though after all I'm being too curious, having determined to think no more about politics.

We have inspected Terentia's forest. All I can say is that only the oak of Dodona[5] is lacking to make us feel that we own Epirus itself. We shall be at either Formiae or Pompeii around the Kalends. If we are not at Formiae do *please* come to Pompeii. That will be very agreeable for us and not much out of the way for you.

About the wall, I have told Philotimus not to put any obstacle in the way of your wishes. But I advise you to

[5] Zeus' oracle at Dodona in Epirus was originally located in a sacred oak.

Vettium. his temporibus, tam dubia vita optimi cuiusque, magni aestimo unius aestatis fructum palaestrae Palatinae, sed ita tamen ut nihil minus velim quam Pomponiam et puerum versari in timore ruinae.

25 (II.5)

Scr. Antii paulo post superiorem

CICERO ATTICO SAL.

1 Cupio equidem et iam pridem cupio Alexandriam reliquamque Aegyptum visere et simul ab hac hominum satietate nostri discedere et cum aliquo desiderio reverti; sed hoc tempore et his mittentibus 'αἰδέομαι Τρῶας καὶ Τρῳάδας ἑλκεσιπέπλους.' quid enim nostri optimates, si qui reliqui sunt, loquentur? an me aliquo praemio de sententia esse deductum? 'Πουλυδάμας μοι πρῶτος ἐλεγχείην ἀναθήσει,' Cato ille noster, qui mihi unus est pro centum milibus. quid vero historiae de nobis ad annos DC praedicarint? quas quidem ego multo magis vereor quam eorum hominum qui hodie vivunt rumusculos. sed, opinor, excipiamus et exspectemus. si enim deferetur, erit quaedam nostra potestas et tum deliberabimus. etiam hercule est in non accipiendo non nulla gloria. qua re si quid Θεοφάνης tecum forte contulerit, ne omnino repudiaris.

---

[1] Cicero was expecting to be offered an appointment as special envoy to Ptolemy XII ('the Piper') of Egypt, who had been recognized as king and ally.

[2] I.e., 'I am afraid of respectable public opinion.' The quotation (a favourite with Cicero) is from *Iliad,* 22.105.

consult Vettius. In these times, when life is so uncertain for men of light and leading, I set store on a single summer's enjoyment of my palaestra on the Palatine, but at the same time the last thing I want is for Pomponia and the boy to live in fear of falling masonry.

25 (II.5)

Antium, shortly after 24 (II.4)

CICERO TO ATTICUS

Yes, I am eager, and have been for long enough, to visit Alexandria[1] and the rest of Egypt, and at the same time to get away from this part of the world where people are tired of me and to come back when they have begun to miss me a little. But at the present time, and the authors of the mission being who they are, 'I fear the Trojans and their long-gowned wives.'[2] What will our optimates say, if there are any left? Perhaps that I have been somehow bribed to change my news. 'Polydamas will cry me shame the first'—our friend Cato, who is 'one worth a hundred thousand'[3] in my eyes. And what will history say of me a thousand years hence? I am far more in awe of that than of the tittle-tattle of my contemporaries. But I think I had better wait and see. If the offer is made, that will give me some sort of latitude and then will be the time to deliberate. Also, dash it all, there is some glory in not accepting. So if Theophanes happens to say something to you, don't turn it down out of hand.

[3] Deriving from a Greek saying from the philosopher Heraclitus; 'For me one man counts as ten [sic] thousand, if he is the best.'

2 De istis rebus exspecto tuas litteras, quid Arrius narret, quo animo se destitutum ferat, et qui consules parentur, utrum, ut populi sermo, Pompeius et Crassus, an, ut mihi scribitur, cum Gabinio Ser. Sulpicius, et num quae novae leges et num quid novi omnino, et, quoniam Nepos proficiscitur, cuinam auguratus deferatur, quo quidem uno ego ab istis capi possum—vide levitatem meam! sed quid ego haec, quae cupio deponere et toto animo atque omni cura φιλοσοφεῖν? sic, inquam, in animo est; vellem ab initio, nunc vero, quoniam quae putavi esse praeclara expertus sum quam essent inania, cum omnibus Musis rationem habere cogito.

3 Tu tamen de †Tutio†[1] ad me rescribe certius et num[2] quis in eius locum paretur, et quid de P. Clodio fiat, et omnia, quem ad modum polliceris, ἐπὶ σχολῆς scribe. et quo die Roma te exiturum putes velim ad me scribas, ut certiorem te faciam quibus in locis futurus sim, epistulamque statim des de iis rebus de quibus ad te scripsi. valde enim exspecto tuas litteras.

26 (II.6)

Scr. Antii paulo post superiorem

CICERO ATTICO SAL.

1 Quod tibi superioribus litteris promiseram, fore ut opus exstaret huius peregrinationis, nihil iam magno opere

[1] *al.* cutio *vel sim.* [2] nunc (*Manutius*)

---

[4] Arrius had had hopes of the Consulship.

[5] A vacancy in the College of Augurs had been created by the

I expect to hear from you about affairs in Rome. What does Arrius say and how does he like being thrown over?[4] What Consuls are in preparation—Pompey and Crassus as the general rumour goes or, as a correspondent writes to me, Gabinius and Ser. Sulpicius? Is there any new legislation? Or any news at all? And who, since Nepos is leaving, is being offered the Augurate?[5] That's the one bait they might catch me with—you see what an irresponsible fellow I am! But why ask all these questions, when I want to put all such matters aside and concentrate my whole time and energy on study? Yes, that is what I intend. I wish I had done so from the first. Now, having discovered by experience the emptiness of the things I prized most highly, I mean to concern myself with all the Muses.

All the same, tell me definitely in your reply about * and whether they are getting someone in his place and what is happening about P. Clodius. Write me everything, as you promise, in leisurely style. And would you please write to me when you think you will be leaving Rome so that I can let you know where I am going to be? Please send me a letter right away about the points I have mentioned. I am eagerly expecting to hear from you.

26 (II.6)

Antium, shortly after 25 (II.5)

CICERO TO ATTICUS

I promised you in an earlier letter that there would be work to show for this spell away from home, but I am no longer

death of Metellus Celer. His brother Nepos would have been a natural successor, but was leaving to govern a province.

confirmo; sic enim sum complexus otium ut ab eo divelli non queam. itaque aut libris me delecto, quorum habeo Anti festivam copiam, aut fluctus numero (nam ad lacertas captandas tempestates non sunt idoneae); a scribendo prorsus abhorret animus. etenim γεωγραφικὰ quae constitueram magnum opus est. ita valde Eratosthenes, quem mihi[1] proposueram, a Serapione et ab Hipparcho reprehenditur. quid censes si Tyrannio accesserit? et hercule sunt res difficiles ad explicandum et ὁμοειδεῖς nec tam possunt ἀνθηρογραφεῖσθαι quam videbantur et, quod caput est, mihi quaevis satis iusta causa cessandi est; qui etiam dubitem an hic Anti considam et hoc tempus omne consumam, ubi quidem ego mallem duumvirum quam Romae fuisse. tu vero sapientior Buthroti domum parasti. sed, mihi crede, proxima est illi municipio haec Antiatium civitas. esse locum tam prope Romam ubi multi sint qui Vatinium numquam viderint, ubi nemo sit praeter me qui quemquam ex viginti viris vivum et salvum velit, ubi me interpellet nemo, diligant omnes! hic, hic nimirum πολιτευτέον. nam istic non solum non licet sed etiam taedet. itaque ἀνέκδοτα a nobis, quae tibi uni legamus, Theopompio genere aut etiam asperiore multo pangentur. neque aliud iam quicquam πολιτεύομαι nisi odisse improbos, et id ipsum nullo cum stomacho sed potius cum aliqua †scribendi† voluptate.

2

Sed ut ad rem, scripsi ad quaestores urbanos de Quinti fratris negotio. vide quid narrent, ecquae spes sit denari an

[1] mihi auctorem *coni. SB*

---

[1] One of the two chief magistrates of Antium, corresponding to the Consuls in Rome.

very positive on the point. I have taken so kindly to idleness that I can't tear myself away from it. So I either amuse myself with books, of which I have a goodly store at Antium, or I count the waves—the weather is unsuitable for fishing mackerel. To writing I feel a downright repugnance. The Geography which I had purposed is really a big undertaking. Eratosthenes, whom I had meant to follow, is sharply censured by Serapion and Hipparchus. What if Tyrannio joins in? And really the material is hard to set out, monotonous, not so easy to embellish as it looked, and (the main point) I find any excuse good enough for doing nothing. I am even considering whether I might not settle down here at Antium and see this whole period through. I had sooner have been *duovir*[1] here than Consul in Rome. You were wiser than I in getting a house in Buthrotum. Yet I can assure you there is not much to choose between that town and this community of Antium. One can hardly believe that there could be a place so near Rome where many of the inhabitants have never seen Vatinius, where no member of the Board of Twenty[2] has a single well-wisher besides myself, where nobody disturbs me and everybody likes me. Yes, this is surely the place to practise politics. In Rome that is impossible, and what is more I am sick of it. So I shall compose *histoires inédites* which I shall read to nobody but you, in the vein of Theopompus or a lot more savage even. And my sole form of political activity now is to hate the rascals, and even that I do without spleen—rather with a certain relish in *.

But to come to business, I have written to the City Quaestors about Quintus' affair. See what they have to say,

[2] Commission set up by Caesar to supervise land distribution.

cistophoro Pompeiano iaceamus. praeterea de muro statue quid faciendum sit. aliud quid? etiam: quando te proficisci istinc putes fac ut sciam.

27 (II.7)

Scr. Antii paulo post superiorem

CICERO ATTICO SAL.

1 De geographia etiam atque etiam deliberabimus. orationes autem me duas postulas; quarum alteram non libebat mihi scribere †qui absciram†, alteram ne laudarem eum quem non amabam. sed id quoque videbimus. denique aliquid exstabit, ne tibi plane cessasse videamur.

2 De Publio quae ad me scribis sane mihi iucunda sunt, eaque etiam velim omnibus vestigiis indagata ad me adferas cum venies, et interea scribas si quid intelleges aut suspicabere, et maxime de legatione quid sit acturus. equidem ante quam tuas legi litteras [in] hominem ire cupiebam, non mehercule ut differrem cum <eo> vadimonium (nam mira sum alacritate ad litigandum), sed videbatur mihi, si quid esset in <eo> populare quod plebeius factus esset, id amissurus. quid enim? 'ad plebem transisti ut Tigranem ires salutatum? narra mihi, reges Armenii patricios resalutare non solent?' quid quaeris? acueram <me> ad exagitandam hanc eius legationem. quam si ille contemnit et si, ut scribis, bilem id commovet

[3] The question was whether Q. Cicero was to be paid his allowances as governor in Roman or Asiatic currency.

[1] Which these were is uncertain.

whether there is any hope of denarii or whether we must let ourselves be foisted off with Pompey's cistophores.[3] Also make up your mind what's to be done about the wall. What else? Oh yes, let me know when you think of leaving Rome.

27 (II.7)

Antium, shortly after 26 (II.6)

CICERO TO ATTICUS

I shall think and think again about the Geography. You ask me for two speeches.[1] One of them I did not care to write out because I *, the other because I did not want to praise a man whom I did not like. But there too we shall see. Anyhow there will be *something* to show you that I have not been entirely idle.

I find what you write to me about Publius very amusing reading, and I will go so far as to ask you to follow every track and bring the results to me when you come, and in the meantime write anything you gather or suspect, especially what he is going to do about the embassy. For my part, before I read your letter, I was anxious for him to go, not, I assure you, to put off my appointment with him in court (I am as keen as could be to commence proceedings), but it looked to me as though he would thus forfeit any popularity he might have acquired by becoming a plebeian. Imagine it! 'Was it to go and pay your respects to Tigranes that you joined the plebs? Tell me, are their Armenian Majesties in the habit of cutting patricians dead?' Yes, I had sharpened my axe to chop up this embassy of his. But if he scorns it and that ruffles, as you say, the

et latoribus et auspicibus legis curiatae, spectaculum egregium.

3 ‹Et›[1] hercule, verum ut loquamur, subcontumeliose tractatur noster Publius, primum qui, cum domi Caesaris quondam unus vir fuerit, nunc ne in viginti quidem esse potuerit; deinde alia legatio dicta erat, alia data est. illa opima ad exigendas pecunias Druso, ut opinor, Pisaurensi an epuloni Vatinio reservatur; haec ieiuna tabellari legatio datur ei cuius tribunatus ad istorum tempora reservatur. incende hominem, amabo te, quoad potest. una spes est salutis istorum inter ipsos dissensio; cuius ego quaedam initia sensi ex Curione. iam vero Arrius consulatum sibi ereptum fremit; Megabocchus et haec saginaria[2] iuventus inimicissima est. accedat vero, accedat etiam ista rixa auguratus. spero me praeclaras de istis rebus epistulas ad te saepe missurum.

4 Sed illud quid sit scire cupio quod iacis obscure, iam etiam ex ipsis quinque viris loqui quosdam. quidnam id est? si est enim aliquid, plus est boni quam putarem.[3] atque haec sic velim existimes, non me abs te κατὰ τὸ πρακτικὸν quaerere, quod gestiat animus aliquid agere in re publica. iam pridem gubernare me taedebat etiam cum licebat;

[1] *add. Watt* [2] sanguinaria (ς) [3] *al.* putaram

---

[2] A law (see Glossary) moved by Caesar as Chief Pontiff to sanction Clodius' adoption by a plebian. Pompey assisted as Augur. [3] See Letter 25, note 1. Ptolemy owed vast sums to Roman creditors and the envoy would unofficially have the lucrative job of collecting it.

[4] The allusion is obscure but evidently contemptuous.

[5] *Epulo*, one of a college of seven members in charge of sacri-

feathers of the movers and witnesses of the *lex curiata*,[2] that will really be a sight to see.

Indeed, to be candid, our Publius is being treated a trifle cavalierly. To begin with, after having once been the one and only member in Caesar's house, he has now been refused membership of the Board of Twenty. And then he was promised one embassy and given another. The fat one, for levying money,[3] is kept in reserve for Drusus of Pisaurum,[4] I fancy, or perhaps for Feast-Priest[5] Vatinius, while the man whose Tribunate is kept in reserve for when their lordships happen to want it gets this skinny errand-boy's job. Do as a favour to me stoke him up as much as may be. Our only hope of salvation lies in their falling out among themselves, of which I sensed certain germs from Curio. But now Arrius is fuming at having his Consulship snatched out of his mouth, and Megabocchus and all our pampered juniors are at daggers drawn. If only, if *only* that fight over the Augurate would come to cap the rest. I hope I shall have occasion to send you many fine letters on these matters.

But I want to know the meaning of the veiled hint you throw out that there are murmurs even among the Board of Five.[6] What's this? If there's anything to it, it's better than I should have hoped for. But please understand that I don't ask you these questions for any practical reason, because I am itching to play a part in public life. I had long grown tired of playing skipper, even when that was in my

ficial banquets. But the description seems to be facetious, alluding to an incident at which Vatinius had arrived at a dinner party wrongly dressed.

6 Perhaps a judicial committee of the Board of Twenty.

nunc vero, cum cogar exire de navi non abiectis sed ereptis gubernaculis, cupio istorum naufragia ex terra intueri, cupio, ut ait tuus amicus Sophocles,

κἂν ὑπὸ στέγῃ
πυκνῆς ἀκούειν ψακάδος εὑδούσῃ φρενί.

5 De muro, quid opus sit videbis. Castricianum mendum nos corrigemus; et tamen ad me Quintus HS[4] CCIↃↃ IↃↃ scripserat, non, ‹ut›[5] ad sororem tuam, HS †XXX a†.[6] Terentia tibi salutem dicit. Cicero tibi mandat ut Aristodemo idem de se respondeas quod de fratre suo, sororis tuae filio, respondisti. de Amalthea quod me admones non neglegemus. cura ut valeas.

28 (II.8)

Scr. Antii XV, *ut vid., Kal. Mai. an. 59 (§ 1)*

CICERO ATTICO SAL.

1 Epistulam cum a te avide exspectarem ad vesperum, ut soleo, ecce tibi nuntius pueros venisse Roma. voco, quaero ecquid litterarum. negant. 'quid ais?' inquam, 'nihilne a Pomponio?' perterriti voce et vultu confessi sunt se accepisse sed excidisse in via. quid quaeris? permoleste tuli. nulla enim abs te per hos dies epistula inanis aliqua re utili

4 di *vel* dicunt *vel sim.* (*Wesenberg*)
5 *add. Malaespina* 6 XXXV *coni. SB, alii alia*

7 The passage, from a lost play of Sophocles (*Tympanistae*), runs 'Ah, what greater joy could you have than, having touched dry land, to hear the rain falling densely, you under shelter with your mind asleep?'

power. Now, when I have—not abandoned the helm, but had it snatched out of my hands and am forced to leave the ship, I want to watch the wreck they're making from terra firma. I want, as your friend Sophocles puts it,

> beneath my roof
> With mind asleep to hear the pattering shower.[7]

About the wall, you will see what needs doing. I shall correct the Castricius mistake, though Quintus did write HS 15,000 to me, not, as he did to your sister, 35,000 (?). Terentia sends you her love. Marcus charges you to give Aristodemus[8] the same answer about him as you gave about his cousin, your nephew. I shall not neglect your reminder about Amalthea. Take care of yourself.

28 (II.8)

Antium, 16 (?) April 59

CICERO TO ATTICUS

As usual, I was avidly expecting a letter from you towards evening, when along comes word that some boys have arrived from Rome. I call them in and ask whether they have any letters for me. They say not. 'What,' say I, 'nothing from Pomponius?' Frightened by my tone and look they confessed that they *had* been given one but had lost it on the way. As you can imagine I was very much put out. Every one of the letters you have sent me lately has con-

[8] Presumably the boys' tutor. A person of this name taught Pompey's sons and later the geographer Strabo.

et suavi venerat. nunc, si quid in ea epistula quam a. d. XVI Kal. Mai. dedisti fuit historia dignum, scribe quam primum ne ignoremus; sin nihil praeter iocationem, redde id ipsum.

Et scito Curionem adulescentem venisse ad me salutatum. valde eius sermo de Publio cum tuis litteris congruebat. ipse vero mirandum in modum 'reges odisse superbos.' peraeque narrabat incensam esse iuventutem neque ferre haec posse. bene habemus nos, si in his spes est; opinor, aliud agamus. ego me do historiae. quamquam, licet me Saufeium putes esse, nihil me est inertius.

2 Sed cognosce itinera nostra, ut statuas ubi nos visurus sis. in Formianum volumus venire Parilibus. inde, quoniam putas praetermittendum nobis esse hoc tempore Cratera illum delicatum, Kal. Mai. de Formiano proficiscemur, ut Anti simus a. d. V Non. Mai. ludi enim Anti futuri sunt ex a. d. IIII [Kal.] ad prid. Non. Mai. eos Tullia spectare vult. inde cogito in Tusculanum, deinde Arpinum, Romam ad Kal. Iun. te aut in Formiano aut Anti aut in Tusculano cura ut videamus.

Epistulam superiorem restitue nobis et appinge aliquid novi.

---

[1] From Lucilius, more fully in another letter (117): 'Granius now / knew his own worth and hated proud grandees.' Granius was

tained something useful and charming. There it is. If the letter you despatched on 15 April had anything in it worth chronicling, write at once so that I am not left in ignorance. If on the other hand it was all badinage, why, I am entitled to that too.

You may be interested to hear that young Curio has called on me to pay his respects. What he had to say about Publius chimed in very well with your letter. He himself 'hates proud grandees'[1] quite remarkably. He told me that the younger set generally are no less incensed and impatient of the present regime. A fine predicament we are in if our hopes rest on them! I think we may as well find other things to think about. *I* am devoting myself to history—except that, though you are welcome to think me a Saufeius, I am the idlest of mortals.

Now here is our itinerary, so that you can make up your mind where to meet us. I want to get to Formiae on Shepherds' Day. Then, as you think I had better forgo that Bay of Luxury at the present time, we shall leave Formiae on the Kalends of May so as to be at Antium on the 3rd. There are to be some games at Antium from the 4th to the 6th which Tullia wants to watch. From there I propose to go to Tusculum, then to Arpinum, returning to Rome by the Kalends of June. Be sure to let us see you either at Formiae or at Antium or at Tusculum.

Please restore me your earlier letter and append something new.

an auctioneer, celebrated for his tart answers to the great men of the day. By *reges* (literally 'kings') Lucilius meant simply 'great persons,' but Cicero uses it with intent of Rome's present despots, the 'Triumvirs.'

29 (II.9)

Scr. Antii XV *vel* XIV *Kal. Mai., ut vid., an. 59*

CICERO ATTICO SAL.

1 Subito cum mihi dixisset Caecilius quaestor puerum se Romam mittere, haec scripsi raptim ut tuos mirificos cum Publio dialogos, cum eos de quibus scribis tum illum quem abdis et ais longum esse quae ad ea responderis perscribere, * * *;[1] illum vero qui nondum habitus est, quem illa Βοῶπις, cum e Solonio redierit, ad te est relatura, sic velim putes, nihil hoc posse mihi esse iucundius. si vero quae de me pacta sunt ea non servantur, in caelo sum, ut sciat hic noster Hierosolymarius traductor ad plebem quam bonam meis puti‹di›ssimis[2] orationibus gratiam rettulerit; quarum exspecta divinam παλινῳδίαν. etenim, quantum coniectura auguramur, si erit nebulo iste cum his dynastis in gratia, non modo de 'cynico consulari' sed ne de istis quidem 'piscinarum Tritonibus' poterit se iactare. non enim poterimus ulla esse invidia spoliati opibus et illa senatoria potentia. sin autem ab iis dissentiet, erit absurdum in nos invehi. verum tamen invehatur. festive, mihi crede, et minore sonitu quam putaram orbis hic in re publica est conversus, citius omnino quam potuit. id culpa

[1] iucundissimos mihi fuisse ostenderem *vel sim. excidisse coni. SB* [2] *add. Turnebus*

---

[1] Clodius. [2] The Greek word *boōpis* is a stock Homeric epithet of Hera. Cicero uses it as a nickname for Clodia (see Letter 21, note 4), who *had* large, brilliant eyes; also Hera was the wife of her brother Zeus.

29 (II.9)

Antium, 16 or 17 (?) April 59

CICERO TO ATTICUS

I write this in haste, as Quaestor Caecilius has suddenly told me that he is sending a boy to Rome. I want to thank you (?) for those wonderful dialogues with Publius,[1] both those of which you write and the one you hide and say it would take too long to set out your answer to what was said. As for the one that has not yet taken place, which our Lady of the Ox Eyes[2] is to report to you when she gets back from Solonium, do understand that nothing can delight me more. If however the bargain as respects myself is not observed, I am *in excelsis*—just wait till our friend from Jerusalem,[3] who manufactures plebeians so easily, learns what a fine return he has made for my toadying speeches! You may expect a superlative palinode. Indeed, as far as I can forecast, if that scamp is going to be in favour with our dynasts he won't be able to make play any more with 'Ex-Consul Tear-em'[4] or even with your Tritons of the fish ponds. Once stripped of our power and 'senatorial dominance' we can't be unpopular. On the other hand, if he is going to quarrel with them, it won't make sense for him to attack me. But let him! Amusing, isn't it, how this political wheel has with less noise than I had expected come full circle, more rapidly to be sure than might have been? That

[3] Pompey, whose troops captured Jerusalem in 63. As Augur he had assisted in Clodius' adoption.

[4] Cicero himself. R. Y. Tyrrell thus translated Clodius' description 'the Cynic Consular' ('Cynic' being derived from the Greek word for 'dog') by 'the sobriquet given to the late Mr Roebuck in the House of Commons.'

Catonis, sed rursus improbitate istorum, qui auspicia, qui Aeliam legem, qui Iuniam et Liciniam, qui Cae<ci>liam[3] et Didiam neglexerunt, qui omnia remedia rei publicae

2 effuderunt, qui regna qu<as>i[4] praedia tetrarchis, qui immanis pecunias paucis dederunt. video iam quo invidia transeat et ubi sit habitatura. nihil me existimaris neque usu neque a Theophrasto didicisse, nisi brevi tempore desiderari nostra illa tempora videris. etenim, si fuit invidiosa senatus potentia, cum ea non ad populum sed ad tris homines immoderatos redacta sit, quid iam censes fore? proinde isti licet faciant quos volunt consules, tribunos pl., denique etiam Vatini strumam sacerdoti διβάφῳ vestiant, videbis brevi tempore magnos non modo eos qui nihil titubarunt sed etiam illum ipsum qui peccavit, Catonem.

3 Nam nos quidem, si per istum tuum sodalem Publium licebit, σοφιστεύειν cogitamus; si ille cogit, at [tantum][5] dumtaxat nos defendere, et, quod est proprium artis huius, ἐπαγγέλλομαι 'ἄνδρ' ἀπαμύνεσθαι ὅτε τις πρότερος χαλεπήνῃ.' patria propitia sit. habet a nobis, etiam si non plus quam debitum est, plus certe quam postulatum est. male vehi malo alio gubernante quam tam ingratis vectoribus bene gubernare. sed haec coram commodius.

4 Nunc audi quod quaeris. Antium me ex Formiano recipere cogito a. d. v Non. Mai. Antio volo Non. Mai. pro-

[3] *add. Manutius* [4] qui (*R. Klotz*) [5] *del. Gronovius*

[5] These laws prescribed certain requirements in connection with legislation which Caesar and Vatinius had disregarded.

[6] As worn by Augurs (in two colours).

[7] From *Iliad*, 24.369. Sophists (see Glossary) would answer questions in public but not take the initiative.

has happened through Cato's fault, and then again through the rascality of our rulers, who have disregarded the auspices and the Lex Aelia and the Junia-Licinia and the Caecilia-Didia,[5] and poured our whole stock of political medicines out of the window, lavishing kingdoms on tetrarchs like private estates and enormous sums of money on a handful of individuals. It is plain enough to me now to what quarter the wind of unpopularity is veering and where it will set. You can say I have learned nothing from experience and nothing from Theophrastus if you don't soon see people regretting the old days when I was in the saddle. For if the dominance of the Senate was unpopular, what do you think the reaction is going to be now that power has been brought down not to the people but to three exorbitant individuals? So let them make Consuls and Tribunes whom they please, let them drape Vatinius' scrofulous back with a priest's double-dyed toga[6]—you will soon see not only those who never put a foot wrong but Cato himself, the one who blundered, emerge as national heroes.

As for myself, if your *copain* Publius allows me, I mean to sophisticize; but if he forces me, then to defend myself only, nothing more. In fact I profess, as befits the Sophist's *métier*, 'him to resist who offers first offence.'[7] May my country be with me! I have given her, if no more than was due, yet more at any rate than was demanded. I prefer to make a bad voyage under another pilot than to steer a good course with such ungrateful passengers. But of this better when we meet.

Now let me answer your question. I propose to return to Antium from Formiae on 3 May. From Antium I want

ficisci in Tusculanum. sed cum e Formiano rediero (ibi esse usque ad prid. Kal. Mai. volo) faciam statim te certiorem. Terentia tibi salutem *καὶ Κικέρων ὁ μικρὸς ἀσπάζεται Τίτον τὸν Ἀθηναῖον.*

30 (II.12)

Scr. Tribus Tabernis XII *Kal. Mai. an.* 59 *(§ 4)*

CICERO ATTICO SAL.

1 Negent illi Publium plebeium factum esse? hoc vero regnum est et ferri nullo pacto potest. emittat ad me Publius qui obsignent; iurabo Gnaeum nostrum, collegam Balbi Ati,[1] mihi narrasse <se> in auspicio fuisse. o suavis epistulas tuas uno tempore mihi datas duas! quibus *εὐαγγέλια* quae reddam nescio, deberi quidem plane fateor.

2 Sed vide *συγκύρημα*. emerseram commodum ex Antiati in Appiam ad Tris Tabernas ipsis Cerialibus, cum in me incurrit Roma veniens Curio meus. ibidem ilico puer abs te cum epistulis. ille ex me, nihilne audissem novi. ego negare. 'Publius' inquit 'tribunatum pl. petit.' 'quid ais?' 'et inimicissimus quidem Caesaris, et ut omnia' inquit 'ista rescindat.' 'quid Caesar?' inquam. 'negat se quicquam de illius adoptione tulisse.' deinde suum, Memmi, Metelli Nepotis exprompsit odium. complexus iuvenem dimisi

[1] anti(i) (*C. L. Smith*)

---

[8] The phrase in Greek was perhaps added by the boy himself to show his progress in the language. See end of next letter.

[1] C. Atius Balbus was Caesar's brother-in-law. Perhaps he was expected to get the vacant Augurate, in which case Pompey is called his colleague in ironic anticipation. [2] 19 April.

to leave for Tusculum on the Nones of May. But when I get back from Formiae—I want to be there until 29 April—I shall let you know at once. Terentia sends her love. *Le petit Cicéron salue Tite l' Athénien.*[8]

30 (II.12)

Tres Tabernae, 19 April 59

CICERO TO ATTICUS

What, deny that Publius has been made a plebeian? There's tyranny if you like, absolutely intolerable! Let Publius send me some witnesses—I'll make an affidavit that our friend Gnaeus, colleague of Atius Balbus,[1] told me that he assisted at the auspices. What delightful letters!—the two were handed to me together. What good news I can give you in return I don't know, but I fully admit that some is due to you.

Now observe a coincidence. I had just come out of the Antium district and joined the Appian Way at Tres Tabernae, on Ceres' Day[2] actually, when my young friend Curio runs into me on his way from Rome. At that very point along comes a boy from you with letters. Curio asked me whether I had heard the news. I said no. 'Publius,' says he, 'is standing for Tribune.' 'No, really?' 'Yes, and as Caesar's deadly enemy, and means to undo everything they've done.' 'What about Caesar?' 'Says he had nothing to do with proposing Publius' adoption.' He went on to declare his own hostility and Memmius' and Metellus Nepos'. I bade the young fellow an affectionate good-bye, in a hurry

properans ad epistulas. ubi sunt qui aiunt ζώσης φωνῆς? quanto magis vidi ex tuis litteris quam ex illius sermone quid ageretur, de rumitatione[2] cottidiana, de cogitatione Publi, de lituis Βοώπιδος, de signifero Athenione, de litteris missis ad Gnaeum, de Theophanis Memmique sermone! quantam porro mihi exspectationem dedisti convivi istius ἀσελγοῦς! sum in curiositate ὀξύπεινος, sed tamen facile patior te id ad me συμπόσιον non scribere; praesentem audire malo.

3 Quod me ut scribam aliquid hortaris, crescit mihi quidem materies ut dicis, sed tota res etiam nunc fluctuat, κατ' ὀπώρην τρύξ.[3] quae si desederit,[4] magis erunt liquata[5] quae scribam. quae si statim a me ferre non poteris, primus habebis tamen et aliquamdiu solus.

4 Dicaearchum recte amas. luculentus homo est et civis haud paulo melior quam isti nostri ἀδικαίαρχοι.

Litteras scripsi hora decima Cerialibus, statim ut tuas legeram, sed eas eram daturus, ut putabam,[6] postridie ei qui mihi obviam venisset. Terentia delectata[7] est [et] tuis litteris. impertit tibi multam salutem, καὶ Κικέρων ὁ φιλόσοφος τὸν πολιτικὸν Τίτον ἀσπάζεται.

[2] ruminatione (*SB*)
[3] τραχύς *vel sim.* (*Bosius*)
[4] decesserit (*Manutius*)
[5] iudicata (*Orelli*)
[6] putaram (*Wesenberg*)
[7] adf(i)ectata (*Victorius*)

to get to the letters. What nonsense that is about the living voice! I got an infinitely better idea from your letter than from his talk of what is going on—the daily rumormongering, Publius' plans, with Lady Ox Eyes to blow the bugle and Athenio[3] carrying the flag, the letter to Gnaeus, Theophanes' and Memmius' talk. And how you excite my expectations about that *ripaille*![4] I'm ravenous with curiosity. All the same, I don't mind your not setting out that symposium in writing—I'd rather hear it from your own lips.

You urge me to write something. My material grows, as you say, but the whole business is still in ferment, must at the vintage. When it settles down, what I write will be better clarified. If you don't get it just yet, at any rate you shall be the first one to have it, and for some time to come the only one.

You are right to admire Dicaearchus. He's an admirable fellow and a better citizen by half than those unjust rulers[5] of ours.

I write this letter at 4 o'clock in the afternoon of Ceres' Day immediately after reading yours, but I thought I would send it tomorrow by the first man I meet. Terentia was pleased by your letter. She sends you much love *et Cicéron le philosophe salue Tite le politique*.

[3] Leader of a Sicilian slave revolt in 104-100. Here a nickname for Clodius' gang-lieutenant Sex. Cloelius. An old patrician family of Cloelii bore the *cognomen* Siculus ('Sicilian').

[4] Literally 'licentious' (in Greek) 'dinner party.'

[5] The name Dicaearchus means 'just ruler.'

31 (II.10)

Scr. Appii Fori XI *Kal. Mai. an. 59*

CICERO ATTICO SAL.

Volo ames meam constantiam. ludos Anti spectare non placet. est enim ὑποσόλοικον, cum velim vitare omnium deliciarum suspicionem, repente ἀναφαίνεσϑαι non solum delicate sed etiam inepte peregrinantem. qua re usque ad Non. Mai. te in Formiano exspectabo. nunc fac ut sciam quo die te visuri simus.

Ab Appi Foro hora quarta. dederam aliam paulo ante a Tribus Tabernis.

32 (II.11)

Scr. in Formiano c. VIII *Kal. Mai., an. 59*

CICERO ATTICO SAL.

1 Narro tibi, plane relegatus mihi videor postea quam in Formiano sum. dies enim nullus erat, Anti cum essem, quo die non melius scirem Romae quid ageretur quam ii qui erant Romae. etenim litterae tuae non solum quid Romae sed etiam quid in re publica, neque solum quid fieret verum etiam quid futurum esset indicabant. nunc, nisi si quid ex praetereunte viatore exceptum est, scire nihil possumus. qua re, quamquam iam te ipsum exspecto, tamen isti puero, quem ad me statim iussi recurrere, da ponderosam aliquam epistulam plenam omnium non modo actorum sed etiam opinionum tuarum, ac diem quo Roma sis exiturus cura ut sciam.

2 Nos in Formiano esse volumus usque ad prid. Non. Mai. eo si ante eam diem non veneris, Romae te fortasse

31 (II.10)

Forum Appii, 20 April 59

CICERO TO ATTICUS

I invite you to admire my steadiness of purpose. I think I had better *not* attend the games at Antium. It would be a bit incongruous, when I want to avoid the suspicion of any kind of pleasure-seeking, to turn up suddenly as a holiday-maker amusing myself, and in so silly a fashion too. So I shall wait for you at Formiae until the Nones of May. Now let me know when we shall see you.

Appii Forum, 10 a.m. I dispatched another letter a little while ago from Tres Tabernae.

32 (II.11)

Formiae, ca. 23 April 59

CICERO TO ATTICUS

I can tell you, I feel quite an exile now that I am at Formiae. When I was at Antium, never a day passed but I was better informed of what went on in Rome than those on the spot. Your letters used to give me not only the news of the town but of the state as well, and not only of the past but the future too. Now, unless I pick up something from a passing wayfarer, I must remain in total darkness. So, though I expect you in person pretty soon, do give this boy (I've told him to hurry back to me at once) a massive letter, full of news and also of your own comment, and mind you let me know what day you are leaving Rome.

We want to stay at Formiae until 6 May. If you don't come before then, perhaps I shall see you in Rome. No use

videbo; nam Arpinum quid ego te invitem?

τρηχεῖ', ἀλλ' ἀγαθὴ κουροτρόφος, οὔτ' ἄρ' ἔγωγε
ἧς γαίης δύναμαι γλυκερώτερον ἄλλο ἰδέσθαι.

haec igitur, et cura ut valeas.

33 (II.13)

Scr. in Formiano c. VII Kal. Mai. an. 59

CICERO ATTICO SAL.

1 Facinus indignum! epistulam *αὐθωρεὶ* tibi a Tribus Tabernis rescriptam ad tuas suavissimas epistulas neminem reddidisse! at scito eum fasciculum quo illam conieceram domum eo ipso die latum esse quo ego dederam et ad me in Formianum relatum esse. itaque tibi tuam epistulam iussi referri, ex qua intellegeres quam mihi tum illae gratae fuissent.

2 Romae quod scribis sileri, ita putabam. at hercule in agris non siletur, nec iam ipsi agri regnum vestrum ferre possunt. si vero in hanc *Τηλέπυλον* veneris *Λαιστρυγονίην*, Formias dico, qui fremitus hominum! quam irati animi! quanto in odio noster amicus Magnus! cuius cognomen una cum Crassi Divitis cognomine consenescit. credas mihi velim, neminem adhuc offendi qui haec tam lente quam ego fero ferret. qua re, mihi crede, *φιλοσοφῶμεν*. iuratus tibi possum dicere nihil esse tanti.

---

[1] From *Odyssey*, 9.27, with reference to the island of Ithaca.

[1] Town in *Odyssey,* 10.82, with which Formiae was identified.

[2] 'Rich.' The person named is not Crassus the 'Triumvir' (who did not have this additional *cognomen*) but a contemporary de-

inviting you to Arpinum.

> Rough land, but breeds good men; and as for me,
> I can see no sight sweeter than my home.[1]

All for now then. Take care of your health.

33 (II.13)

Formiae, ca. 24 April 59

CICERO TO ATTICUS

What a shame! My letter, written to you without delay from Tres Tabernae in reply to your most charming ones, never delivered! I must tell you that the bag in which I threw it was brought to my house in town on the day of dispatch and brought back to me at Formiae. So I am having your letter sent back to you to let you know how much at the time I appreciated those you wrote me.

You say that tongues are silent in Rome. I am not surprised. But my goodness, they are not silent in the country! The very fields cannot put up with your tyrannical regime. But if you come to Laestrygonian Telepylus[1] here, that is to say to Formiae, you will find the place seething with anger and denunciation. How they hate our Great friend! His surname is as flyblown as that of Crassus Dives.[2] Seriously I have not yet met a soul who takes it all as patiently as I do. So take my advice and let us stick to our studies. I can give you my oath that nothing is so rewarding.

scendant of the Crassus referred to in Letter 9. He seems to have gone bankrupt some years later.

Tu si litteras ad Sicyonios habes, advola in Formianum, unde nos prid. Non. Mai. cogitamus.

34 (II.14)

Scr. in Formiano c. v Kal. Mai. an. 59

CICERO ATTICO SAL.

1 Quantam tu mihi moves exspectationem de sermone Bibuli,[1] quantam de colloquio Βοώπιδος, quantam etiam de illo delicato convivio! proinde ita fac venias ‹ut› ad sitientis auris. quamquam nihil est iam quod magis timendum nobis putem quam ne ille noster Sampsiceramus, cum se omnium sermonibus sentiet vapulare et cum has actiones εὐανατρέπτους videbit, ruere incipiat. ego autem usque eo sum enervatus ut hoc otio quo nunc tabescimus malim ἐντυραννεῖσθαι quam cum optima spe dimicare.

2 De pangendo quod me crebro adhortaris, fieri nihil potest. basilicam habeo, non villam frequentia Formianorum †ad quam partem basilicae tribum Aemiliam†. sed omitto vulgus; post horam quartam molesti ceteri non sunt. C. Arrius proximus est vicinus, immo ille quidem iam contubernalis, qui etiam se idcirco Romam ire negat ut hic mecum totos dies philosophetur. ecce ex altera parte Sebosus, ille Catuli familiaris. quo me vertam? statim mehercule Arpinum irem, ni te in Formiano commodissime exspectari viderem, dumtaxat ad prid. Non. Mai. vide enim

[1] Publii *Boot*

---

[1] Ruler of a principality in Syria, hence a nickname for Pompey.

If you have your letter to the Sicyonians, hurry over to Formiae, which we mean to leave on 6 May.

34 (II.14)

Formiae, ca. 26 April 59

CICERO TO ATTICUS

How you whet my appetite about your talk with Bibulus, your discussion with Ox Eyes, and that apolaustic dinner party too! So come expecting thirsty ears. But the most serious danger we now have to fear in my opinion is that when our Sampsiceramus[1] realizes that his name is mud in every man's mouth and sees that these proceedings are very liable to be upset, he may start plunging. For my part I have so lost my manly spirit that I prefer to be tyrannized over in peace and quiet such as is now rotting our fibre than to fight with the rosiest prospect of success.

You are always urging me to composition, but it's out of the question. It's not a country house I have here but a public exchange, so many of the good folk of Formiae come in * * *. But never mind the multitude—after 10 o'clock the common run doesn't bother me. But my closest neighbour is one C. Arrius, or rather roommate, for that is what he has now become. He actually says he won't go to Rome because he wants to philosophize with me here all day long. Then on the other side there is Catulus' friend Sebosus. Where is a man to turn? I would go to Arpinum right away upon my word, only it's clearly most convenient for me to expect you at Formiae—up to 6 May that is, no

quibus hominibus aures sint deditae meae. occasionem mirificam, si qui nunc, dum hi apud me sunt, emere de me fundum Formianum velit! et tamen illud probe, 'magnum quid adgrediamur et multae cogitationis atque oti.' sed tamen satis fiet a nobis neque parcetur labori.

35 (II.15)

Scr. in Formiano c. III *Kal. Mai. an.* 59

CICERO ATTICO SAL.

1 Ut scribis ita video, non minus incerta in re publica quam in epistula tua, sed tamen ista ipsa me varietas sermonum opinionumque delectat. Romae enim videor esse cum tuas litteras lego et, ut fit in tantis rebus, modo hoc modo illud audire. illud tamen explicare non possum quidnam inveniri 2 possit nullo recusante ad facultatem agrariam. Bibuli autem ista magnitudo animi in comitiorum dilatione quid habet nisi ipsius iudicium sine ulla correctione rei publicae? nimirum in Publio spes est. fiat, fiat tribunus pl., si nihil aliud ut eo citius tu ex Epiro revertare. nam ut illo tu careas non video posse fieri, praesertim si mecum aliquid volet disputare. sed id quidem non dubium est quin, si quid erit eius modi, sis advolaturus. verum ut hoc non sit, tamen, sive ruet ‹sive eri›get[1] rem publicam, praeclarum spectaculum mihi propono, modo te consessore spectare liceat.

[1] *add. Corradus*

longer, for look at the kind of people I am condemned to listen to! What a marvellous opportunity for anyone who might be interested in buying my place here while these fellows are on my carpet! And yet you say, and very fine too, 'Let's attack something big, something that needs plenty of thought and time.' However, I shan't disappoint you nor spare my pains.

35 (II.15)

Formiae, ca. 28 April 59

CICERO TO ATTICUS

Evidently it is as you say, things are as uncertain in the political field as in your letter; but it is just this diversity of talk and views that I find so entertaining. When I read a letter of yours I feel I am in Rome, hearing one thing one minute another the next, as one does when big events are toward. One point I can't make out, how a scheme can possibly be devised for providing enough land without exciting opposition. Bibulus' action in holding up the elections may be very noble, but what does it achieve except a personal protest which offers no solution to the country's troubles? Depend upon it, Publius is our only hope. Yes, let him become Tribune, if only to bring you back the sooner from Epirus. I don't see how you can possibly bear to miss him, especially if it turns out that he wants an argument with me. But of course you will hurry back if anything of that sort happens. But even if it doesn't, I promise myself a magnificent show, whether he runs amok or sets the state on its feet again—if only I can watch it with you in the next seat!

3 Cum haec maxime scribebam, ecce tibi Sebosus! nondum plane ingemueram, 'salve' inquit Arrius. hoc est Roma decedere? quos ego homines effugi, cum in hos incidi? ego vero 'in montis patrios et ad incunabula nostra' pergam. denique, si solus non potuero, cum rusticis potius quam cum his perurbanis, ita tamen ut, quoniam tu nihil certi scribis, in Formiano tibi praestoler usque ad III Non. Mai.

4 Terentiae pergrata est adsiduitas tua et diligentia in controversia Mulviana. nescit omnino te communem causam defendere eorum qui agros publicos possideant. sed tamen tu aliquid publicanis pendis, haec etiam id recusat. ea tibi igitur et Κικέρων, ἀριστοκρατικώτατος παῖς, salutem dicunt.

36 (II.16)

Scr. in Formiano prid. Kal. vel Kal. Mai. an. 59 (§ 1)

CICERO ATTICO SAL.

1 Cenato mihi et iam dormitanti prid. Kal. Mai. epistula est illa reddita in qua de agro Campano scribis. quid quaeris? primo ita me pupugit ut somnum mihi ademerit, sed id cogitatione magis quam molestia. cogitanti autem haec fere succurrebant. primum ex eo quod superioribus litteris scripseras, ex familiari te illius audisse prolatum iri aliquid quod nemo improbaret, maius aliquid timueram. hoc mihi eius modi non videbatur. deinde, ut me egomet consoler,

[1] Probably from Ennius.

Just as I was writing these lines—along comes Sebosus! I had hardly finished groaning when 'Good morning to you' says Arrius. And this is getting away from Rome and people! There's the frying pan and here's the fire! Well, I shall go to 'my native hills, the cradle of my birth.'[1] If the worst comes to the worst and solitude is unattainable, better the society of countryfolk than of these hypersophisticates. But I shall wait for you at Formiae till 5 May as you don't say anything definite.

Terentia is most grateful for all your care and trouble over the Mulvius case. To be sure she does not know that you are championing the common cause of public land occupiers. But you do pay something to the tax farmers, she won't even do that. So she and *Cicéron, enfant très aristocrate,* send you their love.

36 (II.16)

Formiae, 29 April or 1 May 59

CICERO TO ATTICUS

Dinner was over and I had already begun to nod when (29 April) I received your letter about the Campanian Domain. In a word, it gave me such a shock at first that sleep became impossible, but rather from activity than distress of mind. The points which occur to me as I turn the matter over are more or less as follows: In the first place, from what you wrote in your previous letter, that you had heard from a friend of Caesar's that something would be proposed which nobody would disapprove of, I had feared something on a pretty large scale. This doesn't have that appearance. Then (I'm comforting myself, you see) all ex-

omnis exspectatio largitionis agrariae in agrum Campanum videtur esse derivata, qui ager, ut dena iugera sint, non amplius hominum quinque milia potest sustinere; reliqua omnis multitudo ab illis abalienetur necesse est. praeterea, si ulla res est quae bonorum animos, quos iam video esse commotos, vehementius possit incendere, haec certe est, et eo magis quod portoriis Italiae sublatis, agro Campano diviso, quod vectigal superest domesticum praeter vicesimam? quae mihi videtur una contiuncula clamore pedisequorum nostrorum esse peritura.

2 Gnaeus quidem noster iam plane quid cogitet nescio:

> *φυσᾷ γὰρ οὐ σμικροῖσιν αὐλίσκοις ἔτι,*
> *ἀλλ’ ἀγρίαις φύσαισι φορβειᾶς ἄτερ,*

qui quidem etiam istuc adduci potuerit. nam adhuc haec *ἐσοφίζετο*, se leges Caesaris probare, actiones ipsum praestare debere; agrariam legem sibi placuisse, potuerit intercedi necne nihil ad se pertinere; de rege Alexandrino placuisse sibi aliquando confici, Bibulus de caelo tum servasset necne sibi quaerendum non fuisse; de publicanis, voluisse illi ordini commodare, quicquid futurum fuerit si Bibulus tum in forum descendisset se divinare non potuisse. nunc vero, Sampsicerame, quid dices? vectigal te nobis in monte Antilibano constituisse, agri Campani

---

[1] A tax on the manumission of slaves.

[2] From Sophocles (fr. 768).

[3] The announcement by a magistrate of his intention to 'watch the skies' (for omens from lightning) was generally regarded as a ban on a prospective assembly, since by reporting an unfavourable omen he could make it illegal for the assembly to transact business. Caesar, however, took no notice of this form of obstruction.

pectation of land allotment seems to have been channelled into the Campanian Domain, and that, at seven acres per man, cannot support more than 5000 grantees; so they are bound to lose the support of the multitude left over. Moreover if anything could further inflame better-class sentiment, roused already as it evidently is, assuredly this will do it; especially since after the abolition of customs duties in Italy and the distribution of the Campanian Domain the only internal revenue left is the five percent[1]—and that will probably be swept away by the shouts of our footmen at a single scratch assembly.

What our friend Gnaeus is up to now I simply do not know:

> On tiny pipes no longer now he blows,
> But, mouthband off, he puffs and blasts amain,[2]

seeing that he's allowed himself to be pushed even to this length. Hitherto he has quibbled, taking the line that he approves of Caesar's legislation, but that Caesar himself must take responsibility for his procedure. Thus he (Pompey) was in favour of the agrarian bill, but whether opportunity was given for a veto or not was no concern of his. He was in favour of settling the King of Egypt's affair at long last, but whether or not Bibulus had been watching the skies[3] at the time it was not his business to inquire. As for the tax farmers, he had wished to oblige the Equestrian Order, but could not be expected to prophesy all that would happen if Bibulus went down to the Forum at that juncture. Very well, my good Sampsiceramus, but what are you going to say now? That you have arranged a revenue for us in Mt Antilibanus and taken away our rents in Cam-

abstulisse? quid? hoc quem ad modum obtinebis? 'oppressos vos' inquit 'tenebo exercitu Caesaris.' non mehercule me tu quidem tam isto exercitu quam ingratis animis eorum hominum qui appellantur boni, qui mihi non modo praemiorum sed ne sermonum quidem umquam fructum

3 ullum aut gratiam rettulerunt. quod si in eam me partem incitarem, profecto iam aliquam reperirem resistendi viam. nunc prorsus hoc statui ut, quoniam tanta controversia est Dicaearcho, familiari tuo, cum Theophrasto, amico meo, ut ille tuus *τὸν πρακτικὸν βίον* longe omnibus anteponat, hic autem *τὸν θεωρητικόν*, utrique a me mos gestus esse videatur. puto enim me Dicaearcho adfatim satis fecisse; respicio nunc ad hanc familiam quae mihi non modo ut requiescam permittit sed reprehendit quia non semper quierim. qua re incumbamus, o noster Tite, ad illa praeclara studia, et eo unde discedere non oportuit aliquando revertamur.

4 Quod de Quinti fratris epistula scribis, ad me quoque fuit '*πρόσθε λέων, ὄπιθεν δὲ*' — quid dicam nescio. nam ita deplorat primis versibus mansionem suam ut quemvis movere possit; ita rursus remittit ut me roget ut annalis suos emendem et edam. illud tamen quod scribit[1] animadvertas velim, de portorio circumvectionis; ait se de consili sententia rem ad senatum reiecisse. nondum videlicet meas litteras legerat, quibus ad eum re consulta et explorata perscripseram non deberi. velim, si qui Graeci iam

[1] scribis (ς)

---

4 Beginning of *Iliad*, 6.181: 'In front a lion, behind a snake, in the middle a goat.' 5 I.e., transferred from one harbour to another and so paying double duty.

pania? How are you going to make that sound convincing? Perhaps the answer will be: 'I'll keep you all under with Caesar's army.' Oh no you won't. It won't be that army of yours that will keep *me* under so much as the ingratitude of the honest men as they are called, who have never made me the slightest return or recompense, material or even verbal. But if I had urged myself in that direction I should surely have found some method of opposition before now. Things being as they are, my mind is made up. Since your crony Dicaearchus and my favourite Theophrastus are so much at loggerheads, your man rating the active life far and away the best and mine the contemplative, I mean to figure as one who has humoured them both. For I think I have done quite enough to satisfy Dicaearchus; now I turn to the other school, which not only permits me to rest from my labours but scolds me for labouring in the first place. So, Titus mine, let me throw myself into my studies, those wonderful studies which I ought never to have left and to which I must now at last return.

You write of my brother Quintus' letter. He wrote to me in the same strain, 'in like a lion, out like a—'[4] well, I don't quite know what to call it. In his opening lines he laments having to stay on in a way that would move a heart of stone; then again he so far relaxes as to ask me to correct and publish his history. But please pay attention to the point about excise duty on transferred goods.[5] He says that he has referred the question to the Senate on the advice of his council. Evidently he had not read my letter in which, after thorough reflection and inquiry, I propounded to him that no tax is due. If any provincials have already come to Rome

Romam ex Asia de ea causa venerunt, videas et, si tibi videbitur, iis demonstres quid ego de ea re sentiam. si possunt[2] decidere,[3] ne causa optima in senatu pereat, ego satis faciam publicanis; εἰ δὲ μή (vere tecum loquar), in hac re malo universae Asiae et negotiatoribus; nam eorum quoque vehementer interest. hoc ego sentio valde nobis opus esse. sed tu id videbis.

Quaestores, autem, quaeso, num etiam de cistophoro dubitant? nam si aliud nihil erit, cum erimus omnia experti, ego ne illud quidem contemnam quod extremum est.

Te in Arpinati videbimus et hospitio agresti accipiemus, quoniam maritimum hoc contempsisti.

37 (II.17)

Scr. in Formiano paulo post superiorem

CICERO ATTICO SAL.

1 Prorsus ut scribis ita sentio, turbat Sampsiceramus. nihil est quod non timendum sit; ὁμολογουμένως τυραννίδα συσκευάζεται. quid enim ista repentina adfinitatis coniunctio, quid ager Campanus, quid effusio pecuniae significant? quae si essent extrema, tamen esset nimium mali; sed ea natura rei est ut haec extrema esse non possint. quid enim eos haec ipsa per se delectare possunt? numquam huc venissent nisi ad alias res pestiferas aditus sibi compararent. verum, ut scribis, haec in Arpinati a. d. VI circiter Id. Mai. — non deflebimus, ne et opera et oleum

[2] possum (*SB*) [3] discedere (*Madvig*)

[1] Pompey's marriage to Caesar's daughter Julia.

from Asia on this matter I should be grateful if you would see them and, if you think fit, explain to them my views on it. If they can reach a settlement, then, to keep the good cause alive in the Senate, I shall not fail the tax farmers. Otherwise, to be frank with you, on this matter my sentiments are rather with the entire province of Asia and the local businessmen, who are also very closely concerned. I feel that this is very important to us. But you will see to it.

Tell me about the Quaestors. Are they boggling even about paying in cistophores? I ask because if nothing else is forthcoming, when we have tried all we know, I shouldn't despise even that last resort.

We shall see you at Arpinum and welcome you in country style since you have scorned our seaside hospitality.

37 (II.17)

Formiae, shortly after 36 (II. 16)

CICERO TO ATTICUS

I am entirely of your opinion. Sampsiceramus is out for trouble. We can expect anything. He is confessedly working for absolute power. What else signifies this sudden marriage connection,[1] or the Campanian Domain, or the pouring out of money? If all this were the end it would be worse than bad enough, but by the nature of the case it cannot be the end. They can't like these measures in and for themselves. They would never have come so far if they were not paving their way to other and disastrous objectives. However, as you say, we shall bewail all this at Arpinum on 10 May or thereabouts, or rather not bewail it, for that would mean that our studies had been a waste of

philologiae nostrae perierit, sed conferemus tranquillo animo. * * *[1] di immortales, neque tam me εὐελπιστία consolatur, ut antea, quam ἀδιαφορία, qua nulla in re tam utor quam in hac civili et publica. quin etiam quod est subinane in nobis et non ἀφιλόδοξον (bellum est enim sua vitia nosse), id adficitur quadam delectatione. solebat enim me pungere ne Sampsicerami merita in patriam ad annos sescentos maiora viderentur quam nostra. hac quidem cura certe iam vacuus sum. iacet enim ille sic ut 'Phocis' Curiana stare videatur. sed haec coram. tu tamen videris mihi Romae fore ad nostrum adventum, quod sane facile patiar si tuo commodo fieri possit. sin ut scribis ita venies, velim ex Theophane expiscere quonam in me animo sit Arabarches. quaeres scilicet κατὰ τὸ κηδεμονικὸν et ad me ab eo quasi ὑποθήκας adferes quem ad modum me geram. aliquid ex eius sermone poterimus περὶ τῶν ὅλων suspicari.

2

3

38 (II.18)

Scr. Romae m. Iun. an. 59

CICERO ATTICO SAL.

1 Accepi aliquot epistulas tuas, ex quibus intellexi quam suspenso animo et sollicito scire averes quid esset novi. tenemur undique, neque iam quo minus serviamus recusamus sed mortem et eiectionem quasi maiora timemus, quae

[1] *lacunam hic ind. SB (ante* neque *Wesenberg) ita fere supplendum:* quo ego quam utor tranquillo

[2] Apparently a play by an otherwise unknown author.

[3] Pompey.

time and trouble, but talk it over in a tranquil spirit. Mine, heaven knows, is tranquil enough (?). Nor is it optimism so much that consoles me, as in time past, as indifference, a state of mind I particularly cultivate in these public and political matters. Indeed a certain foolish vanity to which I am somewhat prone (it's a fine thing to know one's failings) is actually gratified in a way. I used to be piqued by the thought that a thousand years hence Sampsiceramus' services to Rome might be rated higher than mine. I can now rest easy on *that* score. The flop of his reputation makes Curius' 'Woman of Phocis'[2] look like a popular success. But we will talk over all this when we meet. However, it looks to me as though you will still be in Rome when we get back, and I should really just as soon you were if you can conveniently manage it. But if you do come as you say you will, would you kindly fish out of Theophanes how our Arabian Prince[3] is disposed towards me? You will of course make your inquiries as a relative, and bring me a prescription as it were from him on how to conduct myself. We shall be able to get some inkling of the general situation from what he says.

38 (II.18)

Rome, June 59

CICERO TO ATTICUS

I have received several letters of yours from which I could see in what suspense and anxiety you were craving for news. Well, we are held down on all sides. We don't object any longer to the loss of our freedom, but fear death and expulsion as greater evils, which are really far lesser. All

multo sunt minora. atque hic status, qui una voce omnium gemitur, ‹neque facto›[1] neque verbo cuiusquam sublevatur. *σκοπὸς* est, ut suspicor, illis qui tenent nullam cuiquam largitionem relinquere. unus loquitur et palam adversatur adulescens Curio. huic plausus maximi, consalutatio forensis perhonorifica, signa praeterea benevolentiae permulta a bonis impertiuntur. Fufium clamoribus et conviciis et sibilis consectantur. his ex rebus non spes sed dolor est maior, cum videas civitatis voluntatem solutam, virtutem adligatam.

2 Ac ne forte quaeras *κατὰ λεπτὸν* de singulis rebus, universa res eo est deducta spes ut nulla sit aliquando non modo privatos verum etiam magistratus liberos fore. hac tamen in oppressione sermo in circulis dumtaxat et in conviviis est liberior quam fuit. vincere incipit timorem dolor, sed ita ut omnia sint plenissima desperationis. habet etiam Campana lex exsecrationem in contione candidatorum, si mentionem fecerint, quo aliter ager possideatur atque ut ex legibus Iuliis. non dubitant iurare ceteri; Laterensis existimatur laute fecisse quod tribunatum pl. petere destitit ne iuraret.

3 Sed de re publica non libet plura scribere. displiceo mihi nec sine summo scribo dolore. me tueor ut oppressis omnibus non demisse, ut tantis rebus gestis parum fortiter. a Caesare valde liberaliter invitor in legationem illam, sibi ut sim legatus, atque etiam libera legatio voti causa datur.

[1] *add. SB*

with one accord groan of the present state of affairs, yet no one does or says a thing to better it. The object of the people in power, I imagine, is to leave nothing for anybody else to give away. The only one to speak or offer open opposition is young Curio. He gets hearty rounds of applause, a most flattering amount of general salutation in the Forum, and a great many other signs of good will from the honest men. Fufius on the other hand they pursue with catcalls and abuse and hisses. All this doesn't make one more hopeful, but only sadder to see that the sentiment of the community is free while its courage is in chains.

You need not ask for details about this or that. The whole situation has reached a point at which no hope remains of even magistrates, let alone private individuals, ever becoming free men again. Yet in the midst of this suppression of liberty conversation is less inhibited than it used to be, at social gatherings, that is, and over dinner tables. Indignation is beginning to get the upper hand of fear, not however so as to lift the cloud of blank despair. The Campanian law too has a curse clause, to be pronounced upon themselves at a public meeting by all candidates for office, should they moot any form of land ownership not in accordance with the Julian laws. All are taking the oath without demur except Laterensis, who is thought to have made a fine gesture in giving up his candidature for the Tribunate rather than swear it.

But I have no stomach for more about politics. I'm out of humour with myself and writing is most painful. I keep my end up, not too abjectly in view of the general subjugation, but less boldly than befits my past. Caesar is inviting me very handsomely to accept that Commissionership, the one on his staff, and I am also offered a Free Commission

sed haec et praesidi apud pudorem Pulchelli non habet satis et a fratris adventu me ablegat; illa et munitior est et non impedit quo minus adsim cum velim. hanc e<r>go[2] teneo, sed usurum me non puto; neque tamen scit quisquam. non libet fugere, aveo pugnare. magna sunt hominum studia. sed nihil adfirmo; tu hoc silebis.

4 De Statio manu misso et non nullis aliis rebus angor equidem, sed iam prorsus occallui. tu vellem ego vel[3] cuperem adesses; nec mihi consilium nec consolatio deesset. sed ita te para ut, si inclamaro, advoles.

39 (II.19)

Scr. Romae inter Non. et prid. Id. Quint. an. 59

CICERO ATTICO SAL.

1 Multa me sollicitant et ex rei publicae tanto motu et ex his periculis quae mihi ipsi intenduntur. et sescenta sunt, sed mihi nihil est molestius quam Statium manu missum:

> nec meum imperium, ac mitto imperium, non
> simultatem meam
> revereri saltem!

nec quid faciam scio, neque tantum est in re quantus est sermo. ego autem ne irasci possum quidem iis quos valde amo; tantum doleo, ac mirifice quidem. cetera in magnis rebus. minae Clodi contentionesque <quae> mihi pro-

[2] ego (*Orelli*)
[3] ve (*Mueller*)

[1] From Terence's comedy *Phormio*, 232.

in Discharge of Vow. But the protection offered by the latter, resting on Little Beauty's sense of decency, is insufficient, and it takes me away just when my brother will be coming home. The former is safer and does not prevent me being in Rome when I want. So I have this in the bag, but I don't think I shall use it. Still, nobody knows. I have no inclination to run away, I am spoiling for a fight. I have strong public backing. But I make no promises. You will keep this to yourself.

About Statius' manumission and certain other matters, I am distressed of course, but I have become pretty hardened. I could wish, indeed more than wish, you were here. I should then lack neither counsel nor comfort. But do be ready to hurry over if I give the call.

39 (II.19)

Rome, between 7 and 14 July 59

CICERO TO ATTICUS

I have many things on my mind, arising from the grave political crisis and these dangers that menace me personally. They are legion, but nothing distresses me more than Statius' manumission.

> That my commands—no, set commands aside, that
> my displeasure
> Should count with him for nothing![1]

And yet I don't know what to do, and, after all, the talk is more than the thing itself. Moreover I can't even be angry with those I really love. I am only pained, deeply pained. My other troubles are set in great affairs. Clodius' threats

ponuntur modice me tangunt. etenim vel subire eas videor mihi summa cum dignitate vel declinare nulla cum molestia posse. dices fortasse 'dignitatis ἅλις tamquam δρυός! saluti, si me amas, consule.' me miserum! cur non ades? nihil te profecto praeteriret. ego fortasse τυφλώττω et nimium τῷ καλῷ προσπέπονθα.

2 Scito nihil umquam fuisse tam infame, tam turpe, tam peraeque omnibus generibus, ordinibus, aetatibus offensum, quam hunc statum qui nunc est, magis mehercule quam vellem, non modo quam putarem. populares isti iam etiam modestos homines sibilare docuerunt. Bibulus in caelo est, nec qua re scio, sed ita laudatur quasi ‹qui›[1] 'unus homo nobis cunctando restituit rem.' Pompeius, nostri amores, quod mihi summo dolori est, ipse se adflixit. neminem tenent voluntate; an metu necesse sit iis uti vereor. ego autem neque pugno cum illa causa propter illam amicitiam neque adprobo ne omnia improbem quae antea gessi. utor via ‹media›.[2]

3 Populi sensus maxime theatro et spectaculis perspectus est. nam gladiatoribus qua dominus qua advocati sibilis conscissi, ludis Apollinaribus Diphilus tragoedus in nostrum Pompeium petulanter invectus est: 'nostra miseria tu es magnus' miliens coactus est dicere. 'eandem virtutem

[1] *add. Watt* (*post* homo *Wesenberg*)
[2] *add. Wesenberg* (*ante* utor *Koch*)

---

[2] A Greek saying: 'We don't eat acorns any more.' The French rendering (from Voltaire) is due to G. E. Jeans.

[3] Ennius' well-known line on Hannibal's opponent in the Second Punic War, Fabius Cunctator (*Annals*, 370).

and the combats I have to expect give me only moderate concern, for I think I can either face them with all honour or decline them without embarrassment. Perhaps you will say that we have had enough of honour—*le siècle du gland est passé*[2]—and implore me to think of security. Oh dear, why are you not here? Nothing, I am sure, would escape you, whereas I perhaps am blind and hold too fast to that which is good.

The truth is that the present regime is the most infamous, disgraceful, and uniformly odious to all sorts and classes and ages of men that ever was, more so upon my word than I could have wished, let alone expected. These 'popular' politicians have taught even quiet folk to hiss. Bibulus is *in excelsis,* I don't know why, but they laud him as though he were the man who 'singly by delaying saved our all.'[3] My beloved Pompey, to my great sorrow, has been the author of his own downfall. They hold nobody by good will; that they may find it necessary to use terror is what I am afraid of. For my part I do not fight what they are doing on account of my friendship with him, and I do not endorse it, for that would be to condemn all that I did in days gone by. I take a middle way.

Popular sentiment has been most manifest at the theatre and the shows. At the gladiators both the Showmaster and his guests (?)[4] were overwhelmed with hisses. At the Games of Apollo Diphilus the actor attacked poor Pompey quite brutally: 'To our misfortune are you Great'[5] —there were a dozen *encores.*

[4] Probably the Showmaster is Gabinius and his guests are the 'Triumvirs.' [5] This and the following quotations come from an unknown Latin tragedy.

istam veniet tempus cum graviter gemes' totius theatri clamore dixit itemque cetera. nam et eius modi sunt ii versus ut in tempus ab inimico Pompei scripti esse videantur. 'si neque leges neque mores cogunt' et cetera magno cum fremitu et clamore sunt dicta. Caesar cum venisset mortuo plausu, Curio filius est insecutus. huic ita plausum est ut salva re publica Pompeio plaudi solebat. tulit Caesar graviter. litterae Capuam ad Pompeium volare dicebantur. inimici erant equitibus, qui Curioni stantes plauserant, hostes omnibus; Rosciae legi, etiam frumentariae minitabantur. sane res erat perturbata. equidem malueram quod erat susceptum ab illis silentio transire, sed vereor ne non liceat. non ferunt homines quod videtur esse tamen ferendum. sed est iam una vox omnium, magis odio firmata quam praesidio.

4 Noster autem Publius mihi minitatur, inimicus est. impendet negotium, ad quod tu scilicet advolabis. videor mihi nostrum illum consularem exercitum bonorum omnium, etiam satis bonorum, habere firmissimum. Pompeius significat studium erga me non mediocre. idem adfirmat verbum de me illum non esse facturum; in quo non me ille fallit, sed ipse fallitur. Cosconio mortuo sum in eius locum invitatus. id erat vocari in locum mortui. nihil me turpius apud homines fuisset, neque vero ad istam ipsam

[6] A member of Caesar's agrarian Board of Twenty.

[7] Lit. 'a summons into a dead man's place,' seemingly a cant phrase, perhaps with a gladiatorial or military origin; cf. Festus, p. 17 Lindsay: accensi *dicebantur qui in locum mortuorum militum subito subrogabantur.*

But that same manhood bitterly
In time to come shall you lament.

The whole audience vociferated applause as he spoke that, and the rest also. Indeed these lines might seem to have been written for the occasion by an enemy of Pompey. 'If neither law nor custom can constrain,' etc., was recited to a loud accompaniment of shouting and clapping. When Caesar entered, applause was nonexistent. He was followed by Curio junior, who received the sort of ovation that Pompey used to get in the days before freedom fell. Caesar took it badly, and a letter is said to be winging its way to Pompey in Capua. They hate the Knights, who stood up to applaud Curio, they are at war with the whole community. They threaten the Roscian law, even the corn law. It's a pretty kettle of fish. I myself should have preferred their game to run its course in silence, but I am afraid that may not be possible. Public opinion won't endure it any longer, yet endured apparently it must be. But now there is only one universal cry, though with hatred rather than power behind it.

Dear Publius is threatening me, most hostile. The business is looming, and you will naturally make haste back to meet it. I think I have very firm backing in my old consular army of all honest men, including the moderately honest. Pompey signifies good will towards me out of the ordinary. He also assures me that Clodius will not say a word about me, wherein he does not deceive me but is himself deceived. When Cosconius[6] died I was invited to take his place. That was a summons into the breach[7]—a signal public disgrace and worse than useless even as regards 'secu-

ἀσφάλειαν quicquam alienius. sunt enim illi apud bonos invidiosi, ego apud improbos; meam retinuissem invidiam,
5 alienam adsumpsissem. Caesar me sibi vult[3] esse legatum. honestior haec declinatio periculi, sed ego hoc non repudio. quid ergo est? pugnare malo. nihil tamen certi. iterum dico 'utinam adesses!' sed tamen, si erit necesse, arcessemus.

Quid aliud? quid? hoc, opinor: certi sumus perisse omnia. quid enim ἀκκιζόμεθα tam diu?

Sed haec scripsi properans et mehercule timide. posthac ad te aut, si perfidelem habebo cui dem, scribam plane omnia, aut, si obscure scribam, tu tamen intelleges. in iis epistulis me Laelium, te Furium faciam; cetera erunt ἐν αἰνιγμοῖς.

Hic Caecilium colimus et observamus diligenter. edicta Bibuli audio ad te missa. iis ardet dolore et ira noster Pompeius.

40 (II.20)

Scr. Romae m. Quint. an. 59

CICERO ATTICO SAL.

1 Anicato, ut te velle intellexeram, nullo loco defui. Numestium ex litteris tuis studiose scriptis libenter in amicitiam recepi. Caecilium, quibus rebus par est, tueor diligenter. Varro satis facit nobis. Pompeius amat nos carosque habet. 'credis?' inquies. credo; prorsus mihi persuadet, sed quia

[3] volet (*Victorius*)

[8] After C. Laelius Sapiens and L. Furius Philus, friends of the younger Scipio Africanus.

rity.' For they are unpopular with the honest men, I with the rascals. I should have kept my own unpopularity and accepted other people's as well. Caesar wants to have me on his staff. That would be a more respectable evasion of the danger, which however I do not decline. It comes to this, I would rather fight. But my mind is not made up. Again I say, 'If only you were here!' However, if the need arises I shall send for you.

What else now, let me see. This, I think. I am certain that Rome is finished. Why go on mincing words?

But I write this in haste and I am really afraid of saying too much. In future letters I shall either put everything down in plain terms, if I get hold of a thoroughly trustworthy messenger, or else, if I write obscurely, you will none the less understand. In such letters I shall call myself Laelius and you Furius.[8] The rest shall be in veiled language.

I am sedulous here in my attentions to Caecilius. I hear Bibulus' edicts have been sent to you. They have put our Pompey in a passion of rage and chagrin.

40 (II.20)

Rome, ca. mid-July 59

CICERO TO ATTICUS

I have done my utmost for Anicatus, as I saw you wished. After the strong recommendation in your letter I was glad to take Numestius into my circle. Caecilius has my best offices in such matters as call for them. I am well satisfied with Varro. Pompey is my affectionate good friend. Do I believe that? Yes, I do. He quite persuades me of it, but

volo. pragmatici homines omnibus historiis, praeceptis, versibus denique cavere iubent et vetant credere. alterum facio, ut caveam, alterum, ut non credam, facere non possum.

2 Clodius adhuc mihi denuntiat periculum. Pompeius adfirmat non esse periculum, adiurat; addit etiam se prius occisum iri ab eo quam me violatum iri. tractatur res. simul et quid erit certi, scribam ad te. si erit pugnandum, arcessam ad societatem laboris; si quies dabitur, ab Amalthea te non commovebo.

3 De re <publica> breviter ad te scribam; iam enim charta ipsa ne nos prodat pertimesco. itaque posthac, si erunt mihi plura ad te scribenda, *ἀλληγορίαις* obscurabo. nunc quidem novo quodam morbo civitas moritur, ut, cum omnes ea quae sunt acta improbent, querantur, doleant, varietas nulla in re sit aperteque loquantur et iam clare gemant, tamen medicina nulla adferatur. neque enim resisti sine internecione posse arbitramur nec videmus qui finis ce-4 dendi praeter exitium futurus sit. Bibulus hominum admiratione et benevolentia in caelo est. edicta eius et contiones describunt et legunt. novo quodam genere in summam gloriam venit. populare nunc nihil tam est quam odium 5 popularium. haec quo sint eruptura timeo; sed si dispicere quid coepero, scribam ad te apertius.

Tu, si me amas tantum quantum profecto amas, expeditus facito ut sis, si inclamaro, ut accurras; sed do operam

only because I want to be persuaded. Worldly-wise folk tell us in all their histories and maxims, even in their poems, to be on our guard and not to trust others. I follow the one precept, to be on my guard, but the other, not to trust, is beyond me.

Clodius is still threatening trouble. Pompey says there is no danger, he swears it. He even adds that Clodius will attack me only over his dead body. Negotiations proceed. As soon as there is anything definite I shall write to you. If there has to be a fight, I shall send for you to take your share in the work; but if I am let live in peace, I shall not drag you away from Amalthea.

Of the political situation I shall say little. I am terrified by now for fear the very paper may betray us. So henceforward, if I have occasion to write to you at any length, I shall obscure my meaning with code terms. As things are, Rome is dying of a strange malady. Disapproval of what has been done and indignant complaint are universal. Opinion is not divided at any point, there is open grumbling, even to the stage of loud groaning, but nobody comes forward with a remedy. That is because we think resistance is bound to be suicidal, while we see no end to concession except destruction. Bibulus is *in excelsis* with public admiration and favour. They take down his edicts and speeches and read them. He has found a new pathway to glory—nothing is so popular nowadays as hatred of 'popular' politicians. Where all this is going to erupt I dread to think. But if I begin to make anything out I shall write to you more openly.

Now if you love me as much as I am sure you do, you must arrange so that you are free to hurry to my side if I call. But I am doing and shall do my best to avoid the

et dabo ne sit necesse. quod scripseram me Furio scripturum, nihil necesse est tuum nomen mutare; me faciam Laelium et te Atticum, neque utar meo chirographo neque signo, si modo erunt eius modi litterae quas in alienum incidere nolim.

6 Diodotus mortuus est; reliquit nobis HS fortasse $\overline{\text{C}}$.[1] comitia Bibulus cum Archilochio edicto in a. d. XV Kal. Nov. distulit. a Vibio libros accepi. poëta ineptus, et tamen scit nihil; sed est non inutilis. describo et remitto.

41 (II.21)

Scr. Romae post VIII *Kal. Sext. an.* 59 *(§ 3)*

CICERO ATTICO SAL.

1 De re publica quid ego tibi subtiliter? tota periit; atque hoc est miserior quam reliquisti quod tum videbatur eius modi dominatio civitatem oppressisse quae iucunda esset multitudini, bonis autem ita molesta ut tamen sine pernicie, nunc repente tanto in odio est omnibus ut quorsus eruptura sit horreamus. nam iracundiam atque intemperantiam illorum sumus experti, qui Catoni irati omnia perdiderunt, sed ita lenibus uti videbantur venenis ut posse videremur sine dolore interire; nunc vero sibilis vulgi, sermonibus 2 honestorum, fremitu Italiae vereor ne exarserint. equidem sperabam, ut saepe etiam loqui tecum solebam, sic orbem rei publicae esse conversum ut vix sonitum audire, vix im-

[1] centie(n)s (*Constans*)

[1] Probably a slave. As Letter 42 shows, the versifier was Alexander of Ephesus.

necessity. I told you that I should address my letters to 'Furius,' but there is no need to change *your* name. I shall call myself 'Laelius' and you 'Atticus,' and I shall not write in my own hand or use my seal, that is if the letter is such that I should not want it to get into strangers' hands.

Diodotus has died, leaving me perhaps HS 100,000. Bibulus in an Archilochian edict has put off the elections till 18 October. I have received the volumes from Vibius.[1] A tasteless versifier, and yet an ignoramus; but he's *some* use. I am copying them out and returning.

41 (II.21)

Rome, after 25 July 59

CICERO TO ATTICUS

On politics I need not go into detail. The republic is finished. Its plight is all the sadder than when you left because at that time it looked as though the authoritarian regime was agreeable to the masses and, though odious, not actually lethal to their betters; whereas now it is all at once so universally detested that we tremble to think where it will erupt. We know by experience the violent temper and recklessness of these men, who in their rage against Cato have brought Rome to ruin; but they did seem to be using a mild form of poison, so that we might reasonably hope for a painless death. But now I am afraid that what with the hisses of the crowd and the talk of the respectable and the outcry in the country, they are thoroughly exasperated. For my part, as I often remarked to you in conversation as well as in writing, I used to hope that the political wheel had turned so smoothly that we

pressam orbitam videre possemus; et fuisset ita, si homines transitum tempestatis exspectare potuissent. sed cum diu occulte suspirassent, postea iam gemere, ad extremum vero loqui omnes et clamare coeperunt.

3 Itaque ille noster amicus, insolens infamiae, semper in laude versatus, circumfluens gloria, deformatus corpore, fractus animo quo se conferat nescit. progressum praecipitem, inconstantem reditum videt. bonos inimicos habet, improbos ipsos non amicos. ac vide mollitiem animi: non tenui lacrimas cum illum a. d. VIII Kal. Sext. vidi de edictis Bibuli contionantem. qui antea solitus esset iactare se magnificentissime illo in loco summo cum amore populi, cunctis faventibus, ut ille tum humilis, ut demissus erat, ut 4 ipse etiam sibi, non iis solum qui aderant, displicebat! o spectaculum uni Crasso iucundum, ceteris non item! nam quia deciderat ex astris, lapsus potius quam progressus videbatur; et, ut Apelles si Venerem aut Protogenes si Ialysum illum suum caeno oblitum videret, magnum, credo, acciperet dolorem, sic ego hunc omnibus a me pictum et politum artis coloribus subito deformatum non sine magno dolore vidi. quamquam nemo putabat propter Clodianum negotium me illi amicum esse debere, tamen tantus fuit amor ut exhauriri nulla posset iniuria. itaque Archilochia in illum edicta Bibuli populo ita sunt iucunda ut eum lo-

could hardly hear the sound or see the track upon the ground. And so it would have been, if folk had had the patience to wait for the storm to pass over. But after sighing for a long while in secret they at last began to groan, and now finally to cry out in universal protest.

So there is our poor friend,[1] unused to disrepute, his whole career passed in a blaze of admiration and glory, now physically disfigured and broken in spirit, at his wit's end for what to do. He sees the precipice if he goes on and the stigma of a turncoat if he turns back. The honest men are his enemies, the rascals themselves are not his friends. See now how soft-hearted I am. I could not keep back my tears when I saw him addressing a public meeting on 25 July about Bibulus' edicts. How magnificently he used to posture on that platform in other days, surrounded by an adoring people, every man wishing him well! How humble and abject he was then, what a sorry figure he cut in his own eyes, to say nothing of his audience! What a sight! Only Crassus could enjoy it, not so others. He was a fallen star, one looked upon him as a man who had *slid* rather than moved of his own volition. I suppose that if Apelles had seen his Venus or Protogenes his Ialysus[2] daubed with filth, he would have felt a pang as sharp as mine at the sight of this figure, painted and embellished with all the colours of my art, now suddenly made ugly. In view of the Clodius affair nobody expects me to be his friend, yet my affection for him was more than any injury could dissipate. Naturally Bibulus' Archilochian edicts against him are so agreeable to the public that one can't get past the place where

[1] Pompey.

[2] Cicero had seen this painting of a legendary hero in Rhodes.

cum ubi proponunter prae multitudine eorum qui legunt transire nequeamus, ipsi ita acerba ut tabescat dolore, mihi mehercule molesta, quod et eum quem semper dilexi nimis excruciant et timeo tam vehemens vir tamque acer in ferro et tam insuetus contumeliae ne omni animi impetu dolori et iracundiae pareat.

5 Bibuli qui sit exitus futurus nescio. ut nunc res se habet, admirabili gloria est. qui cum comitia in mensem Octobrem distulisset, quod solet ea res populi voluntatem offendere, putarat Caesar oratione sua posse impelli contionem ut iret ad Bibulum. multa cum seditiosissime diceret, vocem exprimere non potuit. quid quaeris? sentiunt se nullam ullius partis voluntatem tenere. eo magis vis nobis est timenda.

6 Clodius inimicus est nobis. Pompeius confirmat eum nihil esse facturum contra me, mihi periculosum est credere. ad resistendum me paro. studia spero me summa habiturum omnium ordinum. te cum ego desidero, tum vero res ad tempus illud vocat. plurimum consili, animi, praesidi denique mihi, si te ad tempus videro, accesserit. Varro mihi satis facit. Pompeius loquitur divinitus. spero nos aut certe cum summa gloria aut etiam sine molestia discessuros.

Tu quid agas, quem ad modum te oblectes, quid cum Sicyoniis egeris, ut sciam cura.

they are posted for the crowd of readers. To their subject they are so painful that his mortification is making him look ill. To me I must say they are unpleasant, both because they torment too savagely a man for whom I have always had a regard and because I am afraid that impetuous as he is, a fierce fighter not accustomed to insults, he may give free rein to his mortification and anger.

Where Bibulus will end up I don't know. As things stand at the moment he is in wonderfully high repute. When he postponed the elections till October, a thing which generally runs counter to the popular wish, Caesar thought he might stir up a public meeting with a speech into going for Bibulus' house. After a long, highly inflammatory harangue he could not raise a murmur. In short, they realize that they have no support in any section of society, which gives us all the more reason to fear violence.

Clodius is hostile. Pompey continues to assure me that he will do nothing against me. It would be dangerous for me to believe that, and I am getting ready to defend myself. I hope to have strong support from all classes. I miss you, and the facts of the case call for your return to meet the crisis. Your presence at the pinch will strengthen me vastly in policy and courage and actual defensive power. I am well satisfied with Varro. Pompey talks marvellously. I hope I shall at least come off with much honour or actually avoid any unpleasantness.

See that you keep me informed on your side of your doings and amusements and your dealings with the good people of Sicyon.

42 (II.22)

Scr. Romae fort. m. Sext. an. 59

CICERO ATTICO SAL.

1 Quam vellem Romae ‹esses›![1] mansisses profecto si haec fore putassemus. nam Pulchellum nostrum facillime teneremus aut certe quid esset facturus scire possemus. nunc se res sic habet: volitat, furit; nihil habet certi, ‹multa›[2] multis denuntiat; quod fors obtulerit id acturus videtur. cum videt quo sit in odio status hic rerum, in eos qui haec egerunt impetum facturus videtur; cum autem rursus opes eorum, vim, exercitus recordatur, convertit se in ‹bo›nos;[3]

2 nobis autem ipsis tum vim tum iudicium minatur. cum hoc Pompeius egit et, ut ad me ipse referebat (alium enim habeo neminem testem), vehementer egit, cum diceret in summa se perfidiae et sceleris infamia fore si mihi periculum crearetur ab eo quem ipse armasset cum plebeium fieri passus esset. sed fidem recepisse sibi et ipsum et Appium de me. hanc si ille non servaret, ita laturum ut omnes intellegerent nihil sibi antiquius amicitia nostra fuisse. haec et in eam sententiam cum multa dixisset, aiebat illum primo sane diu multa contra, ad extremum autem manus dedisse et adfirmasse nihil se contra eius voluntatem esse facturum. sed postea tamen ille non destitit de nobis asperrime loqui. quod si non faceret,tamen ei nihil credere-

[1] *add. SB*
[2] *add. SB*
[3] *add. Wesenberg*

42 (II.22)

Rome, August (?) 59

CICERO TO ATTICUS

Oh, how I wish you were in Rome! No doubt you *would* have stayed if we had expected all this to happen. Then it would be easy enough for us to keep Little Beauty in hand or at least we should be able to find out what he is up to. Now the picture is as follows: he rushes wildly up and down, without any definite programme, threatening numbers of folk with this, that, and the other. Apparently he will take whatever line chance puts in his way. When he notices how the present regime is detested, he makes as though to attack its authors; then again, when he remembers their power and ruthlessness and the armies behind them, he turns upon the honest men. Myself he threatens sometimes with violence, sometimes with the law courts. Pompey has spoken to him, strongly, as he himself informed me (I have no other witness), telling him that he, Pompey, would be branded as a traitor and a villain if I were brought into jeopardy by one whose weapons he had himself furnished in allowing his transfer to the plebs. But both Clodius himself and Appius had given him their words in respect of me. If Clodius did not honour his pledge, he, Pompey, would so react that the preeminent importance of our friendship in his eyes would be obvious to all. To this and more of the same kind, said Pompey, Clodius at first made very considerable demur, but in the end capitulated and gave an assurance that he would take no step contrary to Pompey's wishes. But since that conversation he has continued none the less to use most offensive language about me. Even if he did not, I should not

mus atque omnia, sicut facimus, pararemus.

3 Nunc ita nos gerimus ut in dies singulos et studia in nos hominum et opes nostrae augeantur. rem publicam nulla ex parte attingimus; in causis atque in illa opera nostra forensi summa industria versamur, quod egregie non modo iis qui utuntur opera sed etiam in vulgus gratum esse sentimus. domus celebratur, occurritur, renovatur memoria consulatus, studia significantur. in eam spem adducimur ut nobis ea contentio quae impendet interdum non fugienda videatur.

4 Nunc mihi et consiliis opus est tuis et amore et fide; qua re advola. expedita mihi erunt omnia si te habebo. multa per Varronem nostrum agi possunt quae te urgente erunt firmiora, multa ab ipso Publio elici, multa cognosci quae tibi occulta esse non poterunt, multa etiam—sed absurdum est singula explicare cum ego requiram te ad omnia.

5 unum illud tibi persuadeas velim, omnia mihi fore explicata si te videro; sed totum[4] est in eo, si ante quam ille ineat magistratum. puto Pompeium Crasso urgente * * *[5] si tu aderis, qui per Βοῶπιν ex ipso intellegere possis qua fide ab illis agatur, nos aut sine molestia aut certe sine errore futuros. precibus nostris et cohortatione non indiges. quid mea voluntas, quid tempus, quid rei magnitudo postulet, intellegis.

6 De re publica nihil habeo ad te scribere nisi summum odium hominum in eos qui tenent omnia. mutationis tamen spes nulla. sed, quod facile sentias, taedet ipsum

[4] tantum (*Hervagius*)

[5] vacillare, sed *vel sim. suppletum voluit SB*

trust him a yard and should make all preparations, as I am doing.

My present mode of life is such as daily to increase my popularity and resources. I keep absolutely clear of politics, devoting myself industriously to my cases and forensic work, which I perceive to be a fine road to the favour not only of those who use my services but of the general public as well. My house is thronged with visitors, people come up to me, recalling my Consulship and professing active good will. I am becoming so sanguine that there are times when the impending struggle seems to me something that I ought not to try to avoid.

Now I need your advice and affection and loyalty. So make haste. All will be plain sailing if I have you here. Much can be done through our friend Varro, and more reliably with you to apply the spur, much extracted from Publius himself, much learned which it will be impossible to hide from you, much—but it is absurd to enumerate this and that when I need you for everything. Of one thing I should like you to be convinced, that all will come straight for me once I set eyes on you. But everything depends on your coming before he starts his term of office. I think that Pompey, under pressure from Crassus, may waver, but (?) if you are here, able as you are to gather from Publius himself through Lady Ox Eyes how far they are to be trusted, I shall either escape unpleasantness or at any rate shall know where I stand. You don't need me to entreat or urge you. My wish, the hour, the importance of the issue—you see what they demand.

Of the political situation I have nothing to tell you except the cordial hatred of all men for our all-powerful rulers. No change however is to be hoped for. But as one

Pompeium ‹eum›que[6] vehementer paenitet. non provideo satis quem exitum futurum putem; sed certe videntur haec aliquo eruptura.

7 Libros Alexandri, neglegentis hominis et non boni poëtae sed tamen non inutilis, tibi remisi. Numerium Numestium libenter accepi in amicitiam et hominem gravem et prudentem et dignum tua commendatione cognovi.

43 (II.23)

Scr. Romae fort. m. Sext. an. 59

CICERO ATTICO SAL.

1 Numquam ante arbitror te epistulam meam legisse nisi mea manu scriptam. ex eo colligere poteris quanta occupatione distinear. nam cum vacui temporis nihil haberem et cum recreandae voculae causa necesse esset mihi ambulare, haec dictavi ambulans.

2 Primum igitur illud te scire volo, Sampsiceramum, nostrum amicum, vehementer sui status paenitere restituique in eum locum cupere ex quo decidit, doloremque suum impertire nobis et medicinam interdum aperte quaerere, quam ego posse inveniri nullam puto;[1] deinde omnis illius partis auctores ac socios nullo adversario consenescere, consensionem universorum nec voluntatis nec sermonis maiorem umquam fuisse.

3 Nos autem (nam id te scire cupere certo scio) publicis consiliis nullis intersumus totosque nos ad forensem operam laboremque contulimus. ex quo, quod facile intellegi possit, in multa commemoratione earum rerum quas ges-

[6] *add. SB* [1] post *al.* (*Lambinus*)

can easily perceive, Pompey himself is sick of it all and bitterly unhappy. I cannot well foresee the probable outcome, but some sort of eruption seems inevitable.

I am returning Alexander's book—a careless fellow and not a good poet, but he has his uses. I have been glad to welcome Numerius Numestius into my circle and found him a responsible, discreet sort of person who deserves your recommendation.

43 (II.23)

Rome, August (?) 59

CICERO TO ATTICUS

I believe you have never before read a letter of mine not in my own handwriting. You may gather from that how desperately busy I am. Not having a minute to spare and being obliged to take a walk to refresh my poor voice, I am dictating this while walking.

First then I want you to know that our friend Sampsiceramus is bitterly unhappy about his position and longs to get back to where he stood before his fall; he confides his distress to me and sometimes openly casts about for a remedy, but I don't think there is any to be found. Secondly, that the members and backers of that party are all wilting, though there is no opposition, and that a greater unanimity of sentiment and talk has never been seen.

As for me (a subject on which I am sure you are anxious to be informed), I take no part in political deliberations, devoting myself entirely to court business and work. In consequence, as may easily be supposed, I hear a good

simus desiderioque versamur. sed Boopidis nostrae consanguineus non mediocris terrores iacit atque denuntiat et Sampsiceramo negat, ceteris prae se fert et ostentat. quam ob rem, si me amas tantum quantum profecto amas, si dormis expergiscere, si stas ingredere, si ingrederis curre, si curris advola. credibile non est quantum ego in consiliis ‹et› prudentia tua et, quod maximum est, quantum in amore et fide ponam. magnitudo rei longam orationem fortasse desiderat, coniunctio vero nostrorum animorum brevitate contenta est. permagni nostra interest te, si comitiis non potueris, at declarato illo esse Romae. cura ut valeas.

44 (II.24)

Scr. Romae fort. m. Sext. an. 59

CICERO ATTICO SAL.

1 Quas Numestio litteras dedi, sic te iis evocabam ut nihil acrius neque incitatius fieri posset. ad illam celeritatem adde etiam si quid potes. ac ne sis perturbatus; novi enim te et non ignoro quam sit amor omnis sollicitus atque anxius. sed res est, ut spero, non tam exitu molesta quam aditu.[1]

2 Vettius ille, ille noster index, Caesari, ut perspicimus, pollicitus est sese curaturum ut in aliquam suspicionem facinoris Curio filius adduceretur. itaque insinuav‹i›t[2] in familiaritatem adulescentis et cum eo, ut res indicat, saepe

[1] auditu (*Victorius*)
[2] in sinu aut (*Orelli*)

deal of nostalgic reminiscing on my old exploits. But our Lady Ox Eyes' nearest and dearest flings out formidable threats of wrath to come, denying this to Sampsiceramus but flaunting it ostentatiously before all else. Therefore, if you love me as much as I am sure you do: if you are asleep, wake up! If you are standing still, walk! If you are walking, run! If you are running, fly! You cannot believe how much I rely on your advice and knowledge of the world, and, most valuable of all, your affection and loyalty. The importance of the issue perhaps calls for lengthy exposition, but in the unison of our hearts a few words will suffice. It is of the utmost consequence to me that you should be in Rome—if you can't manage it for the elections then at any rate after he has been returned. Take care of your health.

44 (II.24)

Rome, August (?) 59

CICERO TO ATTICUS

In the letter I dispatched by Numestius I tried to summon you back in the most urgent and imperative language I could muster. Come even faster than I asked if you can. And yet, don't be alarmed—I know you and am well aware how anxious and apprehensive affection makes us. But I hope the business will end less unpleasantly than it has begun.

That man Vettius, my old informer, evidently promised Caesar to find means of bringing Curio junior under suspicion of a felony. So he wormed his way into the young man's friendship and saw a good deal of him, as the facts show. Eventually he brought matters to a head, telling Cu-

congressus est. rem in eum locum deduxit, ut diceret sibi certum esse cum suis servis in Pompeium impetum facere eumque occidere. hoc Curio ad patrem detulit, ille ad

3 Pompeium. res delata ad senatum est. introductus Vettius primo negabat se umquam cum Curione restitisse,[3] neque id sane diu; nam statim fidem publicam postulavit. reclamatum est. tamen[4] exposuit manum fuisse iuventutis duce Curione, in qua Paulus initio fuisset et [Cn.][5] Caepio hic Brutus et Lentulus, flaminis filius, conscio patre; postea C. Septimium, scribam Bibuli, pugionem sibi a Bibulo attulisse. quod totum irrisum est, Vettio pugionem defuisse nisi ei consul dedisset, eoque magis id eiectum est quod a. d. III Id. idem[6] Bibulus Pompeium fecerat certiorem ut caveret insidias, in quo ei Pompeius gratias egerat. introductus Curio filius dixit ad ea quae Vettius dixerat, maximeque in eo tum quidem Vettius est reprehensus quod ‹id›[7] dixerat adulescentium consilium ut in foro [cum][8] gladiatoribus Gabini Pompeium adorirentur; in eo principem Paulum fuisse, quem constabat eo tempore in Macedonia fuisse. fit senatus consultum ut Vettius, quod confessus esset se cum telo fuisse, in vincula coniceretur; qui eum emisisset, eum contra rem publicam esse facturum. res erat in ea opinione ut putarent id esse actum ut Vettius in foro cum pugione et item servi eius comprehenderentur cum telis, deinde ille se diceret indicaturum.

[3] *al.* constitisse [4] tum (*Iunius*) [5] *del. Constans*
[6] diei (*Watt*) [7] *add. SB* [8] *del. Manutius*

---

[1] M. Brutus had been adopted by his uncle Q. Servilius Caepio and is sometimes called Q. Caepio Brutus, though usually by his original name.

rio that he had made up his mind to set upon and kill Pompey with the help of his slaves. Curio took this to his father, and he to Pompey. The matter was brought before the Senate. When Vettius was brought in, he denied at first having ever passed the time of day with Curio, not however for very long; for he presently asked leave to turn state's evidence. There was a roar of protest. None the less Vettius explained that a group of young men had been formed under Curio's leadership, including at the start Paulus, Caepio (Brutus),[1] and Lentulus, the Flamen's son (with his father's knowledge). Later C. Septimius, Bibulus' official secretary, had brought Vettius a dagger from his chief. This was completely scouted—the idea that Vettius could not have come by a dagger unless the Consul had given him one. A further reason for rejecting the tale was that the same Bibulus had sent information to Pompey on the 13th, warning him of a plot, for which Pompey had thanked him. Curio junior was brought into the House and made a reply to what Vettius had said. Fault was then found with Vettius' story on one point in particular. He had stated that the young men's plan had been to attack Pompey in the Forum during Gabinius' gladiator show and that Paulus was the ringleader. Paulus, however, was by general knowledge in Macedonia at that time. The Senate passed a decree that Vettius, since he had confessed to carrying a weapon, should be put in chains, and that any person compassing his release would be acting against the interests of the state. The view generally held is that according to the original plan Vettius was to have been arrested in the Forum with a dagger on his person, and his slaves likewise with weapons. He would then have offered to turn informer.

idque ita actum esset nisi Curiones rem ante ad Pompeium detulissent.

Tum senatus consultum in contione recitatum est. postero autem die Caesar, is qui olim, praetor cum esset, Q. Catulum ex inferiore loco iusserat dicere, Vettium in rostra produxit eumque in eo loco constituit quo Bibulo consuli aspirare non liceret. hic ille omnia quae voluit de re [publica][9] dixit, ut qui illuc factus institutusque venisset. primum Caepionem de oratione sua sustulit, quem in senatu acerrime nominarat, ut appareret noctem et nocturnam deprecationem intercessisse. deinde, quos in senatu ne tenuissima quidem suspicione attigerat, eos nominavit: <L.>[10] Lucullum, a quo solitum esse ad se mitti C. Fannium, illum qui in P. Clodium subscripserat, L. Domitium, cuius domum constitutam fuisse unde eruptio fieret. me non nominavit, sed dixit consularem disertum, vicinum consulis, sibi dixisse Ahalam Servilium aliquem aut Brutum opus esse reperiri. addidit ad extremum, cum iam dimissa contione revocatus a Vatinio fuisset, se audisse ex Curione his de rebus conscium esse Pisonem, generum meum, et M. Laterensem.

4 Nunc reus erat apud Crassum Divitem Vettius de vi et, cum esset damnatus, erat indicium postulaturus; quod si impetrasset, iudicia fore videbantur. ea nos, utpote qui nihil contemnere sole<a>mus,[11] non pertimescebamus.

[9] *del. Manutius* [10] *add. Wesenberg*
[11] *add. Wesenberg*

---

[2] Brutus' mother Servilia was reputed to be Caesar's mistress.

[3] Caesar, whose official residence as Pontifex Maximus lay below Cicero's house on the Palatine.

And that is how it would have gone if the Curios had not carried the matter to Pompey first.

The decree was then read out at a public meeting. The next day Caesar, the man who when he was Praetor once told Q. Catulus to speak from the floor, led Vettius to the Rostra and placed him there—forbidden ground to Consul Bibulus! There Vettius held forth about the affair to his heart's content; obviously he had come ready primed and schooled. To begin with, he left out Caepio, whom he had named very emphatically in the Senate. It was well seen that a night had intervened and that certain intercessions had taken place in the hours of darkness.[2] Secondly, he named persons on whom he had not so much as breathed a suspicion in the Senate—L. Lucullus, who he said was by way of sending C. Fannius (assistant prosecutor in the trial of P. Clodius) to see him, and L. Domitius, from whose house he said the conspirators were to have made their sortie. Me he did not mention by name, but said that a certain eloquent ex-Consul, the Consul's[3] neighbour, had told him that what was now wanted was a Servilius Ahala or a Brutus.[4] Finally, after the meeting had been dismissed and he had been called back by Vatinius, he added that he had heard from Curio that my son-in-law Piso and M. Laterensis were in the plot.

Vettius is now up before Crassus Dives on a charge of violence. After being convicted he will ask leave to turn informer. If that is granted there are likely to be some prosecutions. For one who is not in the habit of making light of any danger I am not overly alarmed. I receive warm

[4] The first Consul.

hominum quidem summa erga nos studia significabantur. sed prorsus vitae taedet; ita sunt omnia omnium miseriarum plenissima. modo caedem timueramus, quam[12] oratio fortissimi senis, Q. Consi<di>, discusserat; †eam†,[13] quam cottidie timere potueramus, subito exorta est. quid quaeris? nihil †me†[14] fortunatius est Catulo cum splendore vitae tum hoc[15] tempore. nos tamen in his miseriis erecto animo et minime perturbato sumus honestissimeque <et salutem>[16] et dignitatem nostram magna cura tuemur.
5 Pompeius de Clodio iubet nos esse sine cura et summam in nos benevolentiam omni oratione significat. te habere consiliorum auctorem, sollicitudinum socium, omni in cogitatione coniunctum cupio. qua re, ut Numestio mandavi tecum ut ageret, item atque eo, si potest, acrius te rogo ut plane ad nos advoles. respiraro si te videro.

45 (II.25)

Scr. Romae fort. m. Sept. an. 59

CICERO ATTICO SAL.

1 Cum aliquem apud te laudaro tuorum familiarium, volam illum scire ex te me id fecisse, ut nuper me scis scripsisse ad te de Varronis erga me officio, te ad me rescripsisse eam rem summae tibi voluptati esse. sed ego mallem ad ipsum[1]

[12] *al.* qu(a)e : quem metum *Madvig* [13] causa *coni. SB*
[14] mehercule *vel* meo iudicio *coni. SB*
[15] mortis *Lambinus* [16] *add. SB* (*post* dignitatem *Alford*)
[1] illum (*Ernesti*)

[5] With reference to an incident during the passage of Caesar's

assurances of general good will. But I am thoroughly sick of life, nothing but misery of every kind wherever you look. A little while back we feared a massacre; brave old Considius' words dispersed it.[5] Suddenly the sort of pretext (?) we had constantly to fear has turned up. In short, to my way of thinking (?) Catulus is supremely to be envied, not only in the dignity of his life but now at this present. However, in all these tribulations I keep my heart up, am not in the least flustered, and have a careful eye, in the most honourable way, both to my security and my dignity. Pompey tells me not to worry about Clodius, and expresses the most cordial sentiments towards me in everything he says. I very much wish to have you with me to advise me on my tactics, to share my anxieties, to join in everything I have in mind. I have asked Numestius to speak to you about this; and myself ask you likewise, if possible more emphatically, to *fly* to my side. I shall breathe again once I see you.

45 (II.25)

Rome, September (?) 59

CICERO TO ATTICUS

When I praise one of your friends to you you may take it that I want you to let him know that I have done so. The other day, you remember, I wrote to you about Varro's good offices towards me, and you wrote back that you were delighted to hear of it. But I would rather you had written to

agrarian laws. Considius told Caesar that he did not stay away from the Senate like the other Senators, who were afraid for their lives, 'because old age makes me fearless.'

scripsisses mihi illum satis facere, non quo faceret sed ut faceret. mirabiliter enim moratus est, sicut nosti, 'ἑλικτὰ καὶ οὐδέν. . .'. sed nos tenemus praeceptum illud, 'τὰς τῶν κρατούντων. . .'. at hercule alter tuus familiaris Hortalus quam plena manu, quam ingenue, quam ornate nostras laudes in astra sustulit cum de Flacci praetura et de illo tempore Allobrogum diceret! sic habeto, nec amantius
2 nec honorificentius nec copiosius potuisse dici. ei te hoc scribere a me tibi esse missum sane volo. sed quid tu scribas? quem iam ego venire atque adesse arbitror; ita enim egi tecum superioribus litteris. valde te exspecto, valde desidero, neque ego magis quam ipsa res et tempus poscit.

His de negotiis quid scribam ad te nisi idem quod saepe? re publica nihil desperatius, iis quorum opera nihil maiore odio. nos, ut opinio et spes et coniectura nostra fert, firmissima benevolentia hominum muniti sumus. qua re advola. aut expedies nos omni molestia aut eris particeps. ideo sum brevior quod, ut spero, coram brevi tempore conferre quae volumus licebit. cura ut valeas.

him that I was well content with him, not that this *was* so but that it might become so. He is a strange person, as you know, 'crooked in mind and naught . . .' But I am holding to the old maxim 'To bear with rulers'. . .'[1] Now your other crony Hortalus, how ungrudgingly and candidly and eloquently he lauded my merits to the stars in speaking of Flaccus' Praetorship and the business of the Allobroges![2] You can take my word for it that no one could have spoken in more friendly, flattering, and ample terms—and I very much hope you will write to him that I have told you so. But why should you write? I expect you are already on your way or nearly home after the appeal in my last letter. I am waiting for you impatiently and miss you sorely, but the facts and the hour demand your return no less loudly than I.

On affairs here I can only repeat what I have so often written. The commonwealth is in truly desperate plight, and the hatred for those responsible is unparalleled. I myself, as I think and hope and forecast, am protected by a powerful bastion of general good will. So make speed. You will either get me out of all unpleasantness or share it. I say less than I might because I hope we shall soon be able to discuss what we want together. Take care of your health.

[1] The two quotations come from Euripides' *Andromache*, 448, and *Phoenissae*, 393. The first runs: 'Thinking crooked thoughts, nothing wholesome, everything devious'; the second: 'We needs must bear with rulers' follies.'

[2] Hortensius and Cicero had recently defended L. Valerius Flaccus on a charge of extortion. As Praetor in 63 Flaccus and a colleague had arrested some Allobrogian envoys who were in communication with the Catilinarians on Cicero's instructions.

46 (III.1)

Scr. in exsilium proficiscens c. XI *Kal. Apr., ut vid., an.* 58

CICERO ATTICO SAL.

Cum antea maxime nostra interesse arbitrabar te esse nobiscum, tum vero, ut legi rogationem, intellexi ad iter id quod constitui nihil mihi optatius cadere posse quam ut tu me quam primum consequare,[1] ut, cum ex Italia profecti essemus, sive per Epirum iter esset faciendum tuo tuorumque praesidio uteremur, sive aliud quid agendum esset certum consilium de tua sententia capere possemus. quam ob rem te oro des operam ut me statim consequare; ‹quod eo› facilius potes quoniam de provincia Macedonia perlata lex est. pluribus verbis tecum agerem nisi pro me apud te res ipsa loqueretur.

47 (III.3)

Scr. in itinere c. IX *Kal. Apr., ut vid., an.* 58

CICERO ATTICO SAL.

Utinam illum diem videam cum tibi agam gratias quod me vivere coëgisti! adhuc quidem valde me paenitet, sed te oro ut ad me Vibonem statim venias, quo ego multis de causis converti iter meum. sed eo si veneris, de toto itinere ac fuga mea consilium capere potero. si id non feceris, mirabor; sed confido te esse facturum.

[1] consequerere *Wesenberg*

---

[1] Brought in by Clodius after Cicero's flight from Rome, exiling him by name.

46 (III.1)

En route into exile, ca. 22 March (?) 58

CICERO TO ATTICUS

Even before I read the bill[1] I felt it was very important to me to have you with me, and now that I have done so I see that nothing could be more desirable with a view to the journey on which I have decided than that you should overtake me as soon as possible, so that when I leave Italy I may have the protection of you and your people if I am to travel through Epirus, or if I am to take some different course I may have your advice in fixing upon a plan. So I beg you to try to overtake me directly. You can do so more easily now that the law about the province of Macedonia[2] has gone through. I should urge you at greater length, but you have the facts and they will speak for me.

47 (III.3)

En route, ca. 24 (?) March 58

CICERO TO ATTICUS

I hope I may see the day when I shall thank you for making me go on living. So far I am heartily sorry you did. But I beg you to come to me as soon as possible at Vibo, where I am going. I have changed direction for many reasons. But if you come there, I shall be able to make a plan for my whole journey and exile. If you do not do that, I shall be surprised; but I am confident you will.

[2] Assigning it to the Consul, L. Piso. Atticus will not have wanted to leave Rome before the appointment of a new governor.

48 (III.2)

Scr. Naribus Lucanis VI *Kal. Apr. an. 58*

CICERO ATTICO SAL.

Itineris nostri causa fuit quod non habebam locum ubi pro meo iure diutius esse possem quam fundum Siccae, praesertim nondum rogatione correcta; et simul intellegebam ex eo loco, si te haberem, posse me Brundisium referre, sine te autem non esse nobis illas partes tenendas propter Autronium. nunc, ut ad te antea scripsi, si ad nos veneris, consilium totius rei capiemus. iter esse molestum scio, sed tota calamitas omnis molestias habet. plura scribere non possum; ita sum animo perculso et abiecto. cura ut valeas.

Data VI Kal.[1] Apr. Narib.[2] Luc.

49 (III.4)

Scr. Vibone, ut vid., III *Non. Apr. an. 58*

CICERO ATTICO SAL.

Miseriae nostrae potius velim quam inconstantiae tribuas quod a Vibone quo te arcessebamus subito discessimus. adlata est enim nobis rogatio de pernicie mea, in qua quod correctum[1] esse audieramus erat eius modi ut mihi ultra quadringenta[2] milia liceret esse, illuc pervenire non liceret. statim iter Brundisium versus contuli ante diem roga-

[1] Id. (*SB*) [2] naris (*R. Klotz*)

[1] *al.* confectum [2] quingenta ς

---

[1] This was near Vibo Valentia in the toe of Italy.

[2] Greece, where Autronius was in exile.

[1] The amended bill allowed Cicero to live at a distance of not

48 (III.2)

Nares Lucanae, 27 March 58

CICERO TO ATTICUS

The reason for my route was that I have no place where I can feel free to stay longer than at Sicca's farm,[1] especially as the bill has not yet been amended. Also I have in mind that if I have you with me I can get back from there to Brundisium, while without you I had best not make for those parts[2] on account of Autronius. Now, as I wrote to you previously, if you join me we shall make a comprehensive plan. I know the journey is troublesome, but the whole disaster is full of all manner of troubles. I cannot write any more, I am too stricken and dejected.

Dispatched 27 March, Nares Lucanae.

49 (III.4)

Vibo (?), 3 April 58

CICERO TO ATTICUS

I hope you will put it down to the misery I am in rather than to fickleness of purpose that I have suddenly left Vibo after I have been asking you to come there. The bill for my destruction has come into my hands, and the correction about which I had heard was to the effect that I am allowed to live at a distance of not less than 400 miles, but am not allowed to get there.[1] I at once changed my course for Brundisium before the bill should become law for fear that

less than 400 (or 500) miles from Rome but provided that his outlawry should begin from the date of its passage. How then was he to reach the assigned limit?

tionis, ne et Sicca, apud quem eram, periret et quod Melitae esse non licebat. nunc tu propera ut nos consequare, si modo recipiemur. adhuc invitamur benigne, sed quod superest timemus. me, mi Pomponi, valde paenitet vivere, qua in re apud me tu plurimum valuisti. sed haec coram. fac modo ut venias.

50 (III.5)

Scr. Thuriis VIII *Id. Apr. an. 58*

CICERO ATTICO SAL.

Terentia tibi et saepe et maximas agit gratias. id est mihi gratissimum. ego vivo miserrimus et maximo dolore conficior. ad te quid scribam nescio. si enim es Romae, iam me adsequi non potes; sin es in via, cum eris me adsecutus, coram agemus quae erunt agenda. tantum te oro ut, quoniam me ipsum semper amasti, ut[1] eodem amore sis; ego enim idem sum. inimici mei mea mihi, non me ipsum ademerunt. cura ut valeas.

Data VIII Id. Apr. Thuri.

51 (III.6)

Scr. in Tarentino XIV *Kal. Mai. an. 58*

CICERO ATTICO SAL.

Non fuerat mihi dubium quin te Tarenti aut Brundisi visurus essem idque ad multa pertinuit, in eis et ut in Epiro

[1] *al. om.* : nunc *Mueller*

my host Sicca might be ruined too and because I cannot stay in Malta. Do make haste to catch me up, that is if I can get anyone to take me in. So far people invite me kindly enough, but I am afraid of what is to follow. For my part, my dear Pomponius, I am heartily sorry to be alive. In that decision you weighed with me most. But of this when we meet. Only do come.

50 (III.5)

Thurii, 6 April 58

CICERO TO ATTICUS

Terentia tells me continually how very thankful she is to you. For that I am most grateful. My life is a misery and I am overwhelmed by profound unhappiness. What to write to you I don't know, for if you are in Rome you cannot catch up with me now, whereas if you are on your way we shall discuss what needs discussing together when you join me. All I beg of you is, since you have always loved me for my own sake, not to change. I am the same man. My enemies have robbed me of what I have, but not of what I am. Take care of your health.

Dispatched 6 April, Thurii.

51 (III.6)

Near Tarentum, 17 April 58

CICERO TO ATTICUS

I had counted on seeing you at Tarentum or Brundisium, and it was from many points of view desirable that I should, for example so that I could stop in Epirus and to have your

consisteremus et de reliquis rebus tuo consilio uteremur. quoniam id non contigit, erit hoc quoque in magno numero nostrorum malorum. nobis iter est in Asiam, maxime Cyzicum. tibi meos commendo. me vix misereque sustento.

Data XIIII Kal. Mai. de Tarentino.

52 (III.7)

Scr. Brundisii prid. Kal. Mai. an. 58 (§ 3)

CICERO ATTICO SAL.

1 Brundisium veni a. d. XIIII Kal. Mai. eo die pueri tui mihi a te litteras reddiderunt, et alii pueri post diem tertium eius diei alias litteras attulerunt. quod me rogas et hortaris ut apud te in Epiro sim, voluntas tua mihi valde grata est et minime nova. <es>set consilium mihi quidem optatum si liceret ibi omne tempus consumere; odi enim celebritatem, fugio homines, lucem aspicere vix possum, esset mihi ista solitudo, praesertim tam familiari in loco, non amara. sed itineris causa ut deverterer, primum est devium, deinde ab Autronio et ceteris quadridui, deinde sine te. nam castellum munitum habitanti mihi prodesset, transeunti non est necessarium. quod si auderem, Athenas peterem. sane ita cadebat ut vellem. nunc et nostri hostes ibi sunt et te non habemus et veremur ne interpretentur illud quoque oppidum ab Italia non satis abesse, nec scribis quam ad diem te exspectemus.

2 Quod me ad vitam vocas, unum efficis ut a me manus

[1] I.e., before his exile.

advice about all other points. Since it has not happened I must include this in the multitude of my misfortunes. My way lies to Asia, Cyzicus for preference. I commend my family to your care. I keep going with difficulty and wretchedness.

Dispatched 17 April, near Tarentum.

52 (III.7)

Brundisium, 29 April 58

CICERO TO ATTICUS

I arrived at Brundisium on 17 April. Your boys gave me a letter from you that day, and others brought me another letter two days later. I am deeply touched and not at all surprised by the kindness of your pressing invitation to stay at your place in Epirus. The idea would be much to my mind if I could spend all the time there—I hate crowds and shun my fellow creatures, I can hardly bear the light of day. The solitude, especially in such a friendly place, would be no hardship to me. But as a stopping place en route, to begin with it's off my road, and then it's only four days' journey from Autronius and the others, and then you would not be there. A fortified place would have its advantages if I were going to live there, but if I am just passing through it isn't necessary. If I dared, I should make for Athens. Certainly as things were falling out[1] I should have wanted to do so. But as it is, I have enemies there, I don't have you, and I am afraid they may make out that even Athens is not far enough away from Italy; and you don't say when I am to expect you.

Your exhortation to me to live is only partially effective.

abstineam, alterum non potes ut me non nostri consili vitaeque paeniteat. quid enim est quod me retineat, praesertim si spes ea non est quae nos proficiscentis prosequebatur? non faciam ut enumerem miserias omnis in quas incidi per summam iniuriam et scelus non tam inimicorum meorum quam invidorum, ne et meum maerorem exagitem et te in eundem luctum vocem; hoc adfirmo, neminem umquam tanta calamitate esse adfectum, nemini mortem magis optandam fuisse. cuius oppetendae tempus honestissimum praetermissum est; reliqua tempora sunt non iam ad medicinam sed ad finem doloris.

3 De re publica video te colligere omnia quae putes aliquam spem mihi posse adferre mutandarum rerum; quae quam‹quam› exigua sunt, tamen, quoniam placet, exspectemus.

Tu nihilominus, si properaris, nos consequere. nam aut accedemus in Epirum aut tarde per Candaviam ibimus. dubitationem autem de Epiro, non inconstantia nostra adferebat sed quod de fratre, ubi eum visuri essemus, nesciebamus; quem quidem ego nec ‹quo› modo visurus nec ut dimissurus sim scio. id est maximum et miserrimum mearum omnium miseriarum.

Ego et saepius ad te et plura scriberem nisi mihi dolor meus cum omnis partis mentis tum maxime huius generis facultatem ademisset. videre te cupio. cura ut valeas.

D.[1] prid. Kal. Mai. Brundisio proficiscens.

[1] data (*SB*)

---

[2] Quintus was returning to Rome from Asia.

You keep me from laying violent hands upon myself, but you cannot keep me from regretting my decision and the fact that I am alive. What is there to hold me, especially if the hope which followed me when I left Rome is no more? I shall not proceed to make a catalogue of all the tribulations on which I have fallen by the signal injury and villainy not so much of those who hated me as of those who were jealous of me. That would only be to stir up my grief and ask you to share my mourning. This I do say flatly, that no one ever suffered so crushing a blow or had greater cause to pray for death. I might have met it with honour, but the moment was let pass. From the time that remains I do not look any longer for a remedy but only for an end to my misery.

I see you are collecting every item in the political news which you think could afford me some hope of a change. They don't amount to much, but, since you wish, let us wait and see.

If you make haste you will catch me up even now, as I shall either go to Epirus or travel slowly through Candavia. My hesitation about Epirus is not due to fickleness of purpose but to uncertainty about my brother,[2] i.e. where I am to meet him—though how I am to meet him or to say good-bye to him I know not. That is the greatest and saddest of all my sorrows.

I should write to you more often and more fully, if it were not that my distress has robbed me of all my mental powers and more particularly of this sort of faculty. I long to see you. Take care of your health.

Dispatched 29 April, on departure from Brundisium.

53 (III.8)

Scr. Thessalonicae IV *Kal. Iun. an. 58 (§ 4)*

CICERO ATTICO SAL.

1 Scripseram ad te quas ob causas in Epirum non essemus profecti, quod et Achaia prope esset plena audacissimorum inimicorum et exitus difficilis haberet cum inde proficisceremur. accessit, cum Dyrrachi essemus, ut duo nuntii adferrentur, unus, classe fratrem Epheso Athenas, alter, pedibus per Macedoniam venire. itaque illi obviam misimus Athenas ut inde Thessalonicam veniret. ipsi processimus et Thessalonicam a.d. X Kal. Iun. venimus, neque de illius itinere quicquam certi habebamus nisi eum ab Epheso ante aliquanto profectum.

2 Nunc istic quid agatur magno opere timeo. quamquam tu altera epistula scribis Id. Mai. audiri fore ut acrius postularet‹ur›,[1] altera iam esse mitiora. sed haec est pridie data quam illa, quo conturbor magis. itaque cum meus me maeror cottidianus lacerat et conficit, tum vero haec addita cura vix mihi vitam reliquam facit.

Sed et navigatio perdifficilis fuit et ille incertus ubi ego essem fortasse alium cursum petivit. nam Phaëtho libertus non vidit; vento reiectus ab Ilio[2] in Macedoniam Pellae mihi praesto fuit. reliqua quam mihi timenda sint video, nec quid scribam habeo et omnia timeo, nec tam miserum est quicquam quod non in nostram fortunam cadere videa-

[1] *add. Malaespina* (?)
[2] illo (ς)

53 (III.8)

Thessalonica, 29 May 58

CICERO TO ATTICUS

I have already written to you the reasons why I did not go to Epirus, namely the proximity of Achaea which is full of enemies who would stop at nothing and the difficulty of getting out of the country when I came to leave it. Furthermore, while I was at Dyrrachium two messages arrived, one to the effect that my brother was travelling by sea from Ephesus to Athens, the other that he was proceeding by land through Macedonia. I therefore sent a messenger to meet him at Athens, to tell him to go from there to Thessalonica. I myself went on and reached Thessalonica on 23 May, but I still have no definite information about his route except that he left Ephesus some time ago.

And now I am very anxious about what is happening in Rome. True, in one of your letters dated the Ides of May you write that according to report he will be vigorously prosecuted, whereas in another you say that the atmosphere has become milder. But that letter was dispatched the day before the other, which makes me doubly uneasy. So with this new anxiety on top of my own chronic grief that tears my heart and wears me down, I am pretty well at the end of my tether.

However, sailing was very difficult, and perhaps in uncertainty of my whereabouts he has taken a different direction. The freedman Phaetho did not see him. He was turned back to Macedonia from Ilium by a contrary wind and reported to me at Pella. Clearly I have every reason for apprehension, but I don't know what to write. I'm afraid of all manner of things, and nothing seems too bad to

tur. equidem adhuc miser in maximis meis aerumnis et luctibus hoc metu adiecto maneo Thessalonicae suspensus nec audeo quicquam.

3 Nunc ad ea quae scripsisti. Tryphonem Caecilium non vidi. sermonem tuum et Pompei cognovi ex tuis litteris. motum in re publica non tantum ego impendere video quantum tu aut vides aut ad me consolandum adfers. Tigrane enim neglecto sublata sunt omnia. Varroni me iubes agere gratias. faciam; item Hypsaeo. quod suades ne longius discedamus dum acta mensis Mai ad nos perferantur, puto me ita esse facturum; sed ubi, nondum statui. atque ita perturbato sum animo de Quinto ut nihil queam statuere; sed tamen statim te faciam certiorem.

4 Ex epistularum mearum inconstantia puto te mentis meae motum videre, qui, etsi incredibili et singulari calamitate adflictus sum, tamen non tam est ex miseria quam ex culpae nostrae recordatione commotus. cuius enim scelere impulsi et proditi simus iam profecto vides; atque utinam ante vidisses neque totum animum tuum maerori mecum simul dedisses! qua re cum me adflictum et confectum luctu audies, existimato me stultitiae meae poenam ferre gravius quam eventi,[3] quod ei crediderim quem esse nefarium non putarim. me et meorum malorum maeror et metus de fratre in scribendo impedit. tu ista omnia vide et

[3] eventum *Wesenberg*

---

[1] Perhaps a freedman of Atticus' uncle Caecilius.

[2] Son of the King of Armenia, taken to Rome by Pompey as a hostage. Clodius had him set free and lives were lost in a resulting scuffle. Cicero's best hope lay in friction between Pompey and Clodius.

happen to us in our present plight. As for my unhappy self, plunged in dire woes and afflictions of my own and now with this added fear, I am staying for the present at Thessalonica, in suspense and not daring to make any move.

Now to answer the points in your letter. I have not seen Caecilius Trypho.[1] I have taken note of your talk with Pompey as recounted in your letter. I perceive no sign of so great a movement in the political situation as you either see coming or profess to see in order to comfort me. If Tigranes[2] has been passed over, it all goes by the board. You tell me to thank Varro; so I shall, and Hypsaeus likewise. I think I shall follow your advice not to go further away until the public transactions for May reach me. But where to go, I have not yet made up my mind. Indeed I am so worried about Quintus that I cannot make up my mind about anything. However, I shall let you know at once.

From the way my letters chop and change I expect you perceive the agitation of my mind, which is not so much caused by unhappiness, smitten though I am by a disaster beyond belief or example, as by the recollection of my own fault. Surely you see now whose[3] villainy it was that urged me on and betrayed me. If only you had seen it sooner and not surrendered your whole soul to grief as I did myself! When therefore you hear of me as plunged in the lowest depths of misery, you are to suppose that the penalty of my folly weighs upon me more heavily than that of the event itself, in that I trusted a man whom I did not think to be a blackguard. Grief for my own troubles and fear on my brother's behalf alike make it hard for me to write. Please

[3] Hortensius is meant.

guberna. Terentia tibi maximas gratias agit. litterarum exemplum quas ad Pompeium scripsi misi tibi.

Data IIII Kal. Iun. Thessalonicae.

54 (III.9)

Scr. Thessalonicae Id. Iun. an. 58 (§ 3)

CICERO ATTICO SAL.

1 Quintus frater cum ex Asia discessisset ante Kal. Mai. et Athenas venisset Id. Mai., valde fuit ei properandum, ne quid absens acciperet calamitatis, si quis forte fuisset qui contentus nostris malis non esset. itaque eum malui properare Romam quam ad me venire; et simul (dicam enim quod verum est, ex quo magnitudinem mearum miseriarum perspicere possis) animum inducere non potui ut aut illum, amantissimum mei, mollissimo animo, tanto in maerore aspicerem aut meas miserias luctu adflictus et perditam fortunam illi offerrem aut ab illo aspici paterer. atque etiam illud timebam, quod profecto accidisset, ne a me digredi non posset. versabatur mihi tempus illud ante oculos cum ille aut lictores dimitteret aut vi avelleretur ex complexu meo. huius acerbitatis eventum altera acerbitate non videndi fratris vitavi. in hunc me casum vos vivendi auctores impulistis. itaque mei peccati luo poenas. quam-

2 quam me tuae litterae sustentant—ex quibus quantum tu ipse speres facile perspicio; [et] quae quidem tamen aliquid habebant solaci ante quam eo venisti a Pompeio:

[1] A prosecution in connection with Quintus' record as governor.

see to everything over there and direct. Terentia says she is most grateful to you. I am sending you a copy of a letter I have written to Pompey.

Dispatched 29 May, Thessalonica.

54 (III.9)

Thessalonica, 13 June 58

CICERO TO ATTICUS

My brother Quintus left Asia before the Kalends of May and reached Athens on the Ides. He had to make great haste for fear a blow[1] might be struck against him in his absence—there might perhaps have been some for whom our present misfortunes are not enough. I therefore thought it better for him to hurry on to Rome rather than to come to me. At the same time (I'll tell the truth, and from it you can gauge the extent of my wretchedness) I could not bring myself to meet him, devoted to me and soft-hearted as he is, in so sad a state, nor yet, bowed in woe as I am, to thrust my misery and ruin in his way or allow him to see it. I was afraid too that he would not have the heart to leave me, nor would he, I am sure. I pictured the moment when he would either have to dismiss his lictors or be torn by force from my arms. This bitter consequence I have avoided by the bitterness of not seeing my brother. Such is the dilemma into which you and others who urged me to live on have pushed me. Well, I am paying for my mistake. Not but what your letter gives me comfort, though I can easily see from it how much hope *you* have! But still it offered some consolation until you got to the point where, after mention of Pompey, you go on: 'And

'nunc Hortensium adlice et eius modi viros.' obsecro, mi Pomponi, nondum perspicis quorum opera, quorum insidiis, quorum scelere perierimus? sed tecum haec coram agemus; tantum dico quod scire te puto: nos non inimici sed invidi perdiderunt. nunc si ita sunt quae speras, sustinebimus nos et spe qua iubes nitemur; sin, ut mihi videntur, ‹in› firma sunt, quod optimo tempore[1] facere non licuit minus idoneo fiet.

3 Terentia tibi saepe agit gratias. mihi etiam unum de malis in metu est, fratris miseri negotium; quod si sciam cuius modi sit, sciam quid agendum mihi sit. me etiam nunc istorum beneficiorum et litterarum exspectatio, ut tibi placet, Thessalonicae tenet. si quid erit novi adlatum, sciam de reliquo quid agendum sit. tu si, ut scribis, Kal. Iun. Roma profectus es, prope diem nos videbis. litteras quas ad Pompeium scripsi tibi misi.

Data Id. Iun. Thessalonicae.

55 (III.10)

Scr. Thessalonicae XIV *Kal. Quint. an. 58 (§ 3)*

CICERO ATTICO SAL.

1 Acta quae essent usque ad VIII Kal. Iun. cognovi ex tuis litteris; reliqua exspectabam, ut tibi placebat, Thessalonicae. quibus adlatis facilius statuere potuero ubi sim. nam si erit causa, si quid agetur, si spem videro, aut ibidem

[1] genere (ς)

now draw in Hortensius and personages of that sort.' For mercy's sake, my dear fellow, don't you *yet* see whose agency, whose treachery and villainy engineered my ruin? But I will take that up with you when we are together. I say only this, and I think you know it is so: it was not enemies but jealous friends who ruined me. As things are, if your hopes are well founded, I shall keep going and trust to the hope which you tell me to trust. If on the other hand they are unreliable, as they seem to me to be, then what I was not allowed to do at the right time shall be done at the wrong.

Terentia often says how grateful she is to you. For me too fear forms one among my troubles, I mean my unfortunate brother's affair. If I could know how that stands, I should know how to proceed. I am still kept at Thessalonica, as you advise, waiting for the good offices and letters you mention. When I get some news I shall be able to plan ahead. If, as you say, you left Rome on the Kalends of June, you will be seeing me soon. I am sending you a letter I have written to Pompey.

Dispatched Ides of June, Thessalonica.

55 (III.10)

Thessalonica, 17 June 58

CICERO TO ATTICUS

Your letter has apprised me of public transactions up to 25 May. I await the rest, as you advised, at Thessalonica. When they arrive I shall be able to decide where to settle. If there's a movement, action, hope in view, I shall either stay where I am or move over to you. If on the other hand

opperiar aut me ad te conferam; sin, ut tu scribis, ista evanuerint, aliquid aliud videbimus. omnino adhuc nihil mihi significatis nisi discordiam istorum; quae tamen inter eos de omnibus potius rebus est quam de me. itaque quid ea mihi prosit nescio. sed tamen quoad me vos sperare vultis, vobis obtemperabo.

2 Nam quod me tam saepe et tam vehementer obiurgas et animo infirmo esse dicis, quaeso, ecquod tantum malum est quod in mea calamitate non sit? ecquis umquam tam ex amplo statu, tam in bona causa, tantis facultatibus ingeni, consili, gratiae, tantis praesidiis bonorum omnium concidit? possum oblivisci qui fuerim? non sentire qui sim, quo caream honore, qua gloria, quibus liberis, quibus fortunis, quo fratre? quem ego, ut novum calamitatis genus attendas, cum pluris facerem quam me ipsum semperque fecissem, vitavi ne viderem, ne aut illius luctum squaloremque aspicerem aut ne me, quem ille florentissimum reliquerat, perditum illi adflictumque offerrem. mitto cetera intolerabilia; etenim fletu impedior. hic utrum tandem sum accusandus quod doleo an quod commisi ut haec aut non[1] retinerem, quod facile fuisset nisi intra parietes meos de mea pernicie consilia inirentur, aut certe vivus non amitterem?

3 Haec eo scripsi ut potius relevares me, quod facis, quam ut castigatione aut obiurgatione dignum putares, eoque ad te minus multa scribo quod et maerore impedior et quod exspectem istinc magis habeo quam quod ipse scribam. quae si erunt adlata, faciam te consili nostri cer-

[1] non aut *Madvig*

those prospects 'fade out,' I shall look elsewhere. To be sure none of you tells me anything so far except the dissension among the powers that be, and as this is about everything under the sun rather than me I hardly see what good I get out of it. But still, as long as you all want me to hope, I shall comply.

When you take me to task, as you so often and so energetically do, and tell me I am lacking in fortitude, I should like to ask you whether there is any misfortune too great to have its place in this disaster of mine. Has any man ever fallen from so fine a position, with so good a cause, so strong in resources of talent, prudence, and influence, and in the support of all honest men? Can I forget what I was, or fail to feel what I am and what I have lost—rank, fame, children, fortune, brother? As to him, mark this novelty in affliction: loving him as I do and ever have done better than myself, I have avoided meeting him so as not to see him in the dress and grief of mourning nor yet to present myself—me, whom he left in the full tide of prosperity—before his eyes, a ruined and broken man. Of other intolerable tribulations I say nothing; indeed tears prevent me. In such circumstances am I really to be blamed for grieving, and not rather for my failure either to keep all these things, as I might easily have done if plans for my undoing had not been hatched under my own roof, or at least to lose them only with life?

I write this so that you may rather lighten my burden, as you do, than think me a proper subject for castigation or scolding; and I do not write more because I am prevented by grief on the one hand and on the other am in the position of waiting for news from Rome rather than having anything to communicate myself. When the news arrives I

tiorem. tu, ut adhuc fecisti, quam plurimis de rebus ad me velim scribas, ut prorsus ne quid ignorem.

Data XIIII Kal. Quint. Thessalonicae.

56 (III.11)

Scr. Thessalonicae IV Kal. Quint. an. 58 (§ 2)

CICERO ATTICO SAL.

1 Me et tuae litterae et quidam boni nuntii, non optimis tamen auctoribus, et exspectatio vestrarum litterarum et quod tibi ita placuerat adhuc Thessalonicae tenebat. si accepero litteras quas exspecto, si spes erit ea quae rumoribus adferebatur, ad te me conferam; si non erit, faciam te certiorem quid egerim.

2 Tu me, ut facis, opera, consilio, gratia iuva. consolari iam desine, obiurgare vero noli; quod cum facis, ut ego tuum amorem et dolorem desidero! quem ita adfectum mea aerumna esse arbitror ut te ipsum consolari nemo possit. Quintum fratrem optimum humanissimumque sustenta. ad me obsecro te ut omnia certa perscribas.

Data IIII Kal. Quint.

57 (III.12)

Scr. Thessalonicae XVI Kal. Sext. an. 58 (§ 3)

CICERO ATTICO SAL.

1 Tu quidem sedulo argumentaris quid sit sperandum et maxime per senatum, idemque caput rogationis proponi

shall let you know my plans. Please write to me, as you have so far been doing, on as many points as you can, so that there may be *nothing* about which I am not informed.

Dispatched 17 June, Thessalonica.

56 (III.11)

Thessalonica, 27 June 58

CICERO TO ATTICUS

Your letter, certain favourable reports (not on the best of authority however), the expectation of letters from yourself and the others, and your earlier advice still keep me in Thessalonica. Once I receive the letters I am expecting, if the hope of which rumours reach me proves real, I shall move over to you; if not, I shall let you know what I do.

On your side, aid me, as you are doing, with effort, advice, and influence. Give up trying to comfort me, but don't scold. When you do this, how I miss your affection and sympathy! I believe you are affected by my misery to the point of being inconsolable yourself. Give a helping hand to Quintus, best and kindest of brothers. I beg you to send me full and reliable news on all matters.

Dispatched 27 June.

57 (III.12)

Thessalonica, 17 July 58

CICERO TO ATTICUS

You are at pains to argue what may be hoped for, particularly through the Senate, and yet you write that the clause in the bill which forbids any reference to the subject in the

scribis qua re in senatu dici nihil liceat. itaque siletur. hic tu me accusas quod me adflictem, cum ita sim adflictus ut nemo umquam, quod tute intellegis. spem ostendis secundum comitia. quae ista est eodem tribuno plebis et inimico consule designato? percussisti autem me etiam de oratione prolata. cui vulneri, ut scribis, medere, si quid potes. scripsi equidem olim iratus quod ille prior scripserat, sed ita compresseram ut numquam emanaturam putarem. quo modo exciderit nescio. sed quia numquam accidit ut cum eo verbo uno concertarem et quia scripta mihi videtur neglegentius quam ceterae, puto ex se <posse>[1] probari non esse meam. id, si putas me posse sanari, cures velim; sin plane perii, minus laboro.

2

3 Ego etiam nunc eodem in loco iaceo sine sermone ullo, sine cogitatione ulla. licet tibi, ut scribis, significarim ut ad me venires, <id> dono tamen et[2] intellego te istic prodesse, hic ne verbo quidem levare me posse. non queo plura scribere nec est quod scribam; vestra magis exspecto.

Data XVI Kal. Sext. Thessalonicae.

[1] ex se *al.* (*SB*)
[2] si donatam ut (*SB* : *similia iam alii*)

Senate is being posted up. So naturally silence reigns. And in these circumstances you take me to task for tormenting myself, when I am tried beyond any mortal that ever was, as you well know. You hold out hope after the elections. What does it amount to, with the same Tribune still in office and my enemy Consul-Designate?[1] Then you have given me a blow about the circulation of that speech.[2] Try, as you say, to patch up the damage if you can. I did write it long ago in a fit of annoyance with him because *he* had written against me, but I suppressed it and never expected it to leak out. How it did get out I don't know. However, as I have never exchanged a contentious word with him in my life and as it seems to me more carelessly written than my other compositions, I think it may be passed off on internal evidence as a forgery. Would you please see to that, if you think my case is curable? If I am past praying for, I don't so much care.

I am still stuck here, with no one to talk to and nothing to think about. I may have suggested to you, as you say, that you should join me; but I give that up, and realize that you are helping me where you are, whereas you could do nothing even verbally to lighten my load here. I can't write any more, nor have I anything to write about. I am rather waiting for news from your side.

Dispatched 17 July, Thessalonica.

1 Clodius would remain in office until 10 December and Metellus Nepos had been or would be elected Consul for 57.

2 A pamphlet in the form of a speech written by Cicero against Clodius and the elder Curio (referred to as 'he') some three years previously. Fragments survive.

58 (III.14)

Scr. Thessalonicae xii *Kal. Sext. an. 58 (§ 2)*

CICERO ATTICO SAL.

1 Ex tuis litteris plenus sum exspectatione de Pompeio, quidnam de nobis velit aut ostendat. comitia enim credo esse habita, quibus absolutis scribis illi placuisse agi de nobis. si tibi stultus esse videor qui sperem, facio tuo iussu †et scio te meis epistulis† potius[1] et mea‹s› spes solitum esse remorari. nunc velim mihi plane perscribas quid videas. scio nos nostris multis peccatis in hanc aerumnam incidisse. ea si qui casus aliqua ex parte correxerit, minus moleste feremus nos vixisse et adhuc vivere.

2 Ego propter viae celebritatem et cottidianam exspectationem rerum novarum non commovi me adhuc Thessalonica. sed iam extrudimur, non a Plancio (nam is quidem retinet) verum ab ipso loco minime apposito ad tolerandam in tanto luctu calamitatem. in Epirum ideo, ut scripseram, non veni quod subito mihi universi nuntii venerant et litterae qua re nihil esset necesse quam proxime Italiam esse. hinc, si aliquid a comitiis audierimus, nos in Asiam convertemus; neque adhuc stabat quo potissimum, sed scies.

Data xii Kal. Sext. Thessalonicae.

[1] et scis te me istis (*Purser*) epistulis sustentare potius *tempt. SB*

---

[1] As Quaestor he took Cicero into his official residence at Thessalonica.

58 (III.14)

Thessalonica, 21 July 58

CICERO TO ATTICUS

After your letter I am all expectation about Pompey, what he means by me or professes to mean. For I suppose that the elections are now over, at the conclusion of which you say he thought my case should be taken up. If you think me a fool to hope, well, I do so at your bidding, and you (?) know that in your letters you have rather been wont to lead me on and keep my hopes alive (?). Now I should be glad if you would let me know the prospects fully and frankly, as you see them. I know that I have fallen into this unhappy plight by my own mistakes, which have been many. If chance in some measure puts them right I shall be less inclined to regret that I was ever born and that I am alive today.

I have not yet moved from Thessalonica because the route is so frequented and because I am waiting from day to day for news of a turn in the situation. But I am now being forced out, not by Plancius,[1] who for his part would like me to stay on, but by the place itself—there could be no less suitable spot in which to bear calamity in such a state of grief as I am in. I have not gone to Epirus, as I wrote that I should, because all at once my letters and reports indicated with one accord that there was no occasion for me to be as near as possible to Italy. From here, once I hear something after the elections, I shall betake myself to Asia, where in particular I am not yet sure, but you shall know.

Dispatched 21 July, Thessalonica.

59 (III.13)

Scr. Thessalonicae Non. Sext. an. 58 (§ 2)

CICERO ATTICO SAL.

1 Quod ad te scripseram me in Epiro futurum, postea quam extenuari spem nostram et evanescere vidi, mutavi consilium nec me Thessalonica commovi, ubi esse statueram quoad aliquid ad me de eo scriberes quod proximis litteris scripseras, fore uti secundum comitia aliquid de nobis in senatu ageretur; id tibi Pompeium dixisse. qua de re quoniam comitia habita sunt tuque nihil ad me scribis, proinde habebo ac si scripsisses nihil esse, meque temporis non longinqui spe ductum esse ‹non›[1] moleste feram. quem autem motum te videre scripseras qui nobis utilis fore videretur, eum nuntiant qui veniunt nullum fore. in tribunis pl. designatis reliqua spes est. quam si exspectaro, non erit quod putes me causae meae, voluntati meorum defuisse.

2 Quod me saepe accusas cur hunc meum casum tam graviter feram, debes ignoscere, cum ita me adflictum videas ut neminem umquam nec videris nec audieris. nam quod scribis te audire me etiam mentis errore ex dolore adfici, mihi vero mens integra est. atque utinam tam in periculo fuisset, cum ego iis quibus meam salutem carissimam esse arbitrabar, inimicissimis crudelissimisque usus sum! qui ut me paulum inclinari timore viderunt, sic impulerunt ut omni suo scelere et perfidia abuterentur ad exitium meum.

[1] *add. Tyrrell*

59 (III.13)

Thessalonica, 5 August 58

CICERO TO ATTICUS

Though I wrote to you that I should stay in Epirus, I changed my mind when I saw that my chances were thinning and fading away, and have not moved from Thessalonica. I had decided to stay there until I heard something from you about what you said in your last letter, namely that some move would be made about my case in the Senate after the elections, Pompey having told you so. Well, the elections are over and you don't write a word to me, so I shall regard that as equivalent to writing that there is nothing doing, and I shall not take it too hard that for no very long time I have been amused by hope. As for the change likely to turn to my advantage which you wrote that you saw coming, those who come from Rome say that nothing of the kind will happen. The remaining hope lies in the Tribunes-Designate. If I wait for that, you will have no reason to think that I have failed in what I owe to my cause and my friends' good will.

You repeatedly take me to task for bearing what has happened to me so hard, but you ought to forgive me when you see how I am tried beyond anything you ever witnessed or heard of. You say you hear that grief has actually disturbed the balance of my mind. No, my mind is sound enough. If only it had been equally so in the hour of danger, when I experienced the cruellest malice from those who I thought cared most about my welfare! The moment they saw me a little unnerved and inclined to waver, they pushed me on, employing all their wickedness and perfidy to bring about my downfall.

Nunc quoniam iam est Cyzicum nobis eundum, quo rarius ad me litterae perferentur,[2] hoc velim diligentius omnia quae putaris me scire opus esse perscribas. Quintum, fratrem meum, fac diligas. quem ego miser si incolumem relinquo, non me totum perisse arbitrabor.

Data Non. Sext.

60 (III.15)

Scr. Thessalonicae XIV *Kal. Sept. an. 58 (§ 8)*

CICERO ATTICO SAL.

1 Accepi Id. Sext. quattuor epistulas a te missas: unam qua me obiurgas et rogas ut sim firmior; alteram qua Crassi libertum ais tibi de mea sollicitudine macieque narrasse; tertiam qua demonstras acta in senatu; quartam de eo quod a Varrone scribis tibi esse confirmatum de voluntate Pompei.

2 Ad primam tibi hoc scribo, me ita dolere ut non modo a mente non deserar sed id ipsum doleam, me tam firma mente ubi utar et quibuscum non habere. nam si tu me uno non sine maerore cares, quid me censes, qui et te et omnibus? et si tu incolumis me requiris, [et] quo modo a me ipsam incolumitatem desiderari putas? nolo commemorare quibus rebus sim spoliatus, non solum quia non ignoras sed etiam ne scindam ipse dolorem meum; hoc confirmo, neque tantis bonis esse privatum quemquam neque in tantas miserias incidisse. dies autem non modo

[2] perferuntur (ς)

As matters stand I must go to Cyzicus, where letters will reach me less often. So I hope you will be all the more careful to send me full reports of everything you think I ought to know. Be good to my brother Quintus. If I leave him out of danger (ah me!), I shall not feel I am altogether lost.

Dispatched Nones of August.

60 (III.15)

Thessalonica, 17 August 58

CICERO TO ATTICUS

On the Ides of August I received four letters from you. In the first you scold me and ask me to show more fortitude. In the second you say that Crassus' freedman has told you how anxious he found me and how I have lost weight. In the third you give an account of transactions in the Senate. The fourth is about the confirmation of Pompey's good will which you say Varro has given you.

In reply to the first, I have this to say. My distress has not affected my mind; on the contrary one of its elements is that, my faculties being as sound as they are, I have neither matter nor company in which to use them. If the loss of my single self causes you some pain, what do you think *my* pain must be in losing you and all besides? And if you, who still enjoy your status in the community, feel my absence, how do you think *I* feel the loss of that very status? I don't propose to rehearse all the good things of which I have been stripped, for you know them already and I don't want to tear my own sore. But I do assert that no man has ever lost so much or fallen into such a pit of

non levat luctum hunc sed etiam auget. nam ceteri dolores mitigantur vetustate, hic non potest non et sensu praesentis miseriae et recordatione praeteritae vitae cottidie augeri. desidero enim non mea solum neque meos sed me ipsum. quid enim sum? sed non faciam ut aut tuum animum angam querelis aut meis vulneribus saepius manus adferam. nam quod purgas eos quos ego mihi scripsi invidisse et in eis Catonem, ego vero tantum illum puto ab isto scelere afuisse ut maxime doleam plus apud me simulationem aliorum quam istius fidem valuisse. ceteros quod

3 purgas, debent mihi probati esse tibi si sunt. sed haec sero agimus.

Crassi libertum nihil puto sincere locutum. in senatu rem probe scribis actam. sed quid Curio? an illam orationem non legit? quae unde sit prolata nescio. sed Axius eiusdem diei scribens ad me acta non ita laudat Curionem. at[1] potest ille aliquid praetermittere; tu, nisi quod erat, profecto non scripsisti. Varronis sermo facit exspectationem Caesaris. atque utinam ipse Varro incumbat in causam! quod profecto cum sua sponte tum te instante faciet.

4 Ego, si me aliquando vestri et patriae compotem fortuna fecerit, certe efficiam ut maxime laetere unus ex omnibus amicis meaque officia et studia, quae parum antea luxerunt (fatendum est enim), sic exsequar ut me aeque

[1] ac (ς)

misery. Time, far from relieving this heartache, actually increases it. Other hurts grow less acute as they grow older, this cannot but increase from day to day from the sense of present misery and the recollection of the life that is past. I mourn the loss not only of the things and persons that were mine, but of my very self. What am I now? But I must refrain from torturing you with complaints or putting my hands too often to my wounds. As for your exculpation of those who I said were jealous of me, among whom you include Cato, I am so far from thinking him guilty of the villainy in question that it is one of my principal regrets that the pretences of others counted more with me than his good faith. As for the rest whom you exculpate, I must approve them if you do. But it's late in the day for us to talk of this.

I imagine that Crassus' freedman spoke only in malice. You say that the debate in the Senate went well. But what of Curio? Or has he not read that speech? How it became public property I can't think. But Axius, in giving me an account of the same day's proceedings, doesn't praise Curio so highly. However, he may be leaving something out, whereas you of course will have written nothing but what was fact. What Varro says gives some hope of Caesar. If only Varro himself would put his shoulder to the wheel! No doubt he will, under pressure from you as well as of his own volition.

If fortune ever gives me back my friends and my country, I promise to see that none of them has so much cause to rejoice as yourself. I shall be so assiduous in friendly offices and tokens of good will, which in the past I must confess have not been sufficiently conspicuous, that you will feel that I am restored to *you* no less than to my

tibi ac fratri et liberis nostris restitutum putes. si quid in te peccavi, ac potius quoniam peccavi, ignosce; in me enim ipsum peccavi vehementius. neque haec eo scribo quo te non meo casu maximo dolore esse adfectum sciam; sed profecto <si> quantum me amas et amasti tantum amare deberes ac debuisses, numquam esses passus me, quo tu abundabas, egere consilio, nec esses passus mihi persuaderi utile nobis esse legem de collegiis perferri. sed tu tantum lacrimas praebuisti dolori meo, quod erat amoris, tamquam ipse ego; quod meritis meis perfectum potuit, ut dies ac noctes quid mihi faciendum esset cogitares, id abs te meo, non tuo scelere praetermissum est. quod si non modo tu sed quisquam fuisset qui me Pompei minus liberali responso perterritum a turpissimo consilio revocaret, quod unus tu facere maxime potuisti, <aut honeste occubuissemus>[2] aut victores hodie viveremus. hic mihi ignosces. me enim ipsum multo magis accuso, deinde te quasi me alterum, et simul meae culpae socium quae<ro>. ac si restituor, etiam minus videbimur deliquisse abs teque certe, quoniam nullo nostro, tuo ipsius beneficio diligemur.

5 Quod te cum Culleone scribis de privilegio locutum, est aliquid, sed multo est melius abrogari. si enim nemo impediet, quid est firmius? sin erit qui ferri non sinat, idem senatus consulto intercedet. nec quicquam aliud opus est

[2] *add. Watt, duce Bruno*

---

[1] A law of Clodius reviving clubs abolished in 64. How it affected Cicero is not clear.

[2] The bill of exile.

brother and our children. If I have treated you badly in any way, or rather *since* I have done so, forgive me. I have treated myself worse. If I write in this strain, it is not that I am unaware how deeply distressed you are by my misfortune. But surely, if now and in the past I had really deserved the affection you felt and feel for me, you would never have let me go short of that good advice of which you have so ample a store, never have let me be persuaded that the passage of the law about the clubs[1] was to my advantage. But you had only tears for my distress, the tribute of affection, just as I had myself. Desert on my part might have gained me something beyond, your daily and nightly meditation as to what it was best for me to do; that, through my delinquency not yours, you did not furnish. If you, or anyone else for that matter, at the time when I was thrown into consternation by Pompey's ungenerous response had held me back from a most discreditable resolution, as you were uniquely in a position to do, I should either have met an honourable death or be living triumphant today. You must forgive me here. I am reproaching myself far more than you, and if I do reproach you it is as my alter ego; also I am looking for someone to share the blame. If I am restored, my fault will come to seem less grave, and you at any rate will care for me, for the sake of what you have done for me since I have done nothing for you.

You say you have talked to Culleo about its being a law[2] ad hominem. There is something in that, but it would be far better to get it repealed. That is the safest way if nobody obstructs. On the other hand, if anyone is going to block a law, he will equally veto a senatorial decree. And there is

[quam][3] abrogari; nam prior lex nos nihil laedebat. quam si, ut est promulgata, laudare voluissemus aut, ut erat neglegenda, neglegere, nocere omnino nobis non potuisset. hic mihi primum meum consilium defuit, sed etiam obfuit. caeci, caeci inquam, fuimus in vestitu mutando, in populo rogando, quod, nisi nominatim mecum agi coeptum esset, fieri perniciosum fuit. sed pergo praeterita, verum tamen ob hanc causam, ut, si quid age[re]tur,[4] legem illam, in qua popularia multa sunt, ne tangatis.

6 Verum est stultum me praecipere quid agatis aut quo modo. utinam modo agatur aliquid! in quo ipso multa occultant tuae litterae, credo ne vehementius desperatione perturber. quid enim vides agi posse aut quo modo? per senatumne? at tute scripsisti ad me quoddam caput legis Clodium in curiae poste fixisse, ne referri neve dici liceret. quo modo igitur Domitius se dixit relaturum? quo modo autem iis quos tu scribis et de re dicentibus et ut referretur postulantibus Clodius tacuit? ac si per populum, poteritne nisi de omnium tribunorum pl. sententia? quid de bonis? quid de domo? poteritne restitui? aut si non poterit, egomet quo modo potero? haec nisi vides expediri, quam in spem me vocas? sin autem spei nihil est, quae est mihi vita? itaque exspecto Thessalonicae acta Kal. Sext., ex quibus statuam in tuosne agros confugiam, ut neque videam homines quos nolim et te, ut scribis, videam et

[3] *del. Schütz*
[4] ageretur (*Lambinus*)

---

[3] Clodius' earlier bill against any person guilty of putting a Roman citizen to death without trial. Although Cicero's name was not mentioned it caused his flight from Rome.

no need for anything else to be repealed, since the first law[3] did not touch me. If I had chosen to welcome it when it was first promulgated or to ignore it as it deserved, it could have done me no harm whatsoever. That was the first point where my judgement let me down, or rather did me down. We were blind, yes, blind, to put on mourning and appeal to the people—a fatal blunder where no proceedings had been taken against me by name. But this is crying over spilt milk. I do it however for a reason, to dissuade you, if any move is to be made, from touching that law, which has many popular features.

But it is fatuous for me to lay down what you people are to do or how you are to do it. If only *something* is done! In that very regard your letters leave many things obscure, I suppose because you are afraid of despair throwing me quite off my balance. For what in your view can be done and how? Through the Senate? But you yourself told me that Clodius posted in the doorway of the Senate House a clause in his law banning 'any motion or mention.' How then could Domitius say that he would make a motion? And how was it that Clodius sat mum while the persons you mention spoke on the subject and demanded that a motion be put to the House? And if it is to go through the Assembly, will that be possible without the unanimous approval of the Tribunes? What about my property, and my house? Can it be restored, and, if not, how can I be? Unless you see solutions to these problems, what sort of a hope are you asking me to entertain? If on the other hand there *is* no hope, what has life to offer me? So I am waiting at Thessalonica for the proceedings of the Kalends of August, in the light of which I shall decide whether to take refuge on your land, where I shall not see anyone I don't want and

propius sim si quid agatur, id quod[5] intellexi cum tibi tum Quinto fratri placere, an abeam Cyzicum.

7 Nunc, Pomponi, quoniam nihil impertisti tuae prudentiae ad salutem meam, quod aut in me ipso satis esse consili decreras aut te nihil plus mihi debere quam ut praesto esses, quoniamque ego proditus, inductus, coniectus in fraudem omnia mea praesidia neglexi, totam Italiam [in me][6] erectam ad me defendendum destitui et reliqui, me, meos tradidi inimicis inspectante et tacente te, qui, si non plus ingenio valebas quam ego, certe timebas minus: si potes, erige adflictos et in eo nos iuva; sin omnia sunt obstructa, id ipsum fac ut sciamus et nos aliquando aut obiurgare aut communiter consolari desine. ego si tuam fidem accusarem, non me potissimum tuis tectis crederem; meam amentiam accuso, quod me a te tantum amari quantum ego vellem putavi. quod si fuisset, fidem eandem, curam maiorem adhibuisses, me certe ad exitium praecipitantem retinuisses, istos labores, quos nunc in naufragiis nostris suscipis, non subisses.

8 Qua re fac ut omnia ad me perspecta et explorata perscribas meque, ut facis, velis esse aliquem, quoniam qui fui et qui esse potui, iam esse non possum, et ut his litteris non te sed me ipsum a me esse accusatum putes. si qui erunt quibus putes opus esse meo nomine litteras dari, velim conscribas curesque dandas.

Data XIIII Kal. Sept.

[5] idque (*R. Klotz*)
[6] *del. Ernesti*

where I shall see you, so you say, and be closer if anything is done, as I understand you and my brother Quintus both think advisable, or go away to Cyzicus.

Now, Pomponius, I appeal to you. You did not give me of your worldly wisdom to save me from ruin, considering perhaps that I was competent to judge for myself or else that you owed me nothing more than your presence. Betrayed, decoyed, trapped as I was, I neglected all my defences, deserted and abandoned the Italy which stood as one man ready to protect me, and surrendered myself and my family to my enemies, while you, my superior in sang-froid if not in mother wit, looked on and said nothing. Now, if it is in your power, raise me from the dust and help me in that. But if all paths are blocked, then tell me so, and don't let us have any more either of scolding or of consolatory commonplace. If I were saying anything against your good faith I should not choose your house for a refuge. It is my own folly that I reproach, in imagining that you felt as warmly towards me as I could have wished. Had that been so you would have brought not better faith indeed but greater solicitude to bear, you would certainly have held me back as I rushed upon destruction, and would have saved yourself the labours you are now undertaking in the wreck of my fortunes.

So please go thoroughly into everything and let me have a full and reliable account. Wish me (as you do) to be *somebody*, since I can no longer be what I was or what I might have been. And please take me as reproaching *myself* in this letter, not you. I should be grateful if you would write letters and arrange for their dispatch to any persons you think ought to be written to in my name.

Dispatched 17 August.

61 (III.16)

Scr. Thessalonicae XII *Kal. Sept. an. 58*

CICERO ATTICO SAL.

Totum iter mihi incertum facit exspectatio litterarum vestrarum Kal. Sext. datarum. nam si spes erit, Epirum, si minus, Cyzicum aut aliud quid sequemur. tuae quidem litterae quo saepius a me leguntur hoc spem faciunt mihi minorem, quod cum ‹diligentius›[1] lectae sunt tum id quod attulerunt ad spem infirmant, ut facile appareat te et consolationi servire et veritati. itaque te rogo plane ut ad me quae sci‹e›s ut erunt, quae putabis ita scribas ut putabis.

Data XII Kal. [April.].[2]

62 (III.17)

Scr. Thessalonicae prid. Non. Sept. an 58 (§ 3)

CICERO ATTICO SAL.

1 De Quinto fratre nuntii nobis tristes nec varii venerant ex a.d. ‹IIII›[1] Non. Iun. usque ad prid. Kal. Sept. eo autem die Livineius, L.[2] Reguli libertus, ad me a Regulo missus venit. is omnino mentionem nullam factam esse nuntiavit, sed fuisse tamen sermonem de C. Clodi filio; isque mihi tum a fratre litteras attulit. sed postridie Sesti pueri venerunt, qui a te litteras attulerunt non tam exploratas a timore quam sermo Livinei fuerat. sane sum in meo infinito

[1] *add. SB*
[2] *del. Baiter*

[1] ante diem non. (*SB* : a.d. III Non. *Hand*)
[2] m *vel* in *vel om.* (*Hervagius*)

61 (III.16)

Thessalonica, 19 August 58

CICERO TO ATTICUS

I am waiting for letters from you and others of date Kalends of August, and that makes my whole plan of travel uncertain. If there is hope, I shall make for Epirus; if not, for Cyzicus or some place or other. The oftener I read your letters the less optimistic they make me. When carefully read they cast doubts on the reasons for optimism which they adduced. It's easy to see that you are trying to combine consolation with honesty. I do ask you therefore to write to me plainly, giving what you know just as it is, and what you think just as you think it.

Dispatched 19th.

62 (III.17)

Thessalonica, 4 September 58

CICERO TO ATTICUS

Gloomy and also consistent reports about my brother Quintus continued to reach me between 2 June and 29 August. On that day however, Livineius, L. Regulus' freedman, arrived, sent to me by Regulus. He told me that nothing had been said publicly, but there had been some talk of C. Clodius' son.[1] He also brought me a letter from my brother. But the following day boys of Sestius' arrived bringing a letter from you which was not quite so reassuring as what Livineius had said. Naturally I feel anxiety,

[1] Appius maior—as Quintus' prosecutor.

maerore sollicitus, et eo magis quod Appi quaestio est.

2 Cetera quae ad me eisdem litteris scribis de nostra spe intellego esse languidiora quam alii ostendunt. ego autem, quoniam non longe ab eo tempore absumus in quo res diiudicabitur, aut ad te conferam me aut etiam nunc circum haec loca commorabor.

3 Scribit ad me frater omnia sua per te unum sustineri. quid te aut horter quod facis aut agam gratias, quod non exspectas? tantum velim fortuna det nobis potestatem ut incolumes amore nostro perfruamur. tuas litteras semper maxime exspecto; in quibus cave vereare[3] ne aut diligentia tua mihi molesta aut veritas acerba sit.

Data prid. Non. Sept.

63 (III.18)

Scr. Thessalonicae c. IV Id. Sept. an. 58

CICERO ATTICO SAL.

1 Exspectationem nobis non parvam attuleras cum scripseras Varronem tibi pro amicitia confirmasse causam nostram Pompeium certe suscepturum et, simul a Caesare ei litterae quas exspectaret remissae essent, actorem etiam daturum. utrum id nihil fuit an adversatae sunt Caesaris litterae an est aliquid in spe? etiam illud scripseras, eun-2 dem 'secundum comitia' dixisse. fac, si vides quantis in malis iaceam et si putas esse humanitatis tuae, me fac de tota causa nostra certiorem. nam Quintus frater, homo

[3] vereri *vel om.* (*Baiter*)

[2] The standing court to try cases of extortion. P. Clodius' brother Appius was now Praetor-Designate.

amid my own infinite distress, and all the more because Appius is President of the Court.[2]

I perceive that the rest of your letter dealing with my own prospects strikes a less sanguine note than what I hear from other correspondents. However, as we are not far away from the time of decision one way or the other, I shall either move to your place or stay yet awhile around here.

My brother writes that you are in everything his sole support and stay. I won't encourage you to do what you are already doing or offer thanks which you do not expect. I can only wish that fortune may grant us to enjoy one another's affection in our native land. I always eagerly await your letters. Don't have any fear that I may find them tediously detailed or painfully candid.

Dispatched 4 September.

63 (III.18)

Thessalonica, ca. 10 September 58

CICERO TO ATTICUS

My expectations were considerably aroused by what you told me about Varro's having assured you as a friend that Pompey would definitely take up my cause, and would further appoint an agent as soon as he had received a letter which he was expecting from Caesar. Did this mean nothing, or was Caesar's letter unfavourable, or is there still a hope? You also wrote that he said 'after the elections.' Do, if you see the trouble I am in and think it becomes the kindness of your heart, do inform me how my whole case stands. My brother Quintus, a wonderful fellow to love me

mirus qui me tam valde amat, omnia mittit spei plena, metuens, credo, defectionem animi mei. tuae autem litterae sunt variae; neque enim me desperare vis nec temere sperare. fac, obsecro te, ut omnia quae perspici a te possunt sciamus.

64 (III.19)

Scr. Thessalonicae XVI *Kal. Oct. an. 58 (§ 3)*

CICERO ATTICO SAL.

1 Quoad eius modi mihi a vobis litterae adferebantur ut aliquid ex iis esset exspectandum, spe et cupiditate Thessalonicae retentus sum; postea quam omnis actio huius anni confecta nobis videbatur, in Asiam ire nolui, quod et celebritas mihi odio est et, si fieret aliquid a novis magistratibus, abesse longe nolebam. itaque in Epirum ad te statui me conferre, non quo mea interesset loci natura qui lucem omnino fugerem, sed et ad salutem libentissime ex tuo portu proficiscar et, si ea praecisa erit, nusquam facilius hanc miserrimam vitam vel sustentabo vel, quod multo est melius, abiecero. ‹ero› cum paucis; multitudinem dimittam.

2 Me tuae litterae numquam in tantam spem adduxerunt quantam aliorum; ac tamen mea spes etiam tenuior semper fuit quam tuae litterae. sed tamen, quoniam coeptum est agi,[1] quoquo modo coeptum est et quacumque de causa, non deseram neque optimi atque unici fratris miseras ac luctuosas preces nec Sesti ceterorumque promissa

[1] ago (*Schütz*)

as he so ardently does, paints everything in rosy colours, fearing, I suppose, that I may otherwise give up altogether. Your letters vary. You don't want me to despair nor yet to hope unwisely. I beg you, let me know everything you can make out.

64 (III.19)

Thessalonica, 15 September 58

CICERO TO ATTICUS

As long as my letters from you and my other friends were such as to arouse some expectation of result, hope and desire kept me at Thessalonica. When it appeared to me that all activity was over for the year, I did not feel like going to Asia because crowds are odious to me, and I did not want to be far away in case something might be done by the new magistrates. So I have decided to betake myself to your place in Epirus; not that the character of the locality makes any difference to me seeing that I shun the light of day altogether, but yours is the harbour from which I shall most gladly set out to my deliverance, or, if that is past praying for, there is nowhere else where I can more easily support this miserable existence, or, what is much better, discard it. I shall have few companions, I shall dismiss the throng.

Your letters have never made me so hopeful as other people's, and yet my hopes have always been even fainter than your letters. However, since a beginning has been made, no matter how or why, I shall not be found wanting. I owe that to my excellent and only brother's piteous, mournful entreaties, and the promises of Sestius and the

nec spem aerumnosissimae mulieris Terentiae nec miserrimae [mulieris][2] Tulliolae obsecrationem et[3] fidelis litteras tuas. mihi Epirus aut iter ad salutem dabit aut quod scripsi supra.

3 Te oro et obsecro, T. Pomponi, si me omnibus amplissimis, carissimis iucundissimisque rebus perfidia hominum spoliatum, si me a meis consiliariis proditum et proiectum vides, si intellegis me coactum ut ipse me et meos perderem, ut me tua misericordia iuves et Quintum fratrem, qui potest esse salvus, sustentes, Terentiam liberosque meos tueare, me, si putas te istic visurum, exspectes, si minus, invisas si potes, mihique ex agro tuo tantum adsignes quantum meo corpore occupari potest, et pueros ad me cum litteris quam primum et quam saepissime mittas.

Data XVI Kal. Oct.

65 (III.20)

Scr. Thessalonicae III Non. Oct. an. 58 (§ 4)

CICERO S. D.[1] Q. CAECILIO
Q. F. POMPONIANO ATTICO

1 Quod quidem ita esse et avunculum tuum functum esse officio vehementissime probo; gaudere me tum dicam si mihi hoc verbo licebit uti. me miserum! quam omnia essent ex sententia, si nobis animus, si consilium, si fides eorum quibus credidimus, non defuisset! quae colligere nolo ne augeam maerorem; sed tibi in mentem venire certo scio quae vita esset nostra, quae suavitas, quae dig-

[2] *del. Schütz*

[3] nec (*Hervagius*)

[1] CICERO ATTICO SALUTEM *vel om.* (*Brunus*)

rest, and the hopes of Terentia, the most unhappy of women, and the pleas of my poor little Tullia, and your loyal letters. Epirus will either set me on the road to safety or—what I said just now.

T. Pomponius, I beg and implore you: you see how the perfidy of others has stripped me of all that I enjoyed in such ample measure, all that I most valued and delighted in, how I have been betrayed and thrown to the wolves by my own advisers. You know how I was made to work my own and my family's ruin. Pity me then and help me. Support my brother Quintus, who can still be saved, look after Terentia and my children, wait for me if you think you are likely to see me in Italy, if not, visit me if you can and assign me so much of your land as will suffice to contain my body. And send me boys with letters as soon and as often as you can.

Dispatched 15 September.

65 (III.20)

Thessalonica, 5 October 58

CICERO TO Q. CAECILIUS Q. F. POMPONIANUS ATTICUS

Well, I heartily approve that it is so and that your uncle has done the proper thing.[1] I shall say I am glad if the time ever comes when I can use that word. Ah me! How well content I should be in every way if courage, judgement, and the good faith of those I trusted had not failed me! I won't make a catalogue, which would add to my distress, but I am sure that the picture of my old life will come to

[1] Caecilius had died leaving Atticus his name and fortune.

nitas. ad quae recuperanda per fortunas incumbe, ut facis, diemque natalem reditus mei cura ut in tuis aedibus amoenissimis agam tecum et cum meis. ego huic spei et exspectationi quae nobis proponitur maxime tamen[2] volui praestolari apud te in Epiro, sed ita ad me scribitur ut putem esse commodius nos eisdem in locis esse.

2 De domo et Curionis oratione, ut scribis ita est. in universa salute, si ea modo nobis restituetur, inerunt omnia: ex quibus nihil malo quam domum. sed tibi nihil mando nominatim, totum me tuo amori fideique commendo. quod te in tanta hereditate ab omni occupatione expedisti, valde mihi gratum est. quod facultates tuas ad meam salutem polliceris, ut omnibus rebus a te praeter ceteros iuver, id quantum sit praesidium video intellegoque te multas partis meae salutis et suscipere et posse sustinere neque ut ita facias rogandum esse.

3 Quod me vetas quicquam suspicari accidisse ad animum tuum quod secus a me erga te commissum aut praetermissum videretur, geram tibi morem et liberabor ista cura, tibi tamen eo plus debebo quo tua in me humanitas fuerit excelsior quam in te mea. velim quid videas, quid intellegas, quid agatur ad me scribas tuosque omnis ad nostram salutem adhortere. rogatio Sesti neque dignitatis satis habet nec cautionis. nam et nominatim ferri oportet

[2] antea *Faber*

your mind, its amenity, its dignity. Try, I beg you, to recover all this, as you are doing, and make it possible for me to celebrate the birthday of my return in your delightful house with you and my family. I *did* want to hold myself in readiness for this proffered hope and expectation on your property in Epirus for preference, but the letters I get suggest that it will be more convenient for me to stay where I am.

About my house and Curio's speech, it is just as you say. Everything will be included in the general restoration of my status, if only that comes about. I care as much about the house as anything. But I don't give you any specific charge, I throw myself entirely on your affection and loyalty. It is very good news that you have freed your hands from business although you have so large an inheritance to think of. I fully appreciate the value of your offer to put all your resources at the service of my restoration and your assurance that in all things you take first place in aiding me. I know that you are taking upon yourself a multiple share of the burden, that you can support it, and that you do not have to be asked to do it.

As you tell me not to imagine that any supposed offence or neglect on my part has made any impression upon your mind, I shall do as you wish and dismiss that worry from my thoughts; but none the less I shall feel all the more indebted to you for showing a more generous spirit towards me than I have shown to you. I hope you will write and tell me what you see and what you gather and what is going on, and encourage all your friends to work for my restoration. Sestius' bill is not satisfactory either from the standpoint of dignity or from that of security. The law should mention my name and be more carefully drafted

et de bonis diligentius scribi, et id animadvertas velim.
Data III Non. Oct. Thessalonicae.

66 (III.21)

Scr. Thessalonicae V *Kal. Nov. an. 58*

CICERO ATTICO SAL.

Triginta dies erant ipsi cum has dabam litteras per quos nullas a vobis acceperam. mihi autem erat in animo iam, ut antea ad te scripsi, ire in Epirum et ibi omnem casum potissimum exspectare. te oro ut si quid erit quod perspicias quamcumque in partem quam planissime ad me scribas et meo nomine, ut scribis, litteras quibus putabis opus esse ut des.

Data V Kal. Nov.

67 (III.22)

Scr. partim Thessalonicae c. XV *Kal. Dec., partim Dyrrachii* VI *Kal. Dec. an. 58 (§ 4)*

CICERO ATTICO SAL.

1 Etsi diligenter ad me Quintus frater et Piso quae essent acta scripserant, tamen vellem tua te occupatio non impedisset quo minus, ut consuesti, ad me quid ageretur et quid intellegeres perscriberes. me adhuc Plancius liberalitate sua retinet iam aliquotiens conatum ire in Epirum. spes homini est iniecta non eadem quae mihi, posse nos

with respect to my property, and I should be grateful if you would pay attention to these points.

Dispatched 5 October, Thessalonica.

66 (III.21)

Thessalonica, 28 October 58

CICERO TO ATTICUS

It is thirty whole days from the time of writing since I heard anything from you. I am now thinking of doing what I said earlier, going to Epirus, and making that the place where I shall await my fate, whatever it is to be. I beg you to write to me in the plainest possible terms of anything that comes within your purview, whatever way it tends, and to write in my name, as you promise, to such persons as you think needful.

Dispatched 28 October.

67 (III.22)

Thessalonica, ca. 16 November, and Dyrrachium, 25 November 58

CICERO TO ATTICUS

Though my brother Quintus and Piso have given me details of what has happened, I could have wished that pressure of business had not prevented you from sending your usual full accounts of what is going on and what you make of it. Plancius' generosity still keeps me where I am, though I have made several moves to get away to Epirus. The good soul is possessed by the hope, which I do not share, that we may be able to leave for home together, and

una decedere, quam rem sibi magno honori sperat fore. sed iam, cum adventare milites dicentur, faciendum nobis erit ut ab eo discedamus, quod cum faciemus ad te statim mittemus ut scias ubi simus.

2 Lentulus suo in nos officio, quod et re et promissis et litteris declarat, spem nobis non nullam adfert Pompei voluntatis; saepe enim tu ad me scripsisti eum totum esse in illius potestate. de Metello scripsit ad me frater quan-3 tum speraret profectum esse per te. mi Pomponi, pugna ut tecum et cum meis mihi liceat vivere, et scribe ad me omnia. premor luctu cum desiderio omnium rerum quae mihi me cariores semper fuerunt. cura ut valeas.

4 Ego quod per Thessaliam si irem in Epirum perdiu nihil eram auditurus et quod [et] mei studiosos habeo Dyrrachinos, ad eos perrexi, cum illa superiora Thessalonicae scripsissem. inde cum ad te me convertam, faciam ut scias, tuque ad me velim omnia quam diligentissime, cuicuimodi sunt, scribas. ego iam aut rem aut ne spem quidem exspecto.

Data VI Kal. Dec. Dyrrachi.

68 (III.23)

Scr. Dyrrachii prid. Kal. Dec. an. 58 (§ 5)

CICERO ATTICO SAL.

1 A. d. V Kal. Dec. tris epistulas a te accepi, unam datam a. d. VIII Kal. Nov., in qua me hortaris ut forti animo mensem

---

[1] Cicero's enemy, the Consul L. Piso, was coming out with troops as governor of Macedonia.

thinks that will be a great feather in his cap. But I shall presently *have* to part from him, as soon as news comes of the soldiers[1] arriving. When I do, I shall send you word at once, so that you know my whereabouts.

Lentulus' friendly attitude, evinced in actions, promises, and letters, makes me somewhat hopeful of Pompey's good will, as you have often told me that he is completely under Pompey's thumb. As to Metellus, my brother has written to me of how much he hopes you have been able to achieve there. Strive, my dear fellow, to win me the right to live with you and my family, and write all to me. I am consumed by grief together with regret for all those things that have always been dearer to me than life itself. Take care of your health.

After writing the above at Thessalonica I proceeded to Dyrrachium, because if I had travelled to Epirus by way of Thessaly I should have heard nothing for a very long time, and because the townspeople are warm friends of mine. When I leave there for your place I shall let you know, and do you please write everything to me, good and bad, in the fullest detail. Results, not hopes, are what I expect now, results or nothing.

Dispatched 25 November, Dyrrachium.

68 (III.23)

Dyrrachium, 29 November 58

CICERO TO ATTICUS

On 26 November I received three letters from you, one dispatched 25 October, in which you urge me to keep my courage up and wait for January; and you go through vari-

Ianuarium exspectem, eaque quae ad spem putas pertinere, de Lentuli studio, de Metelli voluntate, de tota Pompei ratione perscribis. in altera epistula praeter consuetudinem tuam diem non adscribis, sed satis significas tempus; lege enim ab octo tribunis pl. promulgata scribis te eas litteras eo ipso die dedisse, id est a. d. IIII Kal. Nov., et quid putes utilitatis eam promulgationem attulisse perscribis. in quo si iam nostra salus cum hac lege desperata erit, velim pro tuo in me ‹a›more hanc inanem meam diligentiam miserabilem potius quam ineptam putes; sin est aliquid spei, des operam ut maiore diligentia posthac a nostris magistratibus defendamur.

2 Nam ea veterum tribunorum pl. rogatio tria capita habuit; unum de reditu meo, scriptum incaute. nihil enim restituitur praeter civitatem et ordinem; quod mihi pro meo casu satis est, sed quae cavenda fuerint et quo modo te non fugit. alterum caput est tralaticium, de impunitate: 'si quid contra alias leges eius legis ergo factum sit.' tertium caput, mi Pomponi, quo consilio et a quo sit inculcatum vide.

Scis[1] enim Clodium sanxisse ut vix aut omnino non posset nec per senatum nec per populum infirmari sua lex. sed vides numquam esse observatas sanctiones earum legum quae abrogarentur. nam si id esset, nulla fere abrogari posset; neque enim ulla est quae non ipsa se saepiat difficultate abrogationis. sed cum lex abrogatur, illud ipsum abrogatur quo non eam abrogari oporteat. hoc cum et

3

[1] scio *coni. SB*

---

[1] For Cicero's recall. It was vetoed by Clodius or a supporter of his.

ous items which you think have hopeful implications, Lentulus' zeal, Metellus' good will, Pompey's general policy. Your second letter, contrary to your custom, is undated, but you give sufficient indication as to when it was written, for you say you wrote on the very day that the eight Tribunes promulgated their law,[1] i.e. 29 October, and you explain the good you think the promulgation has done. If by this time all hope of my restoration has gone the same way as the bill, I wish you may care enough for me to find my idle solicitude on the subject pitiable rather than foolish. If however there is still hope, I trust you will use your endeavours so that in future the magistrates who are on my side champion me with more circumspection.

That bill of the old Tribunes had three clauses, the first concerning my return. This was carelessly drafted, for it restores nothing except my citizenship and rank. That is enough for me in my present plight, but you must see what points ought to have been provided for and how. The second clause, on impunity, is common form: 'should there be any contravention of other laws in consequence of this law.' As for the third clause—my dear Pomponius, do ask yourself why it was put in and by whom.

Clodius, as you know, attached sanctions to his bill to make it almost or quite impossible for it to be invalidated either by the Senate or by the Assembly. But precedent shows you that such sanctions have never been observed in the case of laws to be repealed. Otherwise it would be virtually impossible to repeal any law, for there is none but protects itself by putting difficulties in the way of repeal. But when a law is repealed, the provision against repeal is repealed at the same time. This being so, not only in fact

re vera ita sit et cum semper ita habitum observatumque sit, octo nostri tribuni pl. caput posuerunt hoc: 'si quid in hac rogatione scriptum est quod per leges plebisve scita' (hoc est, quod per legem Clodiam) 'promulgare, abrogare, derogare, obrogare sine fraude sua non liceat, non licuerit, quodve ei qui promulgavit, ‹abrogavit›, derogavit, ‹obrogavit› ob eam rem poenae multaeve sit, E. H. L. N. R.'

4 Atque hoc in illis tribunis pl. non laedebat; lege enim collegi sui non tenebantur. quo maior est suspicio malitiae alicuius, cum id quod ad ipsos nihil pertinebat, erat autem contra me, scripserunt, ut novi tribuni pl., si essent timidiores, multo magis sibi eo capite utendum putarent. neque id a Clodio praetermissum est. dixit enim in contione a. d. III Non. Nov. hoc capite designatis tribunis pl. praescriptum esse quid liceret. tamen in lege nulla esse eius modi caput te non fallit (quod si opus esset, omnes in abrogando ‹uterentur›), ut Ninnium aut ceteros fugerit, investiges velim, et quis attulerit, et qua re octo tribuni pl. ad senatum de me referre non dubitarint, sibi[2] quod observandum illud caput non putabant, eidem in abrogando tam cauti fuerint ut id metuerent soluti cum essent quod ne iis quidem qui lege tenentur est curandum. id caput sane nolim novos tribunos pl. ferre. sed perferant modo

[2] sive *vel* sine (*SB*)

but in traditional opinion and practice, our eight Tribunes put down the following clause: 'Should there be anything in the terms of this bill, whether in promulgation of a new statute or in repeal or restriction or contravention of an existing statute, which is or was forbidden by or punishable under the laws or the resolutions of the plebs' (which is to say under the lex Clodia) 'or which renders the person responsible for such promulgation or repeal or restriction or contravention liable to penalty or fine, nothing of this is enacted by the present bill.'

Now *those* Tribunes had nothing of the sort to fear, for they were not bound by a law emanating from one of their own body. That makes one all the more suspicious of some malicious intention when one finds them including a provision which did not affect themselves but was contrary to my interest, so that their successors, if timorously disposed, would feel under a much stronger compulsion to adopt the clause. Nor did that escape Clodius. At a meeting on 3 November he remarked that this clause laid down for the Tribunes-Designate how far they might go. And yet you must be aware that no law contains such a clause, though if there were any need for it everyone would have used it in repealing statutes. I should be grateful if you would inquire how it was that Ninnius and the others failed to see this, and who brought the clause in, and why the eight Tribunes, who did not hesitate to make a motion on my case in the Senate (because they did not regard themselves as bound by that clause), pushed caution so far when it came to the repeal that they were afraid of a sanction which did not apply to them and which even those statutorily subject to it are at liberty to ignore. I sincerely hope that the new Tribunes will not propose this clause. However,

quidlibet; uno capite quo revocabor, modo res conficiatur, ero contentus. iam dudum pudet tam multa scribere; vereor enim ne re iam desperata legas, ut haec mea diligentia miserabilis tibi, aliis irridenda videatur. sed si est aliquid in spe, vide legem quam T. Fadio scripsit [T.] Visellius. ea mihi perplacet. nam Sesti nostri, quam tu tibi probari scribis, mihi non placet.

5 Tertia est epistula prid. Id. Nov. data, in qua exponis prudenter et diligenter quae sint quae rem distinere videantur, de Crasso, de Pompeio, de ceteris. qua re oro te ut, si qua spes erit posse studiis bonorum, auctoritate,[3] multitudine comparata rem confici, des operam ut uno impetu perfringatur, in eam rem incumbas ceterosque excites. sin, ut ego perspicio cum tua coniectura tum etiam mea, spei nihil est, oro obtestorque te ut Quintum fratrem ames, quem ego miserum misere perdidi, neve quid eum patiare gravius consulere de se quam expediat sororis tuae filio, meum Ciceronem, cui nihil misello relinquo praeter invidiam et ignominiam nominis mei, tue‹a›re quoad poteris, Terentiam, unam omnium aerumnosissimam, sustentes tuis officiis.

Ego in Epirum proficiscar cum primorum dierum nuntios excepero. tu ad me velim proximis litteris ut se initia dederint perscribas.

Data prid. Kal. Dec.

[3] studiis tribuniciis b- a- *Watt*

let them only put *something* through, never mind what. I shall be satisfied with a single clause recalling me, provided only the thing be done. Already I feel ashamed to be writing at such length, and I fear that by the time you read this the matter may already have been given up as a bad job. In that case my solicitude will seem pitiable to you and ludicrous to others. But if there is anything left to hope for, take a look at the law which Visellius drafted for T. Fadius. It seems admirable to me. Sestius' draft, which you say you approve of, I don't like.

The third letter was dispatched on 12 November. In it you explain, knowledgeably and carefully, the factors which you think are holding matters back, covering Crassus, Pompey, and the rest. If therefore any hope emerges of carrying the business through by the support of the honest men, by influence, by a crowd brought up for the purpose, I beg you to try for a breakthrough at a single push. Put your heart into the effort and rouse the others. But if, as I see to be the case on your forecast and my own too, there is *no* hope, I beg and adjure you to care for my poor brother Quintus, whom I have ruined, unlucky wretch that I am. Don't let him take any decision concerning himself which might be to the injury of your nephew. Protect my Marcus as far as you can. Poor little boy, I am leaving him nothing but my hated and dishonoured name. Support Terentia with your good offices: no woman ever had so much to bear.

I shall go to Epirus when I get news of the first few days. Please write to me in your next letter how the opening moves go.

Dispatched 29 November.

69 (III.24)

Scr. Dyrrachii IV *Id. Dec. an. 58 (§ 2)*

CICERO ATTICO SAL.

1 Antea, cum ad me scripsissetis vestro consensu consulum provincias ornatas esse, etsi verebar quorsum id casurum esset, tamen sperabam vos aliquid aliquando vidisse prudentius; postea quam mihi et dictum est et scriptum vehementer consilium vestrum reprehendi, sum graviter commotus, quod illa ipsa spes exigua quae erat videtur esse sublata. nam si tribuni pl. nobis suscensent, quae potest spes esse? ac videntur iure suscensere, cum et expertes consili fuerint ei[1] qui causam nostram susceperant et nostra concessione omnem vim sui iuris amiserint, praesertim cum ita dicant, se nostra causa voluisse suam potestatem esse de consulibus ornandis, non ut eos impedirent sed ut ad nostram causam adiungerent; nunc, si consules a nobis alieniores esse velint, posse id libere facere; sin velint[2] nostra causa, nihil posse se invitis. nam quod scribis, ni ita vobis placuisset, illos hoc idem per populum adsecuturos fuisse, invitis tribunis pl. fieri nullo modo potuit. ita vereor ne et studia tribunorum amiserimus et, si studia maneant, vinclum illud adiungendorum consulum amissum sit.

2 Accedit aliud non parvum incommodum quod gravis illa opinio, ut quidem ad nos perferebatur, senatum nihil

[1] et (*Orelli*)
[2] vellent (*Ernesti*)

69 (III.24)

Dyrrachium, 10 December 58

CICERO TO ATTICUS

When you and my other supporters wrote to me that the grants for the consular provinces had been authorized with your consent, I had my misgivings about the consequences but I hoped that at some point or other you had seen further than I. Later I was told, both orally and in writing, that your tactics were coming in for strong criticism. I was deeply disturbed, because it looks as if even the faint ray of hope that existed has been extinguished. For if the Tribunes are annoyed with us, what hope can there be? And apparently they have fair reason for annoyance, since those of them who had undertaken to help our cause were not consulted and, through a concession on our part, have lost all the power of their prerogative—more especially as they say it was for our sake that they wanted the Consuls' grants to be under their control, not in order to make difficulties for them but to attach them to our cause. They point out that if the Consuls should now choose to take an unfriendly attitude towards us they are free to do so; whereas, should they be well disposed, they can do nothing against their (the Tribunes') wishes. As for your argument that if you had not agreed the Consuls would have carried their point through the Assembly, that would have been out of the question if the Tribunes had been in opposition. So I am afraid we may have lost the support of the Tribunes and, supposing that remains, I fear the hold we might have had over the Consuls has been let slip.

A further and not negligible disadvantage is that the firm impression (or so it was reported to me) that the

decernere ante quam de nobis actum esset, amissa est, praesertim in ea causa quae non modo necessaria non fuit sed etiam inusitata ac nova (neque enim umquam arbitror ornatas esse provincias designatorum), ut, cum in hoc illa constantia quae erat mea causa suscepta imminuta sit, nihil iam possit non decerni. iam iis ad quos relatum est amicis placuisse non mirum est; erat enim difficile reperire qui contra tanta commoda duorum consulum palam sententiam diceret. fuit omnino difficile non obsequi vel amicissimo homini Lentulo vel Metello, qui simultatem humanissime deponeret. sed vereor ne hos tamen tenere potuerimus, tribunos pl. amiserimus. haec res quem ad modum ceciderit et tota res quo loco sit velim ad me scribas et ita ut instituisti. nam ista veritas, etiam si iucunda non est, mihi tamen grata est.

Data IIII Id. Dec.

70 (III.25)

Scr. Dyrrachii c. med. m. Dec. an. 58

CICERO ATTICO SAL.

Post tuum datae[1] discessum litterae mihi Roma adlatae sunt ex quibus perspicio nobis in hac calamitate tabescendum esse. neque enim (sed bonam in partem accipies), si ulla spes saluti‹s› nostrae subesset, tu pro tuo amore in me hoc tempore discessisses. sed ne ingrati aut ne omnia velle

[1] a me (*Watt*)

Senate was not passing any decrees before my case had been dealt with has been let go by the board, and that for a purpose not merely unnecessary but contrary to custom and precedent (I don't think provincial grants have ever been authorized for Designates). Thus there is nothing to stop any decree, now that the line determined in my interest has been breached in this instance. As for those friends of mine to whom the question was put, it is not surprising that they spoke in favour. It would have been difficult to find anyone prepared to raise his voice publicly against a proposal so much to the advantage of the two Consuls. No doubt it was difficult to refuse such a good friend as Lentulus, or Metellus either when he was so handsomely waiving his grudge against me. But I suspect that we could have held them all the same and that we have lost the Tribunes. I should be grateful if you would tell me how this came about and how the whole matter stands, and do so in your present manner. This frankness of yours may not make for pleasant reading, but I welcome it.

10 December.

70 (III.25)

Dyrrachium ca. mid-December 58

CICERO TO ATTICUS

A letter from Rome, dispatched after you left, has reached me from which I see that I must pine away in this miserable state. And indeed (you won't take this amiss), if there were any lingering hope of my restoration, caring for me as you do you would not have left Rome at this time. But I leave this aside, for fear of appearing ungrateful or of seeming

nobiscum una interire videamur, haec omitto; illud abs te peto, des operam, id quod mihi adfirmasti, ut te ante Kal. Ian. ubicumque erimus sistas.

71 (III.26)

Scr. Dyrrachii, ut vid., med. m. Ian. an. 57

CICERO ATTICO SAL.

Litterae mihi a Quinto fratre cum senatus consulto quod de me est factum adlatae sunt. mihi in animo est legum lationem exspectare; et si obtrectabitur, utar auctoritate senatus et potius vita quam patria carebo. tu, quaeso, festina ad nos venire.

72 (III.27)

Scr. Dyrrachii, ut vid., in. m. Febr. an. 57

CICERO ATTICO SAL.

Ex tuis litteris et ex re ipsa nos funditus perisse video. te oro ut quibus in rebus tui mei indigebunt nostris miseriis ne desis. ego te, ut scribis, cito videbo.

---

[1] A law for Cicero's recall brought before the Assembly on 23 January 57 was blocked by Clodius' gang. Q. Cicero nearly lost his life in the rioting.

to want everything to go to ruin along with myself. I only ask you to try, as you assured me you would, to present yourself wherever I am before the Kalends of January.

71 (III.26)

Dyrrachium, (?), mid-January 57

CICERO TO ATTICUS

I have received a letter from my brother Quintus along with the decree about me passed in the Senate. I propose to wait for the laws to be put to the vote, and if there is opposition I shall avail myself of the Senate's authority and prefer loss of life to that of country. Pray make haste to join me.

72 (III.27)

Dyrrachium (?), early February 57

CICERO TO ATTICUS

From your letter and from the facts themselves I see that I am utterly finished.[1] In matters where my family needs your help I beg you not to fail us in our misery. According to your letter I shall see you soon.[2]

[2] The correspondence here lapses, to be resumed in September after Cicero's return to Italy. The natural conclusion that he and Atticus were together on the latter's Buthrotian estate during the interval is hard to reconcile with para. 2 of Letter 73 and moreover runs counter to a clear implication in *On the Laws* 2.7 that Cicero had never seen the place.

73 (IV.1)

Scr. Romae c. IV *Id. Sept. an.* 57

CICERO ATTICO SAL.

1 Cum primum Romam veni fuit<que> cui recte ad te litteras darem, nihil prius faciendum mihi putavi quam ut tibi absenti de reditu gratularer. cognoram enim, ut vere scribam, te in consiliis mihi dandis nec fortiorem nec prudentiorem quam me ipsum nec etiam propter meam in te observantiam[1] nimium in custodia salutis meae diligentem; eundemque te, qui primis temporibus erroris nostri aut potius furoris particeps et falsi timoris socius fuisses, acerbissime discidium nostrum tulisse plurimumque operae, studi, diligentiae, laboris ad conficiendum reditum meum contulisse. 2 itaque hoc tibi vere adfirmo, in maxima laetitia et exoptatissima gratulatione unum ad cumulandum gaudium conspectum aut potius complexum mihi tuum defuisse. quem semel nactus si umquam dimisero ac nisi etiam praetermissos fructus tuae suavitatis praeteriti temporis omnis exegero, profecto hac restitutione fortunae me ipse non satis dignum iudicabo.

3 Nos adhuc in nostro statu quod difficillime recuperari posse arbitrati sumus, splendorem nostrum illum forensem et in senatu auctoritatem et apud viros bonos gratiam, magis quam opta<ra>mus consecuti sumus; in re autem familiari, quae quem ad modum fracta, dissipata, direpta sit non ignoras, valde laboramus, tuarumque non tam facultatum, quas ego nostras esse iudico, quam consiliorum ad colligendas et constituendas reliquias nostras indigemus.

[1] *locus dubius*

73 (IV.1)

Rome, about 10 September 57

CICERO TO ATTICUS

As soon as I arrived in Rome and came by a suitable person to take a letter to you, I considered it my first duty to congratulate you on my return. I had found you, to be quite frank, neither bolder nor wiser than myself as an adviser, nor, I may add, excessively sedulous in guarding me from harm in default of (?) observances on my part to make you so. But I also found that, having in the early days shared my error, or rather infatuation, and participated in my false alarm, you felt our severance most keenly, and devoted a vast amount of time and zeal and patience and labour to bringing about my return. And so I sincerely assure you that in the plenitude of longed-for joy and congratulation one thing has been wanting to make my cup flow over: to see you, or rather to hold you in my arms. Once I win that happiness, if ever I let it go and if I do not also claim all the arrears of your delightful company that are owing to me, I shall really consider myself hardly worthy of this restitution of my fortunes.

Of my general position it can so far be said that I have attained what I thought would be most difficult to recover, namely my public prestige, my standing in the Senate, and my influence among the honest men, in larger measure than I had dreamed possible. But my private affairs are in a very poor way—you are aware how my property has been crippled and dissipated and pillaged—and I stand in need not so much of your resources, which I count as my own, as of your advice in pulling together what is left and putting it on a sound footing.

4 Nunc, etsi omnia aut scripta esse a tuis arbitror aut etiam nuntiis ac rumore perlata, tamen ea scribam brevi quae te puto potissimum ex meis litteris velle cognoscere.

Prid. Non. Sext. Dyrrachio sum profectus, ipso illo die quo lex est lata de nobis. Brundisium veni Non. Sext. ibi mihi Tulliola mea fuit praesto natali suo ipso die, qui casu idem natalis erat et Brundisinae coloniae et tuae vicinae Salutis; quae res animadversa a multitudine summa Brundisinorum gratulatione celebrata est. a. d. III[2] Id. Sext. cognovi, cum Brundisi essem, litteris Quinti fratris mirifico studio omnium aetatum atque ordinum, incredibili concursu Italiae, legem comitiis centuriatis esse perlatam. inde a Brundisinis honestissime ornatus iter ita feci ut undique ad me cum gratulatione legati convenerint.

5 Ad urbem ita veni ut nemo ullius ordinis homo nomenclatori notus fuerit qui mihi obviam non venerit, praeter eos inimicos quibus id ipsum, se inimicos esse, non liceret aut dissimulare aut negare. cum venissem ad portam Capenam, gradus templorum ab infima plebe completi erant. a qua plausu maximo cum esset mihi gratulatio significata, similis et frequentia ‹et› plausus me usque ad Capitolium celebravit in foroque et in ipso Capitolio miranda multitudo fuit. postridie in senatu, qui fuit dies Non. Sept., senatui gratias egimus.

[2] VI *vel* sex(t) (*O. E. Schmidt*)

[1] The extant speech 'In the Senate after His Return.'

I shall now give you a brief account of such matters as I think you will particularly like to learn from my pen, though I expect you have already been informed of everything in letters from your own people or for that matter by report and general rumour.

I left Dyrrachium on 4 August, the very day on which the law for my recall was put to the vote. I landed at Brundisium on the Nones of August. My little Tullia was there to welcome me. It was her birthday and also, as it happened, the foundation day of the colony of Brundisium and of the temple of your neighbour the Goddess of Weal, a coincidence which attracted popular notice and was joyfully celebrated by the townsfolk. On 11 August (?), while at Brundisium, I learned by letter from Quintus that the law had been carried in the Assembly of Centuries amid remarkable demonstrations of enthusiasm by all ranks and ages and with an extraordinary concourse of country voters. Thence I set out, after receiving the most flattering marks of regard from the townspeople, and as I travelled along I was joined by congratulatory deputations from all quarters.

So I arrived at the outskirts of Rome. Not a man whose name was known to my nomenclator, no matter what his rank, but came out to meet me, except for enemies who could neither conceal nor deny the fact that they were such. When I reached the Porta Capena I found the steps of the temples thronged by the common people, who welcomed me with vociferous applause. Like numbers and applause followed me to the Capitol. In the Forum and on the Capitol itself the crowd was spectacular. In the Senate on the following day, the Nones of September, I made a speech of thanks to the House.[1]

6 Eo biduo, cum esset annonae summa caritas et homines ad theatrum primo, deinde ad senatum concurrissent, impulsu Clodi mea opera frumenti inopiam esse clamarent, cum per eos dies senatus de annona haberetur et ad eius procurationem sermone non solum plebis verum etiam bonorum Pompeius vocaretur idque ipse cuperet multitudoque a me nominatim ut id decernerem postularet, feci et accurate sententiam dixi. cum abessent consulares, quod tuto se negarent posse sententiam dicere, praeter Messallam et Afranium, factum est senatus consultum in meam sententiam ut cum Pompeio ageretur ut eam rem susciperet, lexque ferretur. quo senatus consulto recitato continuo, <cum multitudo>[3] more hoc insulso et novo plausum meo nomine recitando[4] dedisset, habui contionem. <eam>[5] omnes magistratus praesentes praeter unum praetorem et duos tribunos pl. dederunt.

7 Postridie senatus frequens et omnes consulares. nihil Pompeio postulanti negarunt. ille legatos quindecim cum postularet, me principem nominavit et ad omnia me alterum se fore dixit. legem consules conscripserunt qua Pompeio per quinquennium omnis potestas rei frumentariae toto orbe terrarum daretur; alteram Messius, qui omnis pecuniae dat potestatem et adiungit classem et exercitum et maius imperium in provinciis quam sit eorum qui eas obtineant. illa nostra lex consularis nunc modesta videtur, haec Messi non ferenda. Pompeius illam velle se dicit, familiares hanc. consulares duce Favonio fremunt.

[3] *add. SB, Watt* [4] iterando *coni. SB* [5] *add. SB*

---

[2] P. Clodius' brother Appius, and the Tribunes Sex. Atilius Serranus and Q. Numerius Rufus.

Two days later I spoke again. The price of grain had risen very high, and a crowd flocked first to the theatre and then to the Senate, clamouring at Clodius' instigation that the shortage was my doing. The Senate met during those days to consider the grain situation, and there was a general demand, not only from the populace but from the honest men too, that Pompey be asked to take charge of supplies. He himself was eager for the commission, and the crowd called on me by name to propose it. I did so in a full-dress speech. In the absence of all the Consulars except Messalla and Afranius, because, as they alleged, it was not safe for them to speak, the Senate passed a decree as proposed by me, to the effect that Pompey should be asked to undertake the matter and appropriate legislation be introduced. The decree was recited immediately, and the people applauded after the silly newfangled fashion when my name was read out. I then addressed them at the invitation of all magistrates present except for one Praetor and two Tribunes.[2]

The following day there was a large attendance in the House, including all the Consulars. Pompey was given everything he asked. In asking for fifteen Lieutenant Commissioners he named me first, and said that I should be his alter ego for all purposes. The Consuls drafted a law giving Pompey control over all grain supplies throughout the world for a period of five years. Messius proposed an alternative bill which gives him control over all moneys and in addition a fleet, an army, and authority in the provinces superior to that of their governors. Our consular law now looks quite modest; Messius' is felt to be intolerable. According to himself Pompey favours the former, according to his friends the latter. The Consulars are seething, Fa-

nos tacemus, et eo magis quod de domo nostra nihil adhuc pontifices responderant. qui si sustulerint religionem, aream praeclaram habemus, superficiem consules ex senatus consulto aestimabunt; sin aliter, demolientur, suo nomine locabunt, rem totam aestimabunt.

8 Ita sunt res nostrae, 'ut in secundis fluxae, ut in adversis bonae.' in re familiari valde sumus, ut scis, perturbati. praeterea sunt quaedam domestica quae litteris non committo. Quintum fratrem insigni pietate, virtute, fide praeditum sic amo ut debeo. te exspecto et oro ut matures venire eoque animo venias ut me tuo consilio egere non sinas. alterius vitae quoddam initium ordimur. iam quidam qui nos absentis defenderunt incipiunt praesentibus occulte irasci, aperte invidere. vehementer te requirimus.

74 (IV.2)

Scr. Romae in. m. Oct. an. 57

‹CICERO ATTICO SAL.›

1 Si forte rarius tibi a me quam a ceteris litterae redduntur, peto a te ut id non modo neglegentiae meae sed ne occu-

---

[3] Ironical. Favonius' official rank was humble, ex-Quaestor or at most ex-Tribune.

[4] After demolishing Cicero's house on the Palatine Clodius had consecrated part of the site to the goddess Liberty. To allow Cicero to rebuild, this consecration had to be annulled by the Pontiffs and the shrine to Liberty pulled down. Had the Pontiffs maintained the consecration, the temple would still have been pulled down and replaced by another.

vonius at their head.[3] I hold my tongue, a course to which I am the more inclined because the Pontiffs have not yet given any answer about my house. If they lift the religious sanction,[4] I have a splendid site and the Consuls, under senatorial decree, will estimate the value of the building. If not, they will pull down the temple, let out a contract in their own name, and make an estimate for the whole.

So stand my affairs:

'Unsettled,' when our luck is in;
When out, we call it 'fair.'[5]

My financial position, as you know, is in very far from good order. Moreover, there are certain private matters which I don't trust to a letter. My brother is a paragon of affection, courage and loyalty, and I love him as I ought. I am looking forward to seeing you and beg you to make haste; and when you do come, come prepared to give me the benefit of your advice. It is a sort of second life I am beginning. Already, now that I am here, secret resentment and open jealousy are setting in among some of those who championed me when I was away. I need you badly.

74 (IV.2)

Rome, beginning of October 57

CICERO TO ATTICUS

If so be that you hear from me less often than from others, let me ask you not to put it down to pressure of business,

[5] Line from an unknown Latin play. Shuckburgh rendered from Milton 'For happy though but ill, for ill not worst.'

pationi quidem tribuas; quae etsi summa est, tamen nulla esse potest tanta ut interrumpat iter amoris nostri et offici mei. nam ut veni Romam, iterum nunc sum certior factus esse cui darem litteras; itaque has alteras dedi.

Prioribus tibi declaravi adventus noster qualis fuisset et quis esset status atque omnes res nostrae quem ad modum essent, 'ut in secundis fluxae, ut in adversis bonae.' post

2 illas datas litteras secuta est summa contentio de domo. diximus apud pontifices prid. Kal. Oct. acta res est accurate a nobis, et si umquam in dicendo fuimus aliquid, aut etiam si <n>umquam alias fuimus, tum profecto dolor et <rei>[1] magnitudo vim quandam nobis dicendi dedit. itaque oratio iuventuti nostrae deberi non potest; quam tibi, etiam si non desideras, tamen mittam cito.

3 Cum pontifices decressent ita, 'si neque populi iussu neque plebis scitu is qui se dedicasse diceret nominatim ei rei praefectus esset neque populi iussu aut plebis scitu id facere iussus esset,' videri posse sine religione eam partem areae mihi restitui, mihi facta statim est gratulatio (nemo enim dubita<ba>t quin domus nobis esset adiudicata), cum subito ille in contionem escendit quam Appius ei dedit. nuntiat [iam] populo pontifices secundum se decrevisse, me autem vi conari in possessionem venire; hortatur ut se et Appium sequantur et suam Libertatem ut defendant.

[1] dolor et *vel* -ris et *vel* -ris (*Gulielmius*)

---

[1] In the extant speech 'Concerning His House.'

let alone negligence. True, I am extremely busy, but no amount of business can interfere with the course of our affection and the attention I owe you. The fact is, this is the second time since my return to Rome that I have heard of anyone to carry a letter; so this is my second letter.

In the first I gave you an account of the manner of my arrival, my present position, and the whole state of my affairs:

> 'Unsettled,' when our luck is in;
> When out, we call it 'fair.'

After I sent that letter there followed a tremendous struggle over my house. I addressed the Pontiffs on 29 September.[1] I dealt faithfully with my theme, and if ever I amounted to anything as a speaker, or even if I never did at any other time, I think I can say that on that occasion intensity of feeling and the importance of the issue lent me a certain force of eloquence. So our younger generation cannot be kept waiting for the speech. I shall send it to you shortly, even if you are not anxious to have it!

The Pontiffs having found that 'that portion of the site might be restored to me without sacrilege, providing the person claiming to have consecrated it was not commissioned by name thereto by an order of the people or resolution of the plebs, neither ordered so to act by an order of the people or resolution of the plebs,' I was at once congratulated on the result, for nobody doubted that the house had been adjudged to me. Suddenly Clodius got up to address a meeting at Appius' invitation. He announced to the people that the Pontiffs had found in his favour, but that I was attempting to get possession by force, and urged them to follow Appius and himself and defend their

hic cum etiam illi infimi partim admirarentur partim irriderent hominis amentiam (ego statueram illuc non accedere nisi cum consules ex senatus consulto porticum Catuli restituendam locassent), 4 Kal. Oct. habetur senatus frequens. adhibentur omnes pontifices qui erant senatores. a quibus Marcellinus, qui erat cupidissimus mei, sententiam primus rogatus quaesivit quid essent in decernendo secuti. tum M. Lucullus de omnium collegarum sententia respondit religionis iudices pontifices fuisse, legis <es>se[2] senatum; se et collegas suos de religione statuisse, in senatu de lege statu<tur>os cum senatu. itaque suo quisque horum loco sententiam rogatus multa secundum causam nostram disputavit. cum ad Clodium ventum est, cupiit diem consumere, neque ei finis est factus; sed tamen, cum horas tris fere dixisset, odio et strepitu senatus coactus est aliquando perorare. cum fieret senatus consultum in sententiam Marcellini, omnibus praeter unum adsentientibus, Serranus <intercessit. de>[3] intercessione statim ambo consules referre coeperunt. cum sententiae gravissimae dicerentur, senatui placere mihi domum restitui, porticum Catuli locari, auctoritatem ordinis ab omnibus magistratibus defendi, si quae vis esset facta, senatum existimaturum eius opera factam[4] esse qui senatus consulto intercessisset, Serranus pertimuit et Cornicinus ad suam veterem fabulam rediit; abiecta toga se ad generi pedes abiecit. ille noctem sibi postulavit. non concedebant;

[2] *add. Seyffert*
[3] *add. Victorius*
[4] factum (*SB*)

---

[2] Also demolished by Clodius and replaced by one of his own.

Liberty. Even those groundlings were astonished, some of them, while others laughed at his folly—I had decided not to go near the place until the Consuls by decree of the Senate had contracted for the rebuilding of Catulus' portico.[2] On the Kalends of October there was a meeting of the Senate, well attended. All the Pontiffs who were Senators were called in. Marcellinus, who was very strongly on my side, as the first called upon, asked them to give reasons for their decree. M. Lucullus, speaking for all his colleagues, then replied that the Pontiffs had been judges of the religious issue, but the Senate was judge of the law. His colleagues and himself had given their verdict on the former; on the latter they would decide in the Senate, as Senators. Accordingly all of them, as called upon in their turn, spoke at length in favour of my case. When Clodius' turn came he set himself to talk out the sitting and there was no putting a stop to him. However, after holding forth for something like three hours, he was finally forced to wind up by noisy interruptions from the exasperated House. A decree in accordance with Marcellinus' proposal, unanimous apart from one dissentient, was in process of passage when Serranus interposed his veto. Both Consuls immediately set about referring the veto to the Senate. Some very powerful speeches were delivered to the effect that it was the Senate's desire that my house should be restored, a contract for Catulus' portico put in hand, and the authority of the House defended by all magistrates; further, that in case of any violence the person vetoing the decree would be held responsible by the Senate. Serranus took fright, and Cornicinus repeated his old charade—flinging off his toga and throwing himself on his knees before his son-in-law. Serranus asked for a night's

reminiscebantur enim Kal. Ian. vix tamen ei de[5] mea voluntate concessum est.

5 Postridie senatus consultum factum est id quod ad te misi. deinde consules porticum Catuli restituendam locarunt; illam porticum redemptores statim sunt demoliti libentissimis omnibus. nobis superficiem aedium consules de consili sententia aestimarunt HS vicies, cetera valde illiberaliter: Tusculanam villam quingentis milibus, Formianum HS ducentis quinquaginta milibus. quae aestimatio non modo vehementer ab optimo quoque sed etiam a plebe reprehenditur. dices 'quid igitur causae fuit?' dicunt illi quidem pudorem meum, quod neque negarim neque vehementius postularim. sed non est id; nam hoc quidem etiam profuisset. verum iidem, mi T. Pomponi, iidem, inquam, illi, quos ne tu quidem ignoras, qui mihi pinnas inciderant, nolunt easdem renasci. sed, ut spero, iam renascuntur. tu modo ad nos veni; quod vereor ne tardius interventu Varronis tui nostrique facias.

6 Quoniam acta quae sint habes, de reliqua nostra cogitatione cognosce. ego me a Pompeio legari ita sum passus ut nulla re impedirer. quod nisi vellem mihi esset integrum ut,[6] si comitia censorum proximi consules haberent, petere possem, votivam legationem sumpsissem prope omnium fanorum, lucorum; sic enim nostrae rationes [utilitates meae][7] postulabant. sed volui meam potestatem esse vel

[5] tibi de (*SB* : *del. Watt* : et id *coni. idem SB*)
[6] aut (*Hofmann*) [7] *del. Manutius*

[3] When Serranus, one of the two hostile Tribunes of Letter 73.6, had blocked a decree in favour of Cicero's recall by asking for an adjournment.

grace, but the House, remembering the Kalends of January,[3] was unwilling to allow it. However, with much ado and with my good will, the point was conceded him.

On the following day the decree which I send you herewith was passed. The Consuls then signed a contract for the restoration of Catulus' portico, and the contractors immediately demolished the other portico much to everybody's satisfaction. The Consuls with their assessors valued my house, that is the building, at HS 2,000,000 and the other properties at very ungenerous figures—the Tusculan villa at 500,000, the Formian at HS 250,000. The valuation is sharply criticized not only by better-class people but by the populace as well. You may wonder why this happened. *They* say my modesty was the reason, in that I neither refused compensation nor pressed my claim with vigour. But it isn't that. *That* would have been in my favour rather than otherwise. No, my dear T. Pomponius, those same gentry (you don't need me to tell you their names) who formerly clipped my wings don't want to see them grow back to their old size. However, I hope they *are* growing already. Only do come back and join me. I am afraid you may do so less promptly than you would have done, now that your (and my) friend Varro's visit has intervened.

Since you now know what has taken place, let me tell you of my plans for the future. I have let Pompey nominate me one of his Lieutenant Commissioners, but on the understanding that my hands are left quite free. If I did not want to leave it open to myself to stand for the Censorship if next year's Consuls hold an election to that office, I should have taken a votive commission to practically 'every temple and sacred wood.' That is what my interest required. But I wanted to give myself the option of either

petendi vel ineunte aestate exeundi, et interea me esse in oculis civium de me optime meritorum non alienum putavi.

7 Ac forensium quidem rerum haec nostra consilia sunt, domesticarum autem valde impedita. domus aedificatur, scis quo sumptu, qua molestia. reficitur Formianum, quod ego nec relinquere possum nec videre. Tusculanum proscripsi, <etsi>[8] suburbano non facile careo. amicorum benignitas exhausta est in ea re quae nihil habuit praeter dedecus; quod sensisti tu absens, <tui>[9] praesentes. quorum studiis ego et copiis, si esset per meos defensores licitum, facile essem omnia consecutus; quo in genere nunc vehementer laboratur. cetera quae me sollicitant μυστικώτερα sunt. amamur a fratre et a filia. <te>[10] exspectamus.

75 (IV.3)

Scr. Romae IX *Kal. Dec. an. 57* <*§ 5*>

CICERO ATTICO SAL.

1 Avere te certo scio cum scire quid hic agatur tum ea a me scire, non quo certiora sint ea quae in oculis omnium geruntur si a me scribuntur[1] quam cum ab aliis aut scribuntur[2] tibi aut nuntiantur, sed velim perspicias ex meis litteris quo animo ea feram quae geruntur et qui sit hoc tempore aut mentis meae sensus aut omnino vitae status.

[8] *add. Boot* [9] *add. TP* [10] *add. Manutius*
[1] scribantur (*Wesenberg*) [2] scribantur (ς)

---

[4] Probably the hire of roughs to counter Clodius' mob tactics.

standing or leaving at the beginning of next summer, and in the meanwhile I thought it would not be a bad idea to show myself to my fellow countrymen, to whom I owe so much.

Such are my plans as to public affairs. As to my private life, they are in a terrible tangle. My house is being built, you know at what expense and trouble. My Formian villa is being reconstructed, and I cannot bear to let it go nor yet to look at it. I have put up the Tusculan property for sale, though I can't easily do without a place near Rome. The generosity of my friends was exhausted in a matter which yielded nothing but disrepute,[4] as you saw in absence and your people saw on the spot. With their loyalty and resources, if only my defenders had permitted it, I should have had ample for every purpose; whereas now I am greatly embarrassed in this respect. My other anxieties are more *sub rosa*. I have the affection of my brother and daughter.[5] I look forward to seeing you.

75 (IV.3)

Rome, 22 November 57

CICERO TO ATTICUS

I am sure you are dying to know what's afoot here, and also to know it from me—not that news of what goes on in full public view is any more reliable from my pen than when it comes to you from the letters or reports of others, but I should like you to see from a letter of my own how I react to developments, and my attitude of mind and general state of being at the present time.

[5] The omission of Terentia speaks for itself.

2 Armatis hominibus a. d. III Non. Nov. expulsi sunt fabri de area nostra, disturbata porticus Catuli, quae ex senatus consulto consulum locatione reficiebatur et ad tectum paene pervenerat, Quinti fratris domus primo fracta coniectu lapidum ex area nostra, deinde inflammata iussu Clodi inspectante urbe coniectis ignibus, magna querela et gemitu non dicam bonorum, qui nescio an <n>ulli[3] sint, sed plane hominum omnium. ille ve<l ante> demens[4] ruere, post hunc vero furorem nihil nisi caedem inimicorum cogitare, vicatim ambire, servis aperte spem libertatis ostendere. etenim antea, cum iudicium nolebat, habebat ille quidem difficilem manifestamque causam, sed tamen causam; poterat infitiari, poterat in alios derivare, poterat etiam aliquid iure factum defendere: post has ruinas, incendia, rapinas desertus a suis vix iam †Decimum†[5] dissignatorem,[6] vix Gellium retinet, servorum consiliis utitur; videt, si omnis quos vult palam occiderit, nihilo suam causam difficiliorem quam adhuc sit in iudicio futuram.

3 Itaque a. d. III Id. Nov. cum Sacra via descenderem, insecutus est me cum suis. clamor, lapides, fustes, gladii; et haec improvisa omnia. discessi in vestibulum Tetti Damionis. qui erant mecum facile operas aditu prohibuerunt. ipse occidi potuit; sed ego diaeta curare incipio, chirurgiae taedet. ille omnium vocibus cum se non ad iudicium sed ad supplicium praesens trudi[7] videret, omnis Catilinas Acidinos postea reddidit. nam Milonis domum,

[3] *add. Lambinus* [4] vehemens (*SB*) [5] Decium *coni. SB, alii alia* [6] des(s)ig- (*Vetter*) [7] videri (ς)

[1] Street adjoining the north side of the Forum.

[2] A respectable personage, Consul in 179.

On 3 November an armed gang drove the workmen from my site, threw down Catulus' portico which was in process of restoration by consular contract under a senatorial decree and had nearly reached the roof stage, smashed up my brother's house by throwing stones from my site, and then set it on fire. This was by Clodius' orders, with all Rome looking on as the firebrands were thrown, amid loud protest and lamentation—I won't say from honest men, for I doubt whether they exist, but from all and sundry. Clodius was running riot even before, but after this frenzy he thinks of nothing but massacring his enemies, and goes from street to street openly offering the slaves their freedom. Earlier on, when he would not stand trial, he had a difficult, obviously bad case, but still a case. He could have denied the charges or blamed others or even have defended this or that action as legitimate. But after this orgy of wrecking, arson, and loot, his followers have left him. It is all he can do to keep Decius (?) the undertaker or Gellius, and he takes slaves for his advisers. He sees that if he slaughters everybody he chooses in broad daylight, his case, when it comes to court, won't be a jot worse than it is already.

Accordingly, on 11 November as I was going down the Via Sacra,[1] he came after me with his men. Uproar! Stones flying, cudgels and swords in evidence. And all like a bolt from the blue! I retired into Tettius Damio's forecourt, and my companions had no difficulty in keeping out the rowdies. Clodius himself could have been killed, but I am becoming a dietician, I'm sick of surgery. When he found that everyone was calling for him to be bundled off to trial or rather to summary execution, his subsequent behaviour was such as made every Catiline look like an Acidinus.[2] On

eam quae <est in> Cermalo, prid. Id. Nov. expugnare et incendere ita conatus est ut palam hora quinta cum scutis homines et eductis gladiis, alios cum accensis facibus adduxerit. ipse domum P. Sullae pro castris sibi ad eam impugnationem sumpserat. tum ex Anniana Milonis domo Q. Flaccus eduxit viros acris; occidit homines ex omni latrocinio Clodiano notissimo<s>, ipsum cupivit, sed ille †ex interiorem aedium Sulla se in†.[8] senatus postridie Id. domi Clodius. egregius Marcellinus, omnes acres. Metellus calumnia dicendi tempus exemit adiuvante Appio, etiam hercule familiari tuo, de cuius constantia vitae tuae verissimae litterae. Sestius furere. ille postea, si comitia sua non fierent, urbi minari. <Milo>[9] proposita Marcellini sententia, quam ille de scripto ita dixerat ut totam nostram causam areae, incendiorum, periculi mei iudicio complecteretur eaque omnia comitiis anteferret, proscripsit se per omnis dies comitialis de caelo servaturum. contiones turbulentae Metelli, temerariae Appi, furiosissimae Publi; haec tamen summa, nisi Milo in campo obnuntiasset, comitia futura.

4 A. d. XII Kal. Dec. Milo ante mediam noctem cum manu magna in campum venit. Clodius, cum haberet fugitivorum delectas copias, in campum ire non est ausus. Milo permansit ad meridiem mirifica hominum laetitia, summa

[8] se in interiorem μύχον aedium Sullae *tempt. SB*
[9] *add. Tunstall*

[3] Milo inherited this house from his adoptive father T. Annius. It was on the road from the Forum up to the Capitol just across the valley from the Cermalus (the northern height of the Palatine). [4] Hortensius. [5] To the Curule Aedileship, for which Clodius was a candidate. [6] See Letter 36, note 3.

12 November he tried to storm and burn Milo's house in the Cermalus, bringing up fellows with drawn swords and shields and others with lighted firebrands, all in full view at eleven o'clock in the morning. He himself had made P. Sulla's house his assault base. Then out came Q. Flaccus with some stout warriors from Milo's other house, the Anniana,[3] and killed off the most notorious bandits of the whole Clodian gang. He had every wish to kill their principal, but *he* had gone to earth in the recesses (?) of Sulla's house. Senate on the 14th. Clodius at home. Marcellinus first-rate, and the rest backed him up vigorously. But Metellus talked out the time with a filibuster, abetted by Appius and also, I must add, by that friend of yours,[4] about whose consistency of conduct you write most truly. Sestius was beside himself. Clodius later threatened reprisals against the city if his elections[5] were not held. Milo on his side posted up Marcellinus' proposal, which the latter had read out from script, calling for a trial to cover my whole case—the site, the fires, and my own narrow escape, all to take place before the elections. He also put up an announcement that he would watch the skies[6] on all comitial days. Public speeches followed, a seditious one by Metellus, a reckless one by Appius, a quite frantic one by Publius. What it all came to was that, unless Milo declared contrary auspices in the Campus Martius, the elections would be held.

On 19 November Milo went to the Campus before midnight with a large following. Though Clodius had a picked force of runaway slaves at his back, he did not dare go to the Campus. Milo stayed till noon, to the public's enormous glee and his own great *réclame*. The campaign of the

cum gloria. contentio fratrum trium turpis, fracta vis, contemptus furor. Metellus tamen postulat ut sibi postero die in foro obnuntietur; nihil esse quod in campum nocte veniretur; se hora prima in comitio fore. itaque a. d. XI Kal. [Ian.][10] in comitium Milo de nocte venit. Metellus cum prima luce furtim in campum itineribus †prope†[11] deviis currebat; adsequitur inter lucos hominem Milo, obnuntiat. ille se recipit magno et turpi Q. Flacci convicio. a. d. X Kal. nundinae. contio biduo nulla.

5 A. d. VIIII[12] Kal. haec ego scribebam hora noctis nona. Milo campum iam tenebat. Marcellus candidatus ita stertebat ut ego vicinus audirem. Clodi vestibulum vacuum sane mihi nuntiabatur: pauci pannosi sine lanterna. ‹m›eo consilio[13] omnia illi fieri querebantur, ignari quantum in illo hero‹e› esset animi, quantum etiam consili. miranda virtus est. nova quaedam divina mitto,[14] sed haec summa est: comitia fore non arbitror, reum Publium, nisi ante occisus erit, fore a Milone puto; si se in turba ei iam[15] obtulerit, occisum iri ab ipso Milone video. non dubitat facere, prae se fert; casum illum nostrum non extimescit. numquam enim cuiusquam invidi et perfidi consilio est us‹ur›us[16] nec inerti nobili‹tati›[17] crediturus.

[10] *del. Manutius* [11] properans *coni. SB* [12] *al.* XIIII *vel* VIII [13] eo conscio (*Manutius*) [14] mittite (ς)
[15] se uti turb(a)e iam *vel sim.* (*R. Klotz ducibus aliis*)
[16] *add. R. Klotz* [17] *add. SB*

---

[7] Clodius, his brother Appius, and their half-brother Metellus Nepos.

[8] The place called Between Two Woods was on the lower ground between the two heights of the Capitol.

[9] Probably C. Marcellus, Consul in 50.

three brethren[7] became a fiasco. They found their violence outmatched and their fury treated with contempt. However, Metellus asked Milo to declare the auspices to him next day in the Forum. No need, he said, to go at night to the Campus. He himself would be in the Comitium at daybreak. So, on the 20th, in came Milo to the Comitium while it was still dark. As dawn broke, there was Metellus furtively scurrying along the byways to the Campus. Milo caught him up between the Woods[8] and made his declaration, on which Metellus turned tail, to the accompaniment of a deal of coarse jeering from Q. Flaccus. The 21st was marketday, and for a couple of days there was no assembly.

On the morning of the 22nd I am writing this between two and three o'clock. Milo is already in position on the Campus. My neighbour Marcellus (the candidate)[9] is snoring loud enough for me to hear him. I am told that Clodius' forecourt is pretty well deserted—a handful of ragamuffins without a lantern. Clodius' party complain that it's all been my plan. Little do they know our heroic Milo, what a resourceful as well as gallant fellow he is. His spirit is amazing. I pass over certain recent brilliancies, but the sum and substance is as follows: I don't believe there will be any elections. I think Publius will be brought to trial by Milo, unless he is killed first. If he now puts himself in Milo's way in a rough-and-tumble I don't doubt that Milo will dispatch him with his own hands.[10] He has no qualms about doing so, and makes no bones about it. He is not scared of what happened to me, for *he* is never going to follow anybody's envious and treacherous advice or put his trust in a sluggish nobility.

[10] This is practically what happened four years later.

6 Nos animo dumtaxat vigemus, etiam magis quam cum florebamus; re familiari comminuti sumus. Quinti fratris tamen liberalitati pro facultatibus nostris, ne omnino exhaustus essem, illo recusante subsidiis amicorum respondemus. quid consili de omni nostro statu capiamus te absente nescimus. qua re appropera.

76 (IV.4)

Scr. Romae III *Kal. Febr. an.* 56

CICERO ATTICO SAL.

Periucundus mihi Cincius venit[1] a. d. III Kal. Febr. ante lucem; dixit enim mihi te esse in Italia seseque ad te pueros mittere. quos sine meis litteris ire nolui, non quo haberem quod tibi, praesertim iam prope praesenti, scriberem, sed ut hoc ipsum significarem, mihi tuum adventum suavissimum exspectatissimumque esse. qua re advola ad nos eo animo ut nos ames, te amari scias. cetera coram agemus. haec properantes scripsimus. quo die venies, utique ‹fac›[2] cum tuis apud me sis.

77 (IV.7)

Scr. in Arpinati c. Id. Apr. an. 56

CICERO ATTICO SAL.

1 Nihil *εὐκαιρότερον* epistula tua, quae me sollicitum de Quinto nostro, puero optimo, valde levavit. venerat horis duabus ante Chaerippus, mera monstra nuntiarat.

[1] fuit (*Watt*)
[2] *add. Baiter*

My *heart* is high, higher even than in my palmy days, but my purse is low. None the less, with the help of my friends and against his opposition, I am repaying my brother's generosity, so far as my resources allow, so as not to be left entirely penniless. With you away I don't know what line to take as to my position in general. So make haste.

76 (IV.4)

Rome, 28 January 56

CICERO TO ATTICUS

Cincius was a very welcome arrival (before daybreak, 28 January), for he tells me that you are in Italy and that he is sending you boys. I didn't want them to go without a letter from me, not that I have anything to write to you about, especially as you are almost here, but just to tell you that I *am* more than delighted to hear of your return and have been impatiently looking forward to it. We'll deal with other matters when we meet. So hurry to join me, confident in my affection as in your own. I write in haste. The day you get here, don't fail to stay with me and bring your folks.

77 (IV.7)

Arpinum, ca. 13 April 56

CICERO TO ATTICUS

Nothing could have been more *à propos* than your letter, which has greatly relieved my anxiety about our nephew, good boy that he is. Chaerippus had arrived two hours previously with the most horrifying reports.

De Apollonio quod scribis, qui illi di irati, homini Graeco qui conturbat atque idem[1] putat sibi licere quod equitibus Romanis! nam Terentius suo iure. de Metello,
2 'οὐχ ὁσίη φθιμένοισιν,' sed tamen multis annis civis nemo erat mortuus cui equidem . . . tibi nummi meo periculo sint. quid enim vereris? quemcumque heredem fecit, nisi Publium fecit, †verum fecit non improbi quemquam†[2] fuit ipse. quare in hoc thecam nummariam non retexeris, in aliis eris cautior.

3 Mea mandata de domo curabis, praesidia locabis, Milonem admonebis. Arpinatium fremitus est incredibilis de Laterio. quid quaeris? equidem dolui. 'ὁ δὲ οὐκ ἐμπάζετο μύθων.'

Quid superest? etiam. puerum Ciceronem curabis et amabis, ut facis.

78 (IV.4a)

Scr. Antii c. XI *Kal. Quint., ut vid., an. 56*

‹CICERO ATTICO SAL.›

1 Perbelle feceris si ad nos veneris. offendes dissignationem[1] Tyrannionis mirificam librorum meorum, quorum reliquiae multo meliores sunt quam putaram. et velim mihi mittas de tuis librariolis duos aliquos quibus Tyrannio uta-

[1] conturbaret quidem (*Boot*) [2] virum (nimirum *debuit*) fecit non improbiorem quam *Mueller*

[1] desig- (*Vetter*)

[1] His identity and the nature of his financial relations with Atticus are not clear.

As for what you say about Apollonius, the gods confound him! The impudence of a Greek going bankrupt and thinking himself entitled to the same privilege as Roman Knights! Terentius after all is within his rights. As for Metellus,[1] *de mortuis*. All the same, no countryman of ours has died this many years past, of whom for my part . . . Your money is safe enough, I'll guarantee. What are you worrying about? Whoever he's made his heir (unless it be Publius) can't be a greater rascal than he was himself (?), so you won't have to loosen your purse strings on his account, and you'll be more careful next time!

Please remember what I asked you to do about my house, post the guards and say a word to Milo. The people of Arpinum are in an amazing fume about Laterium. Well, there it is! *I* was very sorry, but 'little he recked my rede.'[2]

No more, except to ask you to look after the boy and keep a soft spot in your heart for him, as you do.

78 (IV.4a)

Antium, ca. 20 June (?) 56

CICERO TO ATTICUS

It will be delightful of you to pay us a visit. You will find that Tyrannio has made a wonderful job of arranging my books. What is left of them is much better than I had expected. And I should be grateful if you would send me a couple of your library clerks to help Tyrannio with the

[2] From *Odyssey*, 17.488. Some operation by Q. Cicero on his estate at Laterium, perhaps concerning the diversion of a water course, had annoyed his neighbours.

tur glutinatoribus, ad cetera administris, iisque imperes ut sumant membranulam ex qua indices fiant, quos vos Graeci, ut opinor, σιττύβας[2] appellatis. sed haec, si tibi erit commodum. ipse vero utique fac venias, si potes in his locis adhaerescere, et Piliam adducas;[3] ita enim et aequum est et cupit Tullia.

2 Me dius fidius, ne tu emisti λόχον[4] praeclarum! gladiatores audio pugnare magnifice. si locare voluisses, duobus his muneribus liberasses.[5] sed haec posterius. tu fac venias, et de librariis, si me amas, diligenter.

79 (IV.8)

*Scr. Antii paulo post ep. 78 (IV.4*a*)*

CICERO ATTICO SAL.

1 Multa me in epistula tua delectarunt, sed nihil magis quam patina tyrotarichi. nam de rauduscule[1] quod scribis, 'μήπω μέγ' εἴπῃς πρὶν τελευτήσαντ' ἴδῃς.'

Aedificati tibi in agris nihil reperio. in oppido est quiddam de quo est dubium sitne venale, ac proximum quidem nostris aedibus. hoc scito, Antium Buthrotum esse Romae ut Corcyrae illud tuum. nihil quietius, nihil alsius, nihil amoenius. †ειμηισητω†[2] φίλος <οἶ>κος.[3] postea vero

2 quam Tyrannio mihi libros disposuit, mens addita videtur

[2] sillabos (*Tyrrell*)
[3] adducere (*SB* : adduc(e) *Pius*)
[4] locum (*Bosius*)
[5] te liberasses *Purser*
[1] nam perau(i)dusculo *vel sim.* (*Hervagius*)
[2] ἀεὶ (*SB quoque*) ἄριστος (*G. Schmid*) *Watt*
[3] *add. Corradus*

gluing and other operations, and tell them to bring a bit of parchment for the labels, sittybae as I believe you Greeks call them. But this is if convenient to you. As for yourself, do come without fail, if you can bear to stick down here for a while, and bring Pilia,[1] as is right and proper and as Tullia much wishes.

Well, upon my word you have bought a fine troop! I hear the gladiators are fighting magnificently. If you had cared to hire them out you would have cleared your outlay in these last two shows. But of this later. Do come, and *please* don't forget about the clerks.

79 (IV.8)

Antium, shortly after 78 (IV.4a)

CICERO TO ATTICUS

Many things in your letter delighted me, but the plate of fish au gratin[1] was best of all. As for what you say about the bit of brass, 'boast not before you see the end of all.'

I can't find anything for you in the way of a house in the country. There is something in the town, which may or may not be for sale, and very near our house too. Let me tell you that Antium is the Buthrotum of Rome as your Buthrotum is of Corcyra[2]—the quietest, coolest, pleasantest place in the world. 'Always home sweet home.' And now that Tyrannio has put my books straight, my house seems to

[1] Atticus had married her the previous February.

[1] Salt fish and cheese, a proverbial poor man's dinner. The quotation is from Sophocles' lost *Tyro*.

[2] The town.

meis aedibus. qua quidem in re mirifica opera Dionysi et Menophili tui fuit. nihil venustius quam illa tua pegmata, postquam sittybae libros illustrarunt. vale.

Et scribas mihi velim de gladiatoribus, sed ita bene si rem gerunt; non quaero male si se gesserunt.[4]

80 (IV.5)

Scr. Antii paulo post ep. 79 (IV.8)

CICERO ATTICO SAL.

1 Ain tu? an me existimas ab ullo malle mea legi probarique quam <a> te? cur igitur cuiquam misi prius? urgebar ab eo ad quem misi et non habebam exempla duo.[1] quin[2] etiam (<iam>[3] dudum enim circumrodo quod devorandum est) subturpicula mihi videbatur esse παλινῳδία. sed valeant recta, vera, honesta consilia. non est credibile quae sit perfidia in istis principibus, ut volunt esse et ut essent si quicquam haberent fidei. senseram, noram inductus, relictus, proiectus ab iis. tamen hoc eram animo ut cum iis in re publica consentirem. iidem erant qui fuerant. vix aliquando te auctore resipivi.

2 Dices ea te[nuisse][4] suasisse quae facerem, non etiam ut scriberem. ego mehercule mihi necessitatem volui im-

[4] sit egisse re *vel* sic egisse (*Wesenberg*) : si rem gesserunt *Watt*
[1] exemplare *vel sim.* (*Constans*) [2] quid (*Rinkes*)
[3] *add. Hand* [4] ea tenuisse (*SB*)

[3] The clerks whose services Cicero had requested. Dionysius is to be distinguished from Atticus' learned freedman who figures later in the correspondence.

[1] Probably Pompey. The composition which Cicero calls his

have woken to life. Your Dionysius and Menophilus[3] have worked wonders over that. Those shelves of yours are the last word in elegance, now that the labels have brightened up the volumes. Good-bye.

Oh, and you might let me know about the gladiators, but only if they give a good account of themselves. Otherwise I am not interested.

80 (IV.5)

Antium, soon after 79 (IV.8)

CICERO TO ATTICUS

Come now! Do you really think there is anyone whom I would sooner have read and approve my compositions than yourself? Why then did I send this one to anybody else first? Because the person[1] to whom I sent it was pressing me and I did not have two copies. There was also the fact (I might as well stop nibbling at what has to be swallowed) that I was not exactly proud of my palinode. But good night to principle, sincerity, and honour! You will scarcely credit the treachery of our public leaders, as they set up to be and *would* be if they had a grain of honesty about them. I had seen it, knew it, led on by them as I was, deserted, thrown to the wolves. Yet even so I was disposed to agree with them in politics. They proved to be what they had always been. At long last, and by your advice, I have come to my senses.

You will say that you recommended what I should *do*, not that I should write as well. The truth is, I wanted to

palinode was almost certainly his speech 'On the Consular Provinces,' which lauded Caesar's achievements in Gaul.

ponere huius novae coniunctionis ne qua mihi lice‹re›t[5] ‹re›labi[6] ad illos qui etiam tum cum misereri mei debent non desinunt invidere. sed tamen modici fuimus ἀπο-ϑ‹ϵ›ώσ‹ϵ›ι, ut scrips‹eram›.[7] erimus uberiores, si et ille libenter accipiet et hi subringentur qui villam me moleste ferunt habere quae Catuli fuerat, a Vettio me emisse non cogitant, qui domum negant oportuisse me aedificare, vendere aiunt oportere.[8] sed quid ad hoc si, quibus sententiis dixi quod et‹iam›[9] ipsi probarent, laetati sunt tamen me contra Pompei voluntatem dixisse? finis sit. quoniam qui nihil possunt ii me nolunt amare, demus operam ut ab iis

3 qui possunt diligamur. dices 'vellem iam pridem.' scio te voluisse et me asinum germanum fuisse. sed iam tempus est me ipsum a me amari, quando ab illis nullo modo possum.

Domum meam quod crebro invisis est mihi valde gratum. viaticam[10] Crassipes praeripit. tu 'de via recta in hortos?' videtur commodius. ad te postridie scilicet; quid enim tua? sed viderimus.

Bibliothecam mihi tui pinxerunt cum structione[11] et sittybis. eos velim laudes.

[5] *add. Victorius*
[6] *add. Pluygers*
[7] *add. SB*
[8] oportuisse (*SB*)
[9] et (*SB*) : ei (*Watt*)
[10] viaticum (*SB*)
[11] constr- (*Birt*)

bind myself irrevocably to this new alliance so as to make it quite impossible for me to slip back to those people who won't give up their jealousy even when they ought to be sorry for me. However, I have observed moderation in my 'apotheosis,' as I told you I should. I shall give myself more rein if *he*[2] receives the offering cordially and if, on the other hand, it wrings the withers of certain gentlemen who object to my owning a villa[3] which once belonged to Catulus without recollecting that I bought it from Vettius, and say in the same breath that I ought not to have built my house and that I ought to sell it. But what's that compared with the fact that when I made speeches in the Senate on lines which even they approved they were delighted none the less that I had spoken against Pompey's wishes? *Il faut en finir*. Since the powerless won't be my friends, let me try to make myself liked by the powerful. You will say that I might have thought of that sooner. I know you wanted me to do so, and that I have been a prize donkey. But now it's time for me to love myself since *they* won't love me whatever I do.

Thank you very much for keeping a close eye on my house. Crassipes is forestalling your welcome-home dinner. 'Straight from the road to the suburbs?'[4] Well, it seems more convenient. I'll come to you the next day, naturally. It can't make any odds to you. But we shall see.

Your people have painted my library together with the bookcases and labels. Please commend them.

[2] Caesar.

[3] At Tusculum. Catulus is probably the elder of the two Catuli.

[4] Suburban villas (*horti,* usually translated 'gardens') seem to have been reckoned rather 'fast.'

81 (IV.12)

Scr. Antii ex. m. Iun., ut vid., an. 56

CICERO ATTICO SAL.

Egnatius Romae est, sed ego cum eo de re †Halimeti† vehementer Anti egi. graviter se acturum cum Aquillio confirmavit. videbis ergo hominem si voles. Macroni vix videor praesto esse. Idibus enim auctionem Larini video et biduum praeterea. id tu, quoniam Macronem tanti facis, ignoscas mihi velim. sed si me diligis, postridie Kal. cena apud me cum P[et]ilia. prorsus id facies. Kalendis cogito in hortis Crassipedis quasi in deversorio cenare; facio fraudem senatus consulto. inde domum cenatus, ut sim mane praesto Miloni. ibi te igitur videbo; et praemonebo.[1] domus te nostra tota salutat.

82 (IV.8a)

Scr. Antii vel in Tusculano c. XIV *Kal. Dec., ut vid., an. 56*

<CICERO ATTICO SAL.>

1 †Aperias†[1] vix discesserat, cum epistula. quid ais? putasne fore ut legem non ferat? dic, oro te, clarius; vix enim mihi exaudisse videor. verum statim fac ut sciam, si modo tibi est commodum. ludis quidem quoniam dies est additus, eo

2 etiam melius hic eum diem cum Dionysio conteremus.

[1] promonebo (*Corradus*)

[1] Apellas *Turnebus* : Apenas ς, *edd.* : Apella *coni. SB*

---

[1] Perhaps identical with Thallumetus in Letter 105; both names seem to be corrupt. [2] Probably sumptuary, restricting expenditure on food in public places.

81 (IV.12)

Antium, end of June (?), 56

CICERO TO ATTICUS

Egnatius is in Rome, but I took up Halimetus' (?)[1] affair with him strongly at Antium. He assured me that he would speak seriously to Aquillius. So you will see him if you wish. I hardly think I can oblige Macro. There is the auction, I see, at Larinum on the Ides and for the two days following. As you think such a lot of Macro, I must ask you to forgive me. But don't fail to dine with me on the 2nd with Pilia. You really must. On the Kalends I propose to dine at Crassipes' place in the suburbs in lieu of an inn, and thus cheat the decree![2] Then home after dinner so that I can be ready for Milo in the morning. I shall see you there then, and shall warn you beforehand. All my household wish to be remembered to you.

82 (IV.8a)

Antium or Tusculum, ca. 17 Nov. (?) 56

CICERO TO ATTICUS

Hardly had Apella (?) left when your letter arrived. Are you really saying that you don't think he'll bring the bill[1] to a vote? Please speak a little louder, I don't think I quite caught! But do let me know at once, if you conveniently can that is. As the games are going on for an extra day, I shall be all the happier to be spending that day here with Dionysius.

[1] Nothing is known about this law or its proposer.

De Trebonio, prorsus tibi adsentior. de Domitio,

σύκῳ μὰ τὴν Δήμητρα, σῦκον οὐδὲ ἓν οὕτως ὅμοιον γέγονεν

quam est ista *περίστασις* nostrae, vel quod ab isdem vel quod praeter opinionem vel quod viri boni nusquam; unum dissimile, quod huic merito. nam de ipso casu nescio an illud melius. quid enim hoc miserius quam eum qui tot annos quot habet designatus consul fuerit fieri consulem non posse, praesertim cum aut solus aut certe non plus quam cum altero petat? si vero id est, quod nescio an sit, ut non minus longas iam in codicillorum fastis futurorum consulum paginulas habeant quam factorum, quid illo miserius nisi res publica, in qua ne speratur quidem melius quicquam?

3 De Natta ex tuis primum scivi litteris; oderam hominem. de poëmate quod quaeris, quid si cupiat effugere? quid? sinam?[2] de Fabio Lusco quod eram exorsus, homo peramans nostri semper fuit nec mihi umquam odio. satis enim acutus et permodestus ac bonae frugi. eum, quia non videbam, abesse putabam: audivi ex Gavio hoc Firmano Romae esse hominem et fuisse adsiduum. percussit animum. dices 'tantulane causa?' permulta ad me detulerat

[2] sinat (*SB*)

---

[2] An unplaced fragment of New Comedy.

[3] L. Domitius had been foiled in his candidature for the Consulship of 55. Pompey and Crassus, who were finally elected in January of that year after other competitors, Domitius excepted, had withdrawn, had not put in as candidates at the proper time, and so Cicero does not recognize them. The one competitor about

I quite agree about Trebonius. As for Domitius, 'No pea, by Jove, was e'er so like to pea'[2] as this crisis of his to my own. The same people responsible, the same unexpectedness, the same conspicuous absence of the honest men. The only difference is that he asked for it. As for the actual blow, I dare say I came off the better of the two. Could anything be more lamentable than for a man who has been Consul-Designate from his cradle to be debarred from becoming Consul, especially as he has no competitors, or at any rate no more than one?[3] And if it is true, as I dare say it is, that in the lists in their[4] little notebooks the future Consuls take up as many pages as the past ones, could any condition be more pitiable than his—except the state's, in which no improvement is so much as hoped for?

Your letter gave me first news about Natta.[5] I detested the man. You ask about the poem.[6] Suppose it were to wish to spread its wings, what then? Should I let it? As for Fabius Luscus, as I had started to say, he was always extremely friendly to me and I never had anything against him—a clever fellow enough, very well-behaved and worthy. Well, as I saw nothing of him, I thought he must be out of town, but I heard from Gavius of Firmum (you know) that he was in Rome and had been all the time. That gave me a jolt. You may think it a small thing to trouble about, but he had brought me a lot of reliable information

whom Cicero is doubtful is an unknown; at this time it must have been uncertain whether he would withdraw or not.

[4] The 'Triumvirs' are meant.

[5] Presumably about his death.

[6] Probably 'On His Vicissitudes,' referred to in *Ad Familiares* 20(I.9).23.

non dubia de Firmanis fratribus. quid sit quod se a me remov‹er›it,[3] si modo removit, ignoro.

4 De eo quod me mones, ut et πολιτικῶς me geram et τὴν ἔ‹σ›ω γραμμὴν teneam, ita faciam. sed opus est maiore prudentia, quam a te, ut soleo, petam. tu velim ex Fabio, si quem habes aditum, odorere et istum convivam tuum degustes et ad me de his rebus et de omnibus cottidie scribas. ubi nihil erit quod scribas, id ipsum scribito. cura ut valeas.

83 (IV.6)

Scr. in Cumano c. XIV *Kal. Apr., an.* 55

CICERO ATTICO SAL.

1 De Lentulo scilicet sic fero ut debeo. virum bonum et magnum hominem et in summa magnitudine animi multa humanitate temperatum perdidimus, nosque malo solacio sed non nullo tamen consolamur quod ipsius vicem minime dolemus, non ut Saufeius et vestri, sed mehercule quia sic amabat patriam ut mihi aliquo deorum beneficio videatur ex eius incendio ereptus. nam quid foedius nostra vita, praecipue mea? nam tu quidem, etsi es natura πολι-
2 τικός, tamen nullam habes propriam servitutem, communi

[3] *add. Boot*

[7] This is unexplained. Possibly Pompey and Crassus are meant.

[8] A reference to a game played with pieces on a board. The 'inner line' was a place of safety where the king stood.

[9] Probably someone like Theophanes, in close touch with the dynasts.

about the brethren of Firmum.[7] Why he should have withdrawn himself from me, if he really did, I have no idea.

As for your admonition to behave like a *politique* and to keep to the inner row,[8] I shall do so. But I need greater *expertise*, and that, as usual, I shall ask you to supply. I should be glad if you would pump Fabius, if you have any opportunity, and sample that dinner companion of yours,[9] and write to me about this and all else every day. When you have nothing to say, why, say just that! Take care of your health.

83 (IV.6)

Cumae, about 19 April 55

CICERO TO ATTICUS

The news about Lentulus[1] affects me as it should, naturally. We have lost a good and great man, who combined a really lofty spirit with much grace and kindliness of manner. My consolation, poor enough but still a consolation, is that I feel no sorrow at all on *his* account—I don't say so after the fashion of Saufeius and your co-sectaries,[2] but because upon my soul it seems to me a gift of providence that a man who loved his country as he did should be snatched away from its conflagration. After all what could be more ignominious than the life we lead, I especially? For you, though you are a political animal by nature, are not subject to any peculiar servitude, you have it in com-

[1] L. Lentulus Niger, the Flamen Martialis.

[2] The Epicureans held that death, being the end of personal existence, was no evil. Cicero tended to think the same.

uteris[1] omnium.[2] ego vero, qui, si loquor de re publica quod oportet, insanus, si quod opus est, servus existimor, si taceo, oppressus et captus, quo dolore esse debeo? quo sum scilicet, hoc etiam acriore quod ‹ne›[3] dolere quidem possum ut non in te ingratus videar. quid si cessare libeat et in oti portum confugere? nequiquam; immo etiam in bellum et in castra. ergo erimus *ὀπαδοὶ* qui *ταγοὶ* esse noluimus? sic faciendum est; tibi enim ipsi, cui utinam semper paruissem, sic video placere. reliquum est '*Σπάρταν ἔλαχες, ταύταν κόσμει.*' non mehercule possum et Philoxeno ignosco qui reduci in carcerem maluit. verum tamen id ipsum mecum in his locis commentor ut ista [im]probem, idque tu cum una erimus confirmabis. a te litteras crebro ad me scribi video, sed omnis uno tempore accepi. quae res etiam auxit dolorem meum. casu enim trinas ante legeram quibus meliuscule Lentulo esse scriptum erat. ecce quartae fulmen! sed ille, ut scripsi, non miser, nos vero ferr‹e›i.

3 Quod me admones ut scribam illa Hortensiana, in alia incidi, non immemor istius mandati tui, sed mehercule incipiendo refugi, ne, qui videor stulte illius amici [non][4] intemperiem tulisse, rursus stulte iniuriam illius faciam illustrem si quid scripsero, et simul ne *βαθύτης* mea, quae

[1] fueris (*Boot*) [2] non ne (*Watt*) [3] *add. Brunus*
[4] *secl. SB, qui etiam post* videor *transp. coni.*

---

[3] See Letter 20, note 2.

[4] A poet, sent to prison by Dionysius I, tyrant of Syracuse, for criticizing his tragedies. When brought out and asked to praise them he said: 'Take me back to the quarries.'

[5] To go on living. Lit. 'are made of iron.'

mon with the rest. But as for me, reckoned a madman if I speak on politics as I ought, a slave if I say what is expedient, and a helpless captive if I say nothing—how am I to feel? As I do I suppose, and all the more bitterly because I can't even grieve without seeming ungrateful to you. Suppose I choose to fold my hands and seek a haven of refuge in retirement? Vain thought! On the contrary I must join the fray. Am I then to be a camp follower having refused to be a general? Needs must, for I see that you yourself (if only I had always listened to you!) think it the best course. There is nothing else left except 'Sparta is your portion: embellish it'[3]—no, confound it, I *can't*! I don't blame Philoxenus[4] for preferring to be sent back to gaol. And yet I am trying down here to discipline myself to do just that, to approve their proceedings, and you will strengthen my resolution when we meet. I see you are writing to me often, but I received all your letters in one batch. That actually cost me an extra pang. I happened to open first the three in which you wrote that Lentulus was a trifle better. Then the thunderstroke in the fourth! But, as I have said, he is not to be pitied; *we* have hides of leather.[5]

You remind me about writing the Hortensius piece.[6] I have dropped into other things, but it was not that I had forgotten your injunction. But upon my word, I no sooner got started than I ran back again. I felt that I already looked silly enough for putting up with his unreasonable behaviour when he was my friend, without committing the further folly of drawing attention to his misconduct towards

[6] Atticus had evidently wanted Cicero to write something with a complimentary dedication to Hortensius, with whom Cicero had temporarily fallen out.

in agendo apparuit, in scribendo sit occultior et aliquid
4 satisfactio levitatis habere videatur. sed viderimus. tu modo quam saepissime ad me aliquid.

Epistulam Lucceio quam misi, qua meas res ut scribat rogo, fac ut ab eo sumas (valde bella est) eumque ut approperet adhorteris et quod mihi se ita facturum rescripsit agas gratias, domum nostram quoad poteris invisas, Vestorio aliquid significes. valde enim est in me liberalis.

84 (IV.10)

Scr. in Cumano IX *Kal. Mai. an.* 55 *(§ 2)*

<CICERO ATTICO SAL.>

1 Puteolis magnus est rumor [et] Ptolomaeum esse in regno. si quid habes certius, velim scire. ego hic pascor bibliotheca Fausti. fortasse tu putabas his rebus Puteolanis et Lucrinensibus. ne ista quidem desunt, sed mehercule <ut> a[1] ceteris oblectationibus deseror et voluptat<ibus cum propter aetatem t>um[2] propter rem publicam, sic litteris sustentor et recreor maloque in illa tua sedecula quam habes sub imagine Aristotelis sedere quam in istorum sella curuli tecumque apud te ambulare quam cum eo quocum video esse ambulandum. sed de illa ambulatione fors

[1] *add. Corradus (pro* a *Watt)* [2] *add. SB*

[7] *Ad Familiares* 24 (V.12), asking Lucceius to write a historical monograph on Cicero's Consulship, exile, and restoration.

[1] Ptolemy the Piper, who had lost his throne in 58, had just been restored by Gabinius.

[2] The seafood for which the Bay of Naples was famous. Faus-

me by writing anything. Moreover the self-control I have shown in conduct might not be so apparent in writing, and such an apologia might seem rather lacking in dignity. But we shall see. For your part, write me a line as often as you can.

Mind you get Lucceius to lend you the letter[7] I sent him, asking him to write an account of my doings—a very pretty piece—and urge him to get on with it, and thank him for promising to do so in his reply. Please keep an eye on my house, as far as you can, and say something to Vestorius—he is behaving very handsomely to me.

84 (IV.10)

Cumae, 22 April 55

CICERO TO ATTICUS

At Puteoli there is a strong rumour that Ptolemy is on his throne.[1] If you have more reliable information, I should be glad to know. I am living here on Faustus' library—*you* perhaps think it's on these Puteolan and Lucrine commodities.[2] Well, I have them too. But seriously, while all other amusements and pleasures have lost their charm because of my age and the state of our country, literature relieves and refreshes me. I would rather sit on that little seat you have underneath Aristotle's bust than in our Consuls' chairs of state, and I would rather take a walk with you at your home than with the personage[3] in whose company it appears that walk I must. But as for *that* walk, chance and

tus Sulla may have sold his books to Cicero or Cicero may have been reading them in his villa. [3] Pompey.

2 viderit aut si quis est qui curet deus. nostram ambulationem et Laconicum eaque quae circa sunt velim quod poteris invisas et urgeas Philotimum ut properet, ut possim tibi aliquid in eo genere respondere.

Pompeius in Cumanum Parilibus venit. misit ad me statim qui salutem nuntiaret. ad eum postridie mane vadebam cum haec scripsi.

85 (IV.9)

Scr. Neapoli IV *Kal. Mai an. 55 (§ 2)*

CICERO ATTICO SAL.

1 Sane velim scire num censum impediant tribuni diebus vitiandis (est enim hic rumor) totaque de censura quid agant, quid cogitent. nos hic cum Pompeio fuimus. multum mecum de re publica, sane sibi displicens, ut loquebatur (sic est enim in hoc homine dicendum), Syriam spernens, Hispaniam iactans, hic quoque ut loquebatur — et opinor, usquequaque, de hoc cum dicemus, sit hoc quasi '*καὶ τόδε Φωκυλίδου.*' tibi etiam gratias agebat quod signa componenda suscepisses; in nos vero suavissime mehercule est effusus. venit etiam ad me in Cumanum a. d. VI.[1] nihil minus velle mihi visus est quam Messallam consulatum petere. de quo ipso si quid scis velim scire.

[1] at si *vel* si (*Constans*)

---

[4] A kind of sweat bath. The reference is to work on Cicero's rebuilt house in Rome.

[1] By declaring unfavourable auspices.

[2] Sixth-century author of versified maxims, which he prefaced: 'This also says Phocylides.'

the gods, if any of them is interested, must provide. As for *my* walk and my Laconian bath[4] and its environs, I should be grateful if you would keep an eye on them as far as possible and urge Philotimus to make haste so that I can offer you some sort of return in this respect.

Pompey arrived at his Cuman villa on Shepherds' Day, and at once sent a messenger to me with his compliments. That was yesterday, and I am just going over to him early today as I write this.

85 (IV.9)

Naples, 27 April 55

CICERO TO ATTICUS

I should be very glad to know whether the Tribunes are holding up the census by voiding[1] the days (there is a rumour here to that effect), and what they are doing and proposing to do about the Censorship generally. I have been with Pompey here. He discussed politics with me a good deal, not without much self-dissatisfaction from what he said (one has to put it that way in his case), scorning Syria, spurning Spain—again, from what he said. Indeed, every time we speak of Pompey I think it should be with this refrain, like 'This also says Phocylides.'[2] He further spoke appreciatively of your undertaking to arrange his art collection. Towards myself I must say he was most agreeably effusive. He also paid a visit to my place at Cumae on the 25th. It seemed to me that the last thing he wants is for Messalla to stand for the Consulship. If you know anything on that subject by the way, I should like to know too.

2 Quod Lucceio scribis te nostram gloriam commendaturum et aedificium nostrum quod crebro invisis, gratum. Quintus frater ad me scripsit se, quoniam Ciceronem suavissimum tecum haberes, ad te Non. Mai. venturum. ego me de Cumano movi a. d. v Kal. Mai. eo die Neapoli apud Paetum. a. d. IIII Kal. Mai. iens in Pompeianum bene mane haec scripsi.

86 (IV.11)

Scr. fort. in Tusculano v *Kal. Quint. an.* 55 *(§ 1)*

CICERO ATTICO SAL.

1 Delectarunt me epistulae tuae quas accepi uno tempore duas a. d. v Kal. perge reliqua. gestio scire ista omnia. etiam illud cuius modi sit velim perspicias; potes a Demetrio. dixit mihi Pompeius Crassum a se in Albano exspectari a. d. IIII Kal.; is cum venisset, Romam esse statim venturos ut rationes cum publicanis putarent. quaesivi gladiatoribusne. respondit ante quam inducerentur. id cuius modi sit aut nunc, si scies, aut cum is Romam venerit ad me mittas velim.

2 Nos hic voramus litteras cum homine mirifico (ita mehercule sentio) Dionysio, qui te omnisque vos salutat. 'οὐδὲν γλυκύτερον ἢ πάντ' εἰδέναι.' qua re ut homini curioso ita perscribe ad me quid primus dies, quid secundus, quid censores, quid Appius, quid illa populi Appuleia;

---

[1] Perhaps a facetious reference to a project for provincial tax reform. [2] Quoted from Menander, play uncertain.

[3] Of the gladiator show.

[4] Clodius, called Appuleia (the feminine gender implies im-

Thank you for saying that you will recommend my glory to Lucceius and for keeping a watchful eye on my building. My brother writes to me that as you have our delightful young Quintus with you he will pay you a visit on the Nones of May. I left Cumae on 26 April and stayed the night at Naples with Paetus. I write this very early on 27 April, just off for Pompeii.

86 (IV.11)

Tusculum (?), 26 June 55

CICERO TO ATTICUS

Your two letters which I received together on the 26th gave me much pleasure. Carry on with the good work! I am dying to know everything that goes on. For instance would you find out what this means?—you can, from Demetrius. Pompey told me that he was expecting Crassus at Alba on the 27th, and that when he had arrived they would go to Rome at once, to make up accounts with the tax farmers.[1] 'During the gladiator show?' I asked. He replied, 'Before it starts.' Could you send me word what this is about, either now, if you happen to know, or when he gets to Rome?

Here I am devouring literature with that amazing man (I'm quite serious) Dionysius, who sends his regards to you and all. 'Nothing so sweet as everything to know.'[2] That being so, remember that I am of an inquisitive turn, and tell me in detail about the opening day[3] and the second day and the Censors and Appius and the People's Appuleia.[4]

morality) after an earlier demagogue, L. Appuleius Saturninus. Gladstone used to be known as 'the People's William.'

denique etiam quid a te fiat ad me velim scribas. non enim, ut vere loquamur, tam rebus novis quam tuis litteris delector. ego mecum praeter Dionysium eduxi neminem nec metuo tamen ne mihi sermo desit; ab isto ‹tanto›pere[1] delector. tu Lucceio nostrum librum dabis. Demetri Magnetis tibi mitto statim, ut sit qui a te mihi epistulam referat.

87 (IV.13)

Scr. in Tusculano XVI *vel* XV *Kal. Dec. an. 55 (§ 1)*

CICERO ATTICO SAL.

1 Nos in Tusculanum venisse a. d. XVII Kal. Dec. video te scire. ibi nobis Dionysius praesto fuit. Romae a. d. XIII Kal. volumus esse. quod dico 'volumus,' immo vero cogimur. Milonis nuptiae. Comitiorum non nulla opinio est. ego, etsi * * *, ‹pro re› nata[1] afuisse me in altercationibus quas in senatu factas audio fero non moleste. nam aut defendissem quod non placeret aut defuissem cui non oporteret. sed mehercule velim res istas et praesentem statum rei publicae et quo animo consules ferant hunc σκυλμὸν scribas ad

2 me quantum pote. valde sum ὀξύπεινος et, si quaeris, omnia mihi sunt εὔπεπτα.[2] Crassum quidem nostrum minore dignitate aiunt profectum paludatum quam olim aequalem

[1] abs te opere (*SB*)   [1] etsi irata *vel* et surata (*SB* (*lacunam agnovit F. Schmidt*))   [2] suspecta (*Sedgwick*)

---

[1] Probably concerning Crassus' allowances as governor of Syria.   [2] Probably Crassus, with whom Cicero was now nominally on good terms, rather than Pompey.

[3] L. Aemilius Paulus' departure for Macedonia in 168 was

To finish up with, I should like to hear about your own doings. For to tell the truth, it is not so much the news that gives me pleasure as your letters. I have taken nobody away with me except Dionysius, but I am not afraid of running short of conversation in such delightful company. Please give my book to Lucceius. I am sending you Demetrius of Magnesia's right away, so that you may have somebody to bring me back a letter.

87 (IV.13)

Tusculum, 15 or 16 November 55

CICERO TO ATTICUS

I see you know that I arrived at Tusculum on 14 November. Dionysius was there to meet me. I want to be in Rome on the 18th. I say 'want', but in fact I have to be there—Milo's wedding. There is some expectation of elections. For my part, although * * *, as things stand I am not sorry to have been absent during the altercations[1] which I hear have taken place in the Senate, for I should either have had to support a measure I did not like or to fail a man[2] I ought to support. But I should really be grateful if you would write to me as much as possible about these matters, and the present political situation, and how the Consuls are taking this *tracasserie*. I am quite greedily inquisitive, and, if it's of any interest to you, I can digest anything. They say that our friend Crassus left Rome in general's uniform with rather less *éclat* than his coeval L. Paulus,[3] also Consul for

memorable for the crowds who saw him off. Crassus was now 59 or 60 years old.

eius L. Paulum, item iterum consulem. o hominem nequam!

De libris oratoriis factum est a me diligenter. diu multumque in manibus fuerunt. describas licet. illud etiam <atque etiam>[3] te rogo, τὴν παροῦσαν κατάστασιν τυπωδῶς, ne istuc hospes veniam.

88 (IV.14)

Scr. in Cumano vel Pompeiano med. m. Mai. an. 54

CICERO ATTICO SAL.

1 Vestorius noster me per litteras fecit certiorem te Roma a. d. VI Id. Mai putare profectum esse tardius quam dixeras quod minus valuisses. si iam melius vales, vehementer gaudeo. velim domum ad te scribas ut mihi tui libri pateant non secus ac si ipse adesses, cum ceteri tum Varronis. est enim mihi utendum quibusdam rebus ex his libris ad eos quos in manibus habeo; quos, ut spero, tibi valde probabo.

2 Tu velim, si quid novi forte habes, maxime a Quinto fratre, deinde a C. Caesare, et si quid forte de comitiis, de re publica (soles enim tu haec festive odorari), scribas ad me; si nihil habebis, tamen scribas aliquid. numquam enim mihi tua epistula aut intempestiva aut loquax visa est. maxime autem rogo rebus tuis totoque itinere <feliciter ex>[1] sententiaque confecto nos quam primum revisas. Dionysium iube salvere. cura ut valeas.

[3] *add. Schütz* [1] *add. SB* (ex *iam* ς)

---

[4] The treatise *On the Orator*.

[1] The treatise *On the Republic* (or *State*).

the second time, in days gone by. What a rascal he is!

I have not been idle over the work on oratory.[4] It has been in my hands much and long. You can copy it. May I ask you yet again to give me the present situation *dans les grandes lignes*, so that I shall not come back to Rome like a foreigner?

88 (IV.14)

Cumae or Pompeii, mid-May 54

CICERO TO ATTICUS

Our friend Vestorius has written informing me that he thinks you left Rome on 10 May later than you had told me because you had not been well. If you are now better, I am very glad. I should be grateful if you would write to your house in Rome and tell them to give me free access to your books just as if you were at home yourself, Varro's among the rest. I need certain things in these books for the work I have in hand,[1] which I hope you are going to like more than a little.

If you happen to have any news, from my brother Quintus in the first place and from C. Caesar in the second, or anything about the elections and politics (you are generally pretty good at getting wind of such things), I'd be grateful if you would write to me about it. If you haven't anything, write something or other all the same. Never have I found any letter of yours unseasonable or garrulous. But most of all let me beg you to come back to us as soon as possible, when you have finished your business and your whole trip prosperously and to your satisfaction. Give my regards to Dionysius. Take good care of yourself.

89 (IV.16)

Scr. Romae c. Kal. Quint. an. 54

CICERO ATTICO SAL.

1 Occupationum mearum vel hoc signum erit quod epistula librari manu est. de epistularum frequentia te nihil accuso, sed pleraeque tantum modo mihi nuntiabant ubi esses quod erant abs te, vel etiam significabant recte esse. quo in genere maxime delectarunt duae fere eodem tempore abs te Buthroto datae; scire enim volebam te commode navigasse. sed haec epistularum frequentia non tam ubertate sua quam crebritate delectavit: illa fuit gravis et plena rerum quam mihi M. Paccius, hospes tuus, reddidit. ad eam rescribam igitur, et hoc quidem primum: Paccio et verbis et re ostendi quid tua commendatio ponderis haberet. itaque in intimis est meis, cum antea notus non fuisset.

2 Nunc pergam ad cetera. Varro, de quo ad me scribis, includetur in aliquem locum, si modo erit locus. sed nosti genus dialogorum meorum. ut in oratoriis, quos tu in caelum fers, non potuit mentio fieri cuiusquam ab iis qui disputant nisi eius qui illis notus aut auditus esset, ‹ita›[1] hanc ego de re publica quam institui disputationem in Africani personam et Phili et Laeli ‹et› Manili contuli. adiunxi adulescentis Q. Tuberonem, P. Rutilium, duo Laeli generos, Scaevolam et Fannium. itaque cogitabam, quoniam in singulis libris utor prohoemiis ut Aristoteles in iis quos

[1] *add.* Wesenberg

89 (IV.16)

Rome, about 1 July 54

CICERO TO ATTICUS

The very fact that this letter is in a secretary's hand will show you how busy I am. I have no fault to find with you about the frequency of your letters, but most of them merely tell me your whereabouts in that they carry your address, or give the further information that you are well. I was particularly pleased by two of this sort, dispatched about the same time from your house at Buthrotum, for I wanted to know that you had had a good voyage. But this spate of letters has gratified me more by quantity than quality. Now the one you gave your guest M. Paccius really *was* a substantial epistle, full of matter. So I shall reply to that, and begin by saying that I have shown Paccius both in word and deed how heavily a recommendation from you counts. Accordingly he is in my inner circle, though I had never met him previously.

Now to the other points. Varro, of whom you write to me, shall have a place somewhere, provided there *is* a place. But you know the form of my dialogues. Just as in my work on Oratory, of which you speak so very handsomely, none of those taking part in the discussion could make mention of persons other than those they had known or heard, in the same way I have put this discussion on the State that I have embarked upon into the mouths of Africanus, Philus, Laelius and Manilius, with the addition of some young men, Q. Tubero, P. Rutilius, and Laelius' two sons-in-law, Scaevola and Fannius. So I am thinking of making a suitable occasion to address him in one of the prefaces which I am writing to each book, as Aristotle did

ἐξωτερικοὺς vocat, aliquid efficere ut non sine causa istum appellarem, id quod intellego tibi placere. utinam modo conata efficere possim! rem enim, quod te non fugit, magnam complexus sum et plurimi oti, quo ego maxime egeo.

3 Quod in iis libris quos laudas personam desideras Scaevolae, non eam temere demovi, sed feci idem quod in 'Πολιτείᾳ' deus ille noster Plato. cum in Piraeum Socrates venisset ad Cephalum, locupletem et festivum senem, quoad primus ille sermo habe[re]tur, adest in disputando senex; deinde, cum ipse quoque commodissime locutus esset, ad rem divinam dicit se velle discedere neque postea revertitur. credo Platonem vix putasse satis commodum fore si hominem id aetatis in tam longo sermone diutius retinuisset. multo ego magis[2] hoc mihi cavendum putavi in Scaevola, qui et aetate et valetudine erat ea qua esse meministi et iis honoribus ut vix satis decorum videretur eum pluris dies esse in Crassi Tusculano. et erat primi libri sermo non alienus a Scaevolae studiis; reliqui libri τεχνολογίαν habent, ut scis. huic ioculatorem senem illum, ut noras, interesse sane nolui.

4 De re Piliae[3] quod scribis, erit mihi curae. etenim est luculenta res Aureliani, ut scribis, indiciis, et in eo me etiam Tulliae meae venditabo. Vestorio non desum; gratum enim tibi id esse intellego et ut ille intellegat curo. sed ‹ne›scio[4] qui, cum habeat duo facilis, nihil difficilius.

[2] satis (*Ernesti*) [3] fili(a)e (*Schütz*) [4] scis (*Watt*)

---

[1] His published works, chiefly in dialogue form, now lost.

[2] Scaevola the Augur is a character in the first Book only of the treatise *On the Orator*.

[3] Perhaps a piece of property or an inheritance.

in what he calls his 'exoteric' pieces.[1] I understand that you would favour that. I only hope I can finish what I have undertaken. It's a big subject, as you realize, that I am grasping and an important one, requiring a great deal of time of which I am particularly short.

You say you regret Scaevola's disappearance from the work which you are good enough to praise.[2] I did not drop him casually, but followed the example of our divine Plato in his 'Republic.' Socrates calls on Cephalus, a rich, genial old gentleman, in the Piraeus. During the opening talk the old fellow is present at the discussion, but then, after speaking himself and very nicely too, he says he has to go and attend to a sacrifice, and does not reappear. I imagine that Plato thought it would not be quite *convenable* to keep a man of Cephalus' age too long in so protracted a conversation. I felt this consideration arose for me much more strongly in Scaevola's case, in view of his age and state of health, which were what you remember, and the eminence of his career, which made it seem hardly proper for him to be spending several days in Crassus' Tusculan villa. Moreover the conversation in Book I was sufficiently relevant to Scaevola's interests. The others, as you know, contain technicalities, in which I definitely did not want the old gentleman to participate—you remember how fond he was of his joke.

You write of Pilia's affair.[3] I shall attend to it. From Aurelianus' reports it certainly seems to be of value, as you say. And I shall be making myself popular with my Tullia into the bargain. I am doing my best for Vestorius. I realize that this will please you and am taking care that *he* realizes it. But somehow or other, with two such easygoing fellows to deal with he is the most difficult of mortals.

5 Nunc ad ea <quae> quaeris de C. Catone. lege Iunia et Licinia scis absolutum; Fufia ego tibi nuntio absolutum iri, neque patronis suis tam libentibus quam accusatoribus. is tamen et mecum et cum Milone in gratiam rediit. Drusus reus est factus a Lucretio. iudicibus reiciendis <dies>[5] a. d. v Non. Quint. de Procilio[6] rumores non boni; sed iudicia nosti. Hirrus cum Domitio in gratia est. senatus consultum quod hi consules de provinciis fecerunt, 'quicumque posthac . . .,' non mihi videtur esse valiturum.[7]

6 De Messalla quod quaeris, quid scribam nescio. numquam ego vidi tam paris candidatos. Messallae copias nosti. Scaurum Triarius reum fecit. si quaeris, nulla est magnopere commota *συμπάθεια*, sed tamen habet aedilitas eius memoriam non ingratam et est pondus apud rusticos in patris memoria. reliqui duo pleb<ei>i sic exaequantur [ut][8] Domitius ut valeat amicis, adiuvetur tamen non gratissimo munere, Memmius Caesaris commendet<ur> militibus, Pompei gratia[9] nitatur. quibus si non valuerit, putant fore aliquem qui comitia in adventum Caesaris detrudat, Catone praesertim absoluto.

7 Paccianae epistulae respondi; cognosce cetera. ex fra-

[5] *add. SB et Watt* (dies est dictus *Madvig*)
[6] pr(a)elio (*Manutius*) [7] *de foliorum in archetypo permutatione vide edd.* [8] *del. Sternkopf* [9] gallia (ς)

---

[4] See Letter 16, note 16. C. Cato was prosecuted in connection with electoral disorders in 56.

[5] Charged with collusive prosecution.

[6] Hirrus was a relative and adherent of Pompey, L. Domitius had been Pompey's bitter opponent. Their rapprochement seems to foreshadow Pompey's coming alliance with the optimates.

Now to your inquiries about C. Cato. You know that he has been acquitted of charges under the lex Junia Licinia, and I tell you here and now that he will be acquitted of others under the lex Fufia,[4] and his prosecutors will be happier about the result than his counsel. However, he has made his peace with both Milo and myself. Drusus[5] has been charged by Lucretius; jury to be challenged on 3 July. There are sinister reports about Procilius, but you know the courts. Hirrus and Domitius are friends.[6] The senatorial decree[7] which the present Consuls have passed about the provinces, 'Whosoever henceforth . . .,' seems to me unlikely to work.

I don't know what to say to your question about Messalla. I have never seen candidates so evenly matched. Messalla's resources you know. Scaurus has been prosecuted by Triarius. I may add that no very noticeable sympathy has been aroused on his behalf, but still his Aedileship is not ungratefully remembered and his father's memory counts with the country voters. There remain the two plebeians, who are nicely balanced, Domitius[8] having powerful friends and being helped by his show (not a particularly popular one however), while Memmius is recommended to Caesar's soldiers and relies on Pompey's influence. It is thought that if these advantages do not suffice, someone will be found to stave off the elections until Caesar comes, especially after Cato's acquittal.

The Paccius letter having been answered, let me tell

[7] Provisions unknown.

[8] I.e., Cn. Domitius Calvinus who was finally elected Consul in 53 along with Messalla.

tris litteris incredibilia quaedam de Caesaris in me amore cognovi, eaque sunt ipsius Caesaris uberrimis litteris confirmata. Britannici belli exitus exspectatur; constat enim aditus insulae esse muratos mirificis molibus. etiam illud iam cognitum est, neque argenti scrupulum esse ullum in illa insula neque ullam spem praedae nisi ex mancipiis; ex quibus nullos puto te litteris aut musicis eruditos exspectare.

8 Paulus in medio foro basilicam iam paene texerat[10] isdem antiquis columnis. illam autem quam locavit facit magnificentissimam. quid quaeris? nihil gratius illo monumento, nihil gloriosius. itaque Caesaris amici, me dico et Oppium, dirumparis licet, ‹in› monumentum illud quod tu tollere laudibus solebas, ut forum laxaremus et usque ad atrium Libertatis explicaremus, contempsimus sescenties sestertium; cum privatis non poterat transigi minore pecunia. efficiemus rem gloriosissimam. iam[11] in campo Martio saepta tributis comitiis marmorea sumus et tecta facturi eaque cingemus excelsa porticu ut mille passuum conficiatur. simul adiungetur huic operi villa etiam publica. dices 'quid mihi hoc monumentum proderit?' at quid id laboramus?

[10] texerit (*Corradus*)
[11] nam (*Watt*)

---

[9] Either a mock-poetic phrase or a quotation. Caesar was now making ready for his second invasion of Britain.

[10] The first building was an old basilica (public hall) erected in 179 which Paulus was restoring, the second the magnificent Basilica of Paulus which was completed by his son twenty years later.

you the rest of my news. A letter from my brother contains some quite extraordinary things about Caesar's warm feelings towards me, and is corroborated by a very copious letter from Caesar himself. The result of the war against Britain is eagerly awaited, for the approaches to the island are known to be 'warded with wondrous massy walls.'[9] It is also now ascertained that there isn't a grain of silver on the island nor any prospect of booty apart from captives, and I fancy you won't expect any of *them* to be highly qualified in literature or music!

Paulus has now almost roofed his basilica in the middle of the Forum, using the original antique pillars. The other one,[10] which he gave out on contract, he is constructing in magnificent style. It is indeed a most admired and glorious edifice. So Caesar's friends (I mean Oppius and myself, choke on that if you must) have thought nothing of spending sixty million sesterces on the work which you used to be so enthusiastic about, to widen the Forum and extend it as far as the Hall of Liberty.[11] We couldn't settle with the private owners for a smaller sum. We shall achieve something really glorious. As for the Campus Martius, we are going to build covered marble booths for the Assembly of Tribes and to surround them with a high colonnade, a mile of it in all. At the same time the Villa Publica[12] will be attached to our building. You'll say, 'What good will such a structure be to me?'[13] Now why should we worry ourselves about *that*?

[11] Its exact site is unknown.

[12] Among other uses, foreign envoys were housed here (just north of the Piazza del Gesù).

[13] Perhaps Atticus was not much given to voting at elections.

<Habes> res Romanas. non enim te puto de lustro, quod iam desperatum est, aut de iudiciis quae lege Clodia[12] fiunt[13] quaerere.

9 Nunc te obiurgari patere, si iure. scribis enim in ea epistula quam C. Decimius mihi reddidit Buthroto datam in Asiam tibi eundum esse te arbitrari. mihi mehercule nihil videbatur esse in quo tantulum interesse<t> utrum per procuratores ageres an per te ipsum ut a nobis[14] totiens et tam longe abesses. sed haec mallem integra re tecum egisse; profecto enim aliquid egissem. nunc reprimam susceptam obiurgationem. hoc quod dixi tantum utinam valeat ad celeritatem reditus tui!

Ego ad te propterea minus saepe scribo quod certum non habeo ubi sis aut ubi futurus sis; huic tamen nescio cui, quod videbatur is te[15] visurus esse, putavi dandas esse litteras. tu quoniam iturum te in Asiam esse putas, ad quae tempora te exspectemus facias me certiorem velim, et de Eutychide quid egeris.

[12] coccia *vel* coc(c)ia (*Lange*)
[13] fiant (*Boot*)
[14] mutabis (*Baiter*)
[15] isti (ς : istic te *Madvig*)

Well, there you have the news of Rome—I don't suppose you are interested in the census, which has now been given up as a bad job, or the trials under the lex Clodia.[14]

Now submit to a scolding, if you deserve it. You say in the letter given from Buthrotum which C. Decimius brought me that you think you had better go to Asia. I really must say that I don't see where it makes such a difference whether you act through your agents or in person as to justify your being so long and so far away from us. But I wish I had tackled you about this before you made up your mind. I'm sure I should have made some impression. As it is I'll call a halt to my scolding. I only hope that what I *have* said may have the effect of hastening your return.

I write to you less often than I otherwise should because I am not certain of your present or future whereabouts. But I thought I ought to give a letter to this I don't know who because he seems likely to be seeing you. As you think you will go to Asia, I should be glad to know approximately when we may expect you back, and what you have done about Eutychides.[15]

[14] Clodius had passed a law depriving Censors of the right to expel members from the Senate without trial. It was annulled in 52.

[15] See next letter.